UNIVERSITY OF NORTH CAROLINA
STUDIES IN THE ROMANCE LANGUAGES AND LITERATURES
Number 39

THE SONGS OF
BERNART DE VENTADORN

THE SONGS OF
BERNART DE VENTADORN

(COMPLETE TEXTS, TRANSLATIONS, NOTES, AND GLOSSARY)

EDITED BY

STEPHEN G. NICHOLS, JR.

JOHN A. GALM

AND

A. BARTLETT GIAMATTI

WITH

ROGER J. PORTER

SETH L. WOLITZ

CLAUDETTE M. CHARBONNEAU

CHAPEL HILL

THE UNIVERSITY OF NORTH CAROLINA PRESS

Revised
Copyright 1965, by
The University of North Carolina Press

Depósito Legal: V. 2.408 — 1962

Printed in Spain - Talleres Tipográficos de la Editorial Castalia - Valencia, 1962

CONTENTS

	Page
FOREWORD ...	11
INTRODUCTION ...	13
EDITORIAL NOTE ...	25
VIDA A ...	29
VIDA B ...	33
RAZO C ...	37
RAZO D ...	39
1. Ab joi mou lo vers e·l comens ...	41
2. Amics Bernartz de Ventadorn ...	45
3. Amors, enquera·us preyara ...	48
4. Amors, e que·us es vejaire? ...	51
5. Anc no gardei sazo ni mes ...	54
6. Era·m cosselhatz, senhor ...	56
7. Ara no vei luzir solelh ...	59
8. A, tantas bonas chansos ...	62
9. Bel m'es can eu vei la brolha ...	65
10. Bel m'es qu'eu chan en aquel mes ...	68
11. Bels Monruels, aicel que·s part de vos ...	71
12. Be m'an perdut lai enves Ventadorn ...	72
13. Be·m cuidei de chantar sofrir ...	75
14. Bernart de Ventadorn, del chan ...	78
15. Chantars no pot gaire valer ...	80
16. Conortz, era sai eu be ...	83
17. En cossirer et en esmai ...	86
18. E mainh genh se volv e·s vira ...	89
19. Estat ai com om esperdutz ...	91

		Page
20.	Gent estera que chantes ...	94
21.	Ges de chantar no·m pren talans ...	97
22.	Ja mos chantars no m'er onors ...	100
23.	La dousa votz ai auzida ...	104
24.	Lancan folhon bosc e jarric ...	107
25.	Lancan vei la folha ...	110
26.	Lancan vei per mei la landa ...	114
27.	Lonc tems a qu'eu no chantei mai ...	117
28.	Le gens tems de pascor ...	121
29.	Lo rossinhols s'esbaudeya ...	125
30.	Lo tems vai e ven e vire ...	129
31.	Non es meravelha s'eu chan ...	132
32.	Peirol, com avetz tan estat ...	135
33.	Pel doutz chan que·l rossinhols fai ...	138
34.	Per Dieu, Amor, en gentil loc cortes ...	141
35.	Pel melhs cobrir lo mal pes e·l cossire ...	142
36.	Pois preyatz me, senhor ...	145
37.	Can la frej' aura venta ...	148
38.	Can la verz folha s'espan ...	151
39.	Can l'erba fresch' e·lh folha par ...	153
40.	Can lo boschatges es floritz ...	156
41.	Can par la flors josta·l vert folh ...	160
42.	Can vei la flor, l'erba vert e la folha ...	163
43.	Can vei la lauzeta mover ...	166
44.	Tant ai mo cor ple de joya ...	169
45.	Tuih cil que·m preyon qu'eu chan ...	173

Notes ...	177
Glossary ...	191
Proper names ...	231
Bibliography ...	233

TO

THOMAS G. BERGIN

"tu duca, tu segnore, e tu maestro"
...*Inferno* II, 140

FOREWORD

Ernest Hoepffner, discussing Bernart de Ventadorn and his position in the history of the Provençal lyric, brings his chapter to its conclusion with the following paragraph:

"Par la musicalité de sa langue, simple et harmonieuse, par la fluidité de ses vers et le charme de ses images, et surtout par la justesse et la sincerité de ses sentiments, il se révèle grand poète lyrique, sensible et délicat, d'une grace un peu mélancolique, comme la poésie occitane n'en connaît point d'autre. Il a été vraiment plus que les autres, comme il l'affirme lui-même, le grand chantre de l'amour." *(Les Troubadours,* Paris 1955, p. 59.)

It is to be noted that Professor Hoepffner does not hesitate to use the expression "grand poète", voicing a judgment which most students of old Provençal would enthusiastically endorse. But equally to our point here is the footnote that appears on the same page: "Depuis 1915, il existe une excellente et magnifique édition des chansons de Bernard de Ventadour, établie par les soins de Carl Appel... Un monument digne du grand poète. Il serait souhaitable qu'on eût en France, si ce n'est une édition complète, du moins un choix assez riche de ses oeuvres avec des traductions françaises." And here too Professor Hoepffner speaks for the rest of us who have been privileged to know Bernart; he feels that it is not enough for a truly great poet to have won the scrupulous and sensitive attention of a distinguished scholar; admirable as Appel's edition is, it is in its very thoroughness a somewhat forbidding vestment for the tender and graceful lyrics of a lover poet. (To which one must add as well the practical consideration that it is out of print.) If Bernart is to be at least somewhat better known and known, hopefully, to a wider circle than "the twenty-three readers of Provençal",

Appel's work must be reinforced, on another level and, since not all lovers of poetry read German, in another tongue.

Moved by the same considerations as those that underlie Professor Hoepffner's note, Messrs. Nichols and associates have prepared the present edition. Its virtues for the student of literature, as apart from the Provençal specialist, are several. It presents a translation in good English prose of all the poems of Bernart; it contains a concise introduction, defining the character of the poet's work and commenting on linguistic and stylistic aspects of the poems; it offers a full glossary in English of all the words in the text. The student of comparative literature, for example, will have at his disposal all the necessary equipment for the understanding and appreciation of Bernart's verse. I believe the Provençal specialist will also be grateful for the present edition; it would be presumptuous to speak of it as "supplementing" Appel but it does provide a thoroughly up to date bibliography (much has been done in the last 45 years on Bernart and his milieu) and it contains a number of useful notes on some of the more debated passages in the text. Humblest yet most valuable service of all, both for general reader and specialist, the present work makes available, for those who have never had an opportunity to obtain Appel's edition, a complete and convenient edition of the poems.

The young scholars who have prepared this edition have labored with the enthusiasm of youth itself and the dedication of true scholarship to prepare a work which will be of value to their fellows in the years to come and in so doing to enlarge somewhat the audience of a gifted and original poet. I have been pleased and honored to be associated with their enterprise.

THOMAS G. BERGIN,
Yale University

INTRODUCTION

The poetic tradition of the troubadours was so dominated by the aristocratic milieu which fostered it, that, unless the poets were themselves politically important aristocrats such as Guillaume IX, their identity has practically become effaced. Since they were not politically or socially significant in their own time, it was not until later, when the poets became important as literary figures, that an attempt was made to chronicle their lives. But by the thirteenth century, when the biographies were composed, the anonymous biographers had little more than legends and the content of the poets' own work to guide them. It is for these reasons that despite the relatively large corpus of his work (forty-one poems ascribed to him with certainty), we know so little about the life of Bernart de Ventadorn. There are no contemporary documents which record pertinent information about him, but from several allusions in his work, and from a rather scurrilous stanza of Peire d'Alvernhe,[1] we may be certain that Bernart spent some time at Ventadour, and that he was in England at least once. Whether he was born and reared in Ventadour as the child of a servant couple, we cannot say. It does seem probable that Bernart was associated with the court of Venta-

---

[1] Peire d'Alvernhe, who wrote from 1158-1180, was roughly a contemporary of Bernart. The stanza from the *sirventes. Chantarai d'aquestz trobadors*, reads as follows (text from Hill and Bergin, *Anthology of the Provençal Troubadours*):

> E·l ters: Bernatz de Ventadorn
> qu'es menres de Bornel un dorn;
> en son paire ac bon sirven
> per trair'ab arc manal d'alborn,
> e sa maire calfava·l forn
> et amassava l'issermen.

dour as an apprentice and later as a troubadour, for we do know that Bernart's patron, Lord Eble, whom he mentions in *canso* 30 (line 23), was the head of an important troubadour school, and composed *cansos* himself, though none has been preserved.[2]

Since none of his songs has been preserved, our only interest in this lord of Ventadour lies in the information which our knowledge of his life can provide for Bernart's chronology. To this end, much of the voluminous conjecture with which scholars have tried to reconstruct Bernart's life has been concerned with ascertaining whether the Eble who was Bernart's protector was Eble II or Eble III. Actually, scholars have been as interested in the wife of Eble as in him, for it was with this noblewoman that Bernart was traditionally supposed to have been in love. These questions become highly academic, however, and hardly seem justified even in order to pinpoint more accurately Bernart's dates. For everyone has concurred that Bernart follows the oldest troubadours —Guillaume IX, Cercamon, Jaufré Rudel, Marcabru— and therefore his creatively active period must have been between 1150-1180. The beginning date has varied between 1140 and 1150, but the difference assumes importance only if one is concerned with specific influences on and by Bernart, or with historical questions, highly speculative at best, such as the identification of the women for whom Bernart composed his songs. Whatever the conjecture which may be made about Bernart's life on the basis of his songs, nothing may be said of his later life, when he ceased to write poetry, unless one accepts the undocumented statement of the biographer who reports that the poet

---

[2] Cercamon dedicates his *planh* on the death of Guillaume X of Aquitaine (died April 9, 1137) to Lord Eble in these words:

> Lo plainz es de bona razo
> Que Cercamonz tramet n'Eblo.

Marcabru refers to the poems of Eble in these terms:

> Ja non farai mai plevina
> Ieu per la troba n'Eblo,
> Que sentenssa follatina
> Manten encontra razo.   (xxxi, 73-6)

For further discussion of Eble cf. Jeanroy, *La Poésie lyrique des troubadours* (Paris, 1934), ii, 16ff. Appel, *Bernart von Ventadorn* (Halle, 1915), vii ff.

entered a monastery. In any case, whether Bernart's withdrawal from the world after circa 1180 was a symbolic one to the cloister, or real, he wrote no more after that date at the latest. Even this terminal date is one of convenience rather than a certainty; it is impossible to establish a chronology for Bernart's songs, as he mentions no specific event which would permit us to say that a particular song was composed in conjunction with a datable event.

Ventadour is within the Limousin dialect district, and Bernart might be expected to use Limousin predominantly as his basic language. Our knowledge of Limousin is based on an early translation of Boethius, on an edition of St. John, on law documents and on early religious poetry.[3] A comparison of Bernart's language with these documents indicates that his speech has such common characteristics of Limousin as the vocalization of final -l after -a- which is found in rhymes like *aitau-corau* (21,20, 44); *vau-mau* (13, 38-39) in place of the more classic provençal *aital-coral, val-mal*. Appel, in his rather extensive discussion of Bernart's language (pp. cxxiii-cxli of his edition), concludes that "the poet, to a large extent, does use his own dialect, since the idiosyncrasies of his speech may be explained through Limousin".[4] On the other hand, we are dealing with a technically complex poetic tradition which had already existed for at least fifty years before Bernart. Each troubadour, from Guillaume IX on, contributed something not only to the technique of the troubadour style, but, in so doing, to the language as well: perhaps a new series of rhyme possibilities which his dialect offered. The result of this use of and contribution to the troubadour language by poets from different districts was that the troubadour language became a traditional one with elements of several dialects (such as Gascon: Cercamon, Marcabru; and Limousin: Guillaume IX, Jau-

---

[3] For a description of these documents see C. Chabaneau, "La langue et la littérature du Limousin", *Revue des langues romanes*, XXXV, 379ff. But cf. Jeanroy's qualification of some of Chabaneau's contentions, *op. cit.*, i, 47-52.

[4] "Der dichter bediente sich, dürfen wir glauben, im grossen und ganzen seiner heimatlichen Mundart. Die Eigenheiten, die wir fanden, lassen sich fast alle als Limousinismen erklären, und vielleicht wird sich bei genauerer Kenntnis der Sprachgeographie noch manches als limousinisch ergeben, was wir jetzt nicht mit Sicherheit als solches erkennen." (Apel, cxxxix-cxl).

fré Rudel), which would otherwise have been phonologically inconsistent, existing side by side. Thus we find that in Bernart's language, as in that of Guillaume IX, the closed Latin ę, which remained closed in common Provençal (and in Old Limousin, cf. Chabaneau, *Grammaire limousine,* pp. 25 and 249), became ei, so that words coming from the VL ę were rhymed with words actually ending in ę+y: *crei* [7, 23 *(crę)*], for example, with *sordei, guerrei* (7, 7, 31). This trait has been used to argue a Poitevin influence on the troubadour language which would be quite plausible from the close political ties between Limousin and Poitou, but in Bernart's case it would not be conclusive since his rhyme words show such double forms as *cre* (3,17; 36,26), *crei* (7,23); *fe* (4,15), *fei* (21,10), etc.

Even though Appel found that Bernart's idiosyncrasies could be explained by Limousin, it must be observed that some of Bernart's vocabulary follows laws which hold true for the southwest, but not necessarily for Limousin. Thus in the case of the ǫ- breaking, one finds the southwestern form *nǫih* in Bernart, instead of the Limousin and western form *nüeit,* and similarly *trop* for *trüeb, foc* for *füec.* Other patterns which are generally true for both the west and southwest are also found in Bernart. Thus the closing of the open o (ǫ) before a nasal, characteristic of most dialects of Limousin (cf. Grandgent, *Phonology and Morphology of Old Provençal,* par. 36), is found in Bernart's usage: *Pontem > pǫn* (43, 38); *fontem > fǫn* (5, 3; 43, 24). This rule does not hold true, as one would expect, for *bonem > bǫn,* for which one invariably finds *bo* in the rhyme (*bo-tenso* 32, 9-10; *perdo—m'en son bo* 9, 21, 24), as well as within the line (*bo vers* 8, 2; *bo saber* 10, 18; *bo pretz* 18,10). One could continue citing examples of Bernart's dialectical variety, but such a course would serve only to confirm the capacity of the troubadour language, or rather of the troubadours who used it, to absorb and to use diverse influence.

The variety of forms uncovered by linguistic analysis in Bernart's language attests the importance of words as sounds to troubadour poetry. It is above all a poetry of rhyme where the sound patterns created in a poem almost seem to take precedence over the total meaning to be conveyed by the words. By Bernart's time, the basic rhyming patterns had already been worked out, but he plays an important role as a refiner of the tradition. His most significant contribution to the technical aspect of the prosody is the subtle and varied form which he made of the stanza. Before Bernart's time, the short stanza of three to six lines built either with very long lines or a combination of long and short lines had been common.[5] Bernart was the first to use the eight-line stanza extensively and made greater use of the seven- and nine-line stanzas than had previously been done. At the same time, he replaced the combination of long and short lines [6] within the stanza by a much subtler series of combinations. Bernart uses, for example, an eight-line stanza with four eight-syllable lines, two seven-syllable lines and two ten-syllable lines (no. 1), or he combines seven- and eight-syllable lines in a seven- or eight-line stanza (nos. 2, 7, 17, 19, 21, 24, 26, 27, 29). He uses five- and six-syllable lines in a twelve-line stanza (no. 25); five-, six-, and seven-syllable lines in a twelve-line stanza (no. 44); eight-syllable lines in eight-line stanzas (nos. 31, 40, 43); and seven-syllable lines in a seven-line stanza (nos. 30, 45—the latter carries the symmetry still further by having seven stanzas). The variety of line arrangements within the poems is not haphazard or whimsical, it is almost always related to the rhyme scheme. One of the simplest examples is No. 19 which rhymes a b a b b a a b where the a-lines are eight-syllable and the b-lines are seven-syllable. A more complicated use is seen in the first *canso* (a b b a c c d d) where the first quatrain (abba) is octosyllabic, the c-rhymes seven-syllable, and the d-rhymes ten-syllable. One sometimes finds the line of different length from the rest of the stanza used as a signal for a *rima esparsa*, as in poem 2 (a b b a c d d) which is octosyllabic except for the fifth line in each stanza which is the seven-syllable, c-rhyme line.

In his rhymes, as in his stanza formation, Bernart shows subtlety and finesse. He developed the use of feminine rhyme to a greater

---

[5] The six-line strophe using eleven-and fourteen-syllable lines or eight- and four-syllable lines had been the most common stanza forms: six out of eleven of Guillaume's poems use this form (three others use a three-line stanza); fifteen of Marcabru's poems use it.

[6] Guillaume IX uses eight- and four-syllable lines in four of his eleven poems and eleven- and fourteen-syllable lines in three poems.

extent than had been done before him, [7] and one may attribute the tonal richness of his poems to the fact that only twelve of the forty-one are without any feminine rhyme.

The rhyme-words play a larger role than that of creating intricate sound patterns, however. As the most emphatic words in the line by virtue of the rhyme stress, they are frequently used to emphasize the key ideas of the stanza. Thus in the first stanza of *canso* 1, the rhyme-words, as they are rhythmically associated, sum up the content of the stanza. [8] It is true that the content of the stanza is light, but the theme is central to the whole troubadour philosophy where the joy of creation, the joy of love, and the sheer delight in words are so closely entwined. Content and vehicle become closely related to aid understanding in the oral presentation of the songs. But there is an even more basic reason for the close association of content and vehicle: the form of the poem is also the poem's subject matter — many of Bernart's poems are concerned, as is this one, with the poem itself, for it was through the poem that the lady was attained. So in the first poem, the rhymes alone, in the first quatrain of the first stanza, tell us that the quatrain has as subject the beginning and end of the poems. Similarly, by associating *comensansa - alegransa* in the first couplet of the second quatrain and by making these two lines the shortest, Bernart conveys through rhyme and metrics alone the idea of the quick, joyous beginning expressed by the total content of the couplet. The same technique is used in the last couplet of the stanza which is stretched out to ten-syllable lines more suitable to the moral aphorism with which the poet closes. In this one stanza, he has not only *stated* his creative joy, he has *demonstrated* it rhythmically and metrically.

Although Bernart uses a variety of stanzaic patterns, he generally creates the stanzas in ways which will permit him to link them as *coblas unissonans*, i. e. the same rhymes, in the same order are used in all the stanzas of the poem. He does show, though, a certain

---

[7] Guillaume IX has one poem in which feminine rhyme appears (Jeanroy No. 8). Cercamon uses mixed rhyme in three of his eight poems (Dejeanne 1, 4, 8); Jaufré Rudel in three out of seven (5, 6, 7). Marcabru uses feminine rhymes in thirteen out of forty poems and was the first to use feminine rhymes exclusively in poems (nos. 5, 9, 21, 28, 30, 37).

[8] *Comens, fenis, fis, comensamens, comensansa, alegransa, grazir, fenir.*

INTRODUCTION   19

virtuosity for other means of stanza linking. His *canso* 3, for instance, is the most ambitious example of *coblas dissolutas* in the troubadour tradition up to his time. The poem is rhymed a b c d e e f g h g g and has seven-syllable lines in eleven-line stanzas, the stanzas being linked by the *rimas esparsas* which are not answered within the stanza, but in the same place in the following stanzas. This particular example has a complicated rhyme, further complicated by the length of the stanza. The listener is allowed to orient himself, however, by the couplet ee which comes in the middle of the stanza and by the signal g...gg at the end of the stanza. These tie the stanza together until the next stanza begins to answer the *rimas esparsas*. It should also be remarked that there are further signals for the listener: the *rimas dissolutas* are all feminine and are also tied together within the stanza by a sort of assonance *-ara, -ora*, etc. The fact of having the lines all the same length gives added strength to the stanza for the support of the *rimas dissolutas*.

The sense of symmetry which we saw in the stanzaic patterns may also be observed in the movement of *coblas doblas* and *coblas redondas* as in *cansos* 30 and 31. In the first, *canso* 30, the stanzas are linked in pairs by the repetition of the same rhymes in the same place in each pair of stanzas. So *canso* 30 is really four pairs of stanzas rather than eight individual stanzas. The last line in each stanza, a *rima esparsa*, runs through the whole poem and thus acts to tie the stanza-pairs together. *Canso* 31 is somewhat more complicated, since the stanzas are linked in an endless circle by the repetition of the head and tail rhymes throughout the poem in alternating order.[9] The effect is that of two contiguous circles turning around the axes of the stationary b and d rhymes.

---

[9] In no. 31 the a-rhyme is *-an*; the b-rhyme *-or*; the c-rhyme *-en*; and d-rhyme *-es*. The pattern is:

I	II	III	IV	etc.
-an	-en	-an	-en	
-or	-or	-or	-or	
-or	-or	-or	-or	
-an	-en	-an	-en	
-en	-an	-en	-an	
-es	-es	-es	-es	
-es	-es	-es	-es	
-en	-an	-en	-an	

An interesting variation of the *coblas redondas* is seen in *canso* 44 where the first stationary couplet, which we saw in *canso* 31, is done away with in favor of a progressive *rime croisée* running through the first part of the stanza: a b a b a b a b C c c b. The stanzas are either *capfinadas* (stanzas I and II) or *capcaudadas,* that is the last word or rhyme in the stanza is repeated in the first line of the following one. In effect, a new rhyme is introduced in each stanza (see note 10) and becomes the repeated rhyme in the following stanza. The result is a sort of spiral progression with the stable Ccc-rhymes (further stanza support comes from the repetition of the word *amor* as the C-rhyme) serving as the axis for the spiral. The repeated rhyme from the preceding stanza also helps to orient the listener, while the new rhyme prepares him for the following stanza.[10]

The spiral progression, a going ahead and coming back to the same place, finally comes to a halt with the cch-rhyme of the tornada. This back and forth movement is characteristic of some of the rhetorical games of Bernart. A somewhat different example of the back and forth movement may be seen in the grammatical rhymes of *canso* 9. Here the actual rhyme scheme is a b a b b a a b *(coblas unissonans)*. But the rhyme associations are almost overshadowed by the repetition in each couplet of the same radical-word. The effect is such that we do not associate the matching rhyme-words, *brolha-folha, brolh-folh,* etc., but rather the *ab* couplets of matching radical-words: *brolha-brolh, folha-folh*. In these couplets, the radical-word is varied grammatically, but, be-

---

[10] The effect is somewhat complicated and more easily visualized than described:

I:		II:		III:		IV:		V:		VI:	
joya	a	verdura	b	reciza	d	esperansa	e	ironda	f	afaire	g
desnatura	b	chamiza	d	fiansa	e	aonda	f	aire	g	cossire	h
groya	a	asegura	b	conquiza	d	balansa	e	prionda	f	retraire	g
frejura	b	biza	d	semblansa	e	onda	f	repaire	g	vire	h
ploya	a	desmezura	b	deviza	d	desenansa	e	jauzionda	f	esclaire	g
aventura	b	guiza	d	benanansa	e	esconda	f	amaire	g	dire	h
poya	a	cura	b	viza	d	lansa	e	fonda	f	vejaire	g
melhura	b	enquiza	d	pezansa	e	esponda	f	gaire	g	rire	h
amor	C	amor	C	Amor	C	amor	C	amor	C	amor	C
doussor	c	onor	c	cor	c	amador	c	ador	c	plor	c
flor	c	ricor	c	alhor	c	dolor	c	color	c	sabor	c
verdura	b	Piza	d	Fransa	e	blonda	f	traire	g	sospire	h

cause the radical is the same, we do not feel that there has been an advance to a new word.

At a later period in the troubadour tradition, such technical virtuosity as we have seen in the preceding discussion of Bernart's use of rhyme, might have been an end in itself. But one of the most impressive aspects of Bernart's poetry is the sincerity which one senses through it. This sense of shared lyric feeling springs from the fact that Bernart himself leads us into the rhetorical situation of the poetry, which is always interpreted for us from the perspective of the personal referent of the poetic "I". The subjective character who leads us into the poem is always introduced in, or shortly following, the beginning of the canso. The situation revealed at the beginning of the poems concerns the inability of the principal character, the I, to communicate with some other figure whose existence is felt throughout the poem, but who is not present. The problem posed by the poems is therefore essentially a problem of communication: the difficulty of mediating between the feelings of the principal figure and the object of his emotions, the *domna*. Our belief in the sincerity of the poet almost certainly stems from the fact that we are drawn into this effort of communication. In a real sense we become rhetorical personages ourselves, in as much as, in reading the poem, we become a surrogate figure for the *domna* to whom the poet addresses the poem, but whom he cannot seem to reach.

Bernart does not ask us, or the *domna*, to take his worthiness as a man and as a lover for granted. It is perhaps his most original contribution that he elaborates for the first time in vernacular medieval love lyric the supposition which underlies all love poetry: the feeling that the poet is a superior lover because he is more sensitive to beauty. As may be seen in *canso* 15, the role of poetry in this poetry-love equation is not merely that of a mediator between the love and its object. It is a reason in itself for the superiority of the poet. In as much as he is a superior *cantador*, he is capable of a more sincere love. There is of course a circularity of argument here, since the poetic superiority traditionally stems from the *fins amors* of the poet, but such a circularity serves to underline the inseparability of the ideas of love and poetry in Bernart.

The inseparability of love and poetry is implicit in another important characteristic of Bernart: the treatment of time in his poems. The frequent identification of the love poet with a particular time of the year, the spring season, is the most obvious aspect of the question. But there is a wider, subtler use of time. One example is seen in stanza seven of *canso* 15 where special time, *nadaus* 'Christmas', and duration of time (one special day stretched to equal one hundred ordinary days) are evoked to stress the extraordinary value of a favor from the *domna*. The use of time in this manner is a device which puts at the poet's disposal several possibilities of exploration and exploitation. One possibility concerns the poetry itself. All poems have an implicit temporal duration (one aspect of which we saw in the discussion of metrical stanzaic structure) which is as special a duration of time in relation to ordinary speech as a holiday is to the regualar extent of time. The equation of one special temporal instant with another is a twofold complement in which each stresses the value of the other by comparison with the ordinary situation. This attitude underlies the comparison already referred to in stanza seven of *canso* 15. In *canso* 5, also, to cite only one other example, we see that a temporal moment, consecrated by the awakening of love, becomes a special referent which, by analogy, makes the poet aware of all time:

> Anc no gardei sazo no mes
> ni can flors par ni can s'escon
> ni l'erba nais delonc la fon,
> mas en cal c'oras m'avengues
> d'amor us rics esjauzimens,
> tan me fo bels comensamens
> qu'eu cre c'a quel tems senhorei. (5,1-8)

Here, the awakened awareness of time provokes a recognition of the joy and beauty associated with certain seasons. It has had the effect of reintegrating the poet with nature. The manner of representing this reintegration has also the effect of demonstrating for the benefit of the *domna* that love, so closely allied with nature, is itself natural, and, conversely, that to remain outside of love is to remain outside of nature. It is an implicit threat that the *domna* risks an unnatural act.

On the other hand, the obverse effect from that conveyed by the evocation of the special moment may be stressed, as in *canso* 30:

Lo tems *vai e ven e vire.*

In this line the three alliterating verbs all weigh on the one subject —the pause caused by the two conjuctions lengthens the line still more—to evoke visually and audibly the long duration of ordinary time when no favor is forthcoming from the *domna*. This is the reverse effect of that seen in *canso* 15 since the *cen dias,* which sped by so quickly in comparison with the special moment, are stretched out to convey the *ennui* of waiting. It is characteristic of Bernart's constant analysis of the love situation that he studies the discontent of waiting as well as the joy of the special moment. There is no more graphic a way of expressing this discontent than by equating it with the dull, annihilating march of time.

Within the imposed limitations of a general introduction, there is insufficient space to treat every characteristic contributing to Bernart's superiority. Brief mention, however, should be made of stylistic traits, such as Bernart's tendecy to impart a pseudo-dialectical progression to his arguments by creating a level of general truth, through the use of maxims and proverbs, from which he then proceeds to the personal application in his particular situation. The general truth is posed in order to lend, by analogy, an air of right to the particular situation of the poet. Similarly, the juxtaposition of the subjective and the universal transfers some of the grandeur of the universal to the subjective level: an impression calculated to impress the *domna*. The progression from universal truth to particular manifestation is accomplished stylistically by the large number of causal connectives of which *per so, per que, aisso, si, com* are characteristic. These stylistic traits are extremely important since, by the juxtaposition of the impersonal, general truth with the personal level of the poet's situation, the sense of a personal level *is* created. We feel that we are being admitted to this personal level on intimate terms, and this in turn does much to create an atmosphere of shared experience so important for successful love poetry.

His rhetorical skill reminds us that there are many aspects of Bernart's poetry which give the impression that Bernart is an intellectual rather than a lyric poet. The feeling of intellectual density does not come merely from the finesse with which Bernart succeeds in using rhetorical devices such as that described above. It springs even more from the substitution of poetry for nature as the metaphorical identification for love in Bernart's poems. It is seen in the constant analysis which marks the development of the poet's image as lover. Finally, it is evident in the symmetry seen in the stanzaic form and, on the level of content, in the *va-et-vient* from maxim to personal manifestation. Such a tendency to analyse rather than evoke sets Bernart apart from Guillaume IX and Jaufré. Yet these tendencies should not obscure the real lyric quality of Bernart's work. In *canso* 44, for example, which we have already examined briefly for its interesting rhyme scheme, Bernart shows himself responding spontaneously to a landscape which he has created entirely from his own exuberance. It is in this surrender to his emotions—as in the image of the lark in the first stanza of no. 43—that the *canso* achieves its feeling of spontaneity. And it is in this feeling of spontaneity, in spite of the conventional matter of its parts, that this poem works as a poem, revealing a poetic flight quite different from that of some of the more analytical poems which are important in another way. But in the combination of lyricism and analysis which characterizes Bernart, the way is unquestionably prepared for Chretien de Troyes, Chaucer, and Dante.

S. G. N., Jr.

New Haven, Connecticut
June 1961

EDITORIAL NOTE

In preparing the present edition of Bernart de Ventadorm, we felt that the main aim should be to provide a complete yet relatively inexpensive English edition. We hoped it would be useful for class-work and for those scholars in other fields who might be interested in Bernart's poetry. Neither of these uses would require the extensive critical apparatus which Appel's fine edition offers. In short, our aim was not to try to supersede Appel's critical edition —there is no need for a replacement— but to complement it with a convenient English edition, easily obtainable.

Our debt to Appel's work will be apparent to the reader. We have accepted, for the most part, the texts which he established, and have retained his numbering of the poems to facilitate references. We have not, however, retained Appel's punctuation which, influenced by German syntax, seemed excessive to the American eye. Our glossary is basically a translation for the *Glossar* given at the back of Appel's work, although we have added words where they had been omitted, and corrected line references wherever necessary.

The translations, of course, are our own work, and we have tried to clarify dificult passages with notes which benefit from work done since Appel's edition was published in 1915. In some cases, notably in the articles of Vossler, Schultz-Gora, and Kurt Lewent, we were able to consult observations referring specifically to Appel's comments. Those observations which seemed particularly cogent are found in the notes. References to the notes are indicated in the texts and translations by an asterisk (*).

The problem of translation style is always a difficult one. Briefly, our approach to the problem was to present clear, English prose versions of the Provençal texts. We have followed the Provençal grammar and syntax only when it did not distort the English. The tense of the verbs was especially difficult to follow in English, and we frequently chose to ignore the literal tense value of a Provençal verb in order to conform to a normal English sequence of tenses. Relative clauses, particulary where the pronoun had no specific antecedent, were also cumbersome and were often changed to independent clauses or sentences. The translations, then, represent our understanding of the Provençal and may not be relied upon as a literal representation of the texts.

An undertaking of this nature always involves the asistance of many persons who do not receive direct credit. Our debt to Professor Bergin for his encouragement, for his availability, and for the generous contribution of his knowledge and experience to this work is expressed in the dedication of this book to him. We are especially grateful to professor Henri Peyre for his efforts to secure a research grant toward the preparation of this book, and to the Graduate School of Yale University for awarding us the grant. Our thanks also go to Mrs. Katharine W. Denison for typing the texts.

J. A. G.
S. G. N., Jr.

New Haven, Connecticut
June 1961

BERNART DE VENTADORN

Vida A *

Bernartz de Ventedorn si fo de Limozin, del castel de Ventedorn. Hom fo de paubra generation, fills d'un sirven qu'era forniers, q'escaudava lo forn per cozer lo pan del castel de Ventedorn.

E venc bels hom et adreitz, e saup ben trobar e cantar, et era cortes et enseignatz. E·l vescoms de Ventedorn, lo sieus seigner, s'abellic mout de lui e de son trobar e de son chantar, e fetz li grand' onor. E·l vescoms de Ventedorn si avia moiller bella e gaia e joven e gentil; et abellic se d'en Bernart e de las soas chanssos, et enamoret se de lui et el de lieis, si q'el fetz sos vers e sas chanssos d'ella, de l'amor q'el avia ad ella, e de la valor de la dompna.

Mout duret lonc temps lor amors anz qe·l vescoms, maritz de la dompna, ni las gens s'en aperceubessen. E qan lo vescoms s'en fo aperceubutz, en estraigniet en Bernart de si, e pois fetz la moiller serrar e gardar. Adoncs fetz la dompna dar comjat a'n Bernat, e fetz li dir qe·is partis e·is loignes d'aquella encontrada.

Et el s'en partic et anet s'en a la duqessa de Normandia, q'era joves e de gran valor, e s'entendia mout en pretz et en honor et els benditz de sa lauzor.

E plazion li fort li vers e las chanssos d'en Bernart, don ella lo receup e l'onret e l'acuillic e·l fetz mout grans plazers. Lonc temps estet en la cort de la duqessa, et enamoret se d'ella, e la dompna s'enamoret de lui, don en Bernartz en fetz maintas bonas chanssos.

Mas lo reis Enrics d'Englaterra la pres per moiller, e la trais de Normandia e menet la·n en Englaterra; e'n Bernartz remas adoncs de sai tristz e dolens.

E partic se de Normandia e venc s'en al bon comte Raimon de Toloza, et estet ab lui en sa cort entro qe·l coms mori. E qan lo coms fo mortz, en Bernartz abandonet lo mon e·l trobar e·l chantar e·l solatz del segle, e pois se rendet a l'orden de Dalon; e lai el fenic.

E tot so q'ieu vos ai dich de lui, si me comtet e·m dis lo vescoms n'Ebles de Ventedorn, que fo fills de la vescomtessa q'en Bernartz amet tant.

VIDA A

Bernart de Ventadorn was from Limousin, from the castle of Ventadorn. He was of a poor family, the son of a servant who was a baker, heating the stove to bake bread for the castle. He became a handsome and clever man who knew how to compose verse and sing it well. He was courteous and well-bred besides. The Viscount of Ventadorn, his lord, was greatly charmed with Bernart, and especially with his composing and singing, for which he gave him great honor. The Viscount had a beautiful young wife, gay and gracious. She, too, was charmed with Bernart and his songs so that she fell in love with him, and he with her. Henceforth, he made his verses and songs about her and her excellence.

Their love lasted a very long while before the Viscount, the husband of the lady, perceived it. And when he perceived it, he banished Bernart and then had his wife locked up under guard. He made her bid farewell to Bernart and tell him he had to leave and go far away from that region.

So Bernart left and went to the Duchess of Normandy, who was young and of great excellence, well-versed in matters of fame and honor and appreciative of fine expressions in her praise.

Bernart's songs and verses pleased her greatly, so that she received and welcomed him, honored him, and did him a great many kindnesses. He stayed a long time in the Duchess's court. He fell in love with her, and she with him, and he composed many fine songs about her.

But King Henry of England took her for his wife, and brought her from Normandy to England. Bernart remained on this side of the Channel, sad and smarting.

So he left Normandy to come to the court of the good Count Raimon of Toulouse where he stayed until the Count died. When the Count was dead, Bernart renounced the world, giving up poetry and other temporal pleasures to take orders at Dordogne where he finally died.

Now everything that I have told you of Bernart was related to me by the Viscount Eble de Ventadorn who was the son of the Viscountess whom Bernart loved to greatly.

Vida B

Bernartz de Ventador si fo de Lemoisin, d'un chastel de Ventador, de paubra generation, fils d'un sirven e d'una fornegeira, si con dis Peire d'Alvergne de lui en son chantar, qan dis mal de totz los trobadors:

> E·l ters: Bernartz de Ventadorn, 5
> qu'es menres de Bornel un dorn;
> en son paire ac bon sirven
> per trair' ab arc manal d'alborn,
> e sa maire calfava·l forn
> et amassava l'issermen. 10

Mas de qi q'el fos fils, Dieus li det bella persona et avinen, e gentil cor, don fo el comensamen gentilessa, e det li sen e saber e cortesia e gen parlar; et aveia sotilessa et art de trobar bos motz e gais sons.

Et enamoret se de la vescomtessa de Ventador, moillier de 15 so seingnor. E Dieus li det tant de ventura, per son bel captenemen e per son gai trobar, q'ella li volc ben outra mesura, qe noi gardet sen, ni gentilessa ni honor ni valor ni blasme, mas fugi son sen e segret sa voluntat, si con dis N'Arnautz de Meruoil:

> Consir lo joi et oblit la foudat 20
> E fuc mon sen e sec ma voluntat;

e si dis Gui d'Uisel:

> Q'enaissi s'aven de fin aman,
> Qe·l sens non a poder contra·l talan.

Et el fo honoratz e presiatz per tota bona gen, e sas chansos honoradas e grasidas. E fo vesuz et ausiz e receubuz mout voluntiers e foron li faich grand'honor e gran don per los grans barons e per los grans homes, don el anava en gran arnes et en gran honor.

Mout duret lor amors longa sason enans qe·l vescoms, sos maritz, s'en aperceubes. E qan s'en (fo) aperceubut, mout fo dolens e tris, e mes la vescomtessa, soa moillier, en gran tristessa et en gran doler, e fez dar cumjat a Bernat de Ventador q'el issis de la sua encontrada. Et el s'en issi e s'en anet en Normandia, a la dukessa q'era adonc domna dels Normans, et era joves e gaia e de gran valor e de prez e de gran poder, et entendia mout en honor et en prez. Et ella lo receub con gran plaiser e con grant honor e fo mout alegra de la soa venguda e fetz lo seingnor e maistre de tota la s(o)a cort. Et enaissi con el s'enamoret de la moillier de so seingnor, enaissi s'enamoret de la duchessa, et ella de lui. Lonc temps ac gran joia d'ella e gran benanansa, entro q'ella tolc lo rei Enric d'Angleterra, per marit e qe la·n mena outra lo brac del mar d'Angleterra, si q'el no la vi mai, ni so mesatge.

Don el, puois, de duol e de tristessa qe ac de lei, si se fetz monges en l'abaïa de Dalon, et aqui persevera tro a la fin.

VIDA B

Bernart de Ventadorn was from Limousin, from the castle of Ventadorn. Of low extraction, he was the son of a servant and a bakeress, as Peire d'Alverhne says in the song where he slanders the troubadours:

> The third, Bernart de Ventadorn, who misses
> measuring up to Bornelh by a hand's breadth, had
> in his father a worthy wielder of the laburnum bow.
> And his mother fired the oven, and gathered twigs.

But whoever's son he was, God gave him a beautiful and charming person as well as a noble heart in which the first quality was gentility. God also gave him reason, knowledge, courtliness and fair speech. He had subtlety and skill in composing good words and gay tunes.

Bernart fell in love with the Viscountess of Ventadorn, the wife of his lord. God gave him such good luck in this, because of his good manners and joyful creations, that the Viscountess was most desirous of Bernart. She did not follow her reason, or live up to her nobility, or think of her honor, valor, or shame. Rather, she fled her reason, following her desire, as Arnaut de Meruoil says:

> Entirely preoccupied with joy (forgetting madness),
> I flee my reason and follow my desire.

And as Gui d'Uicel says:

> Thus it happens with true lovers that reason
> does not have power over desire.

Bernart was honored and esteemed by all good people, and his songs were honored and beloved. He was seen, heard, and received most willingly. Great men and barons bestowed gifts and fame on him, wherefore he was able to travel in great equipage as well as in great honor.

The love of Bernart and the Viscountess lasted for a long time before the Viscount, her husband, perceived it. And when he perceived it, he was sad and grieved. He caused the Viscountess, his wife, great sorrow and grief, making her take leave of Bernart de Ventadorn, who left the region. Bernart set forth and went to Normandy, to the Duchess who was then mistress of the Normans. She was young and gay and of great valor, fame, and power, being well-versed in honor and fame. She received him with great pleasure and honor. She was cheered by his coming, making him lord and master of her court. And as he had fallen in love with the wife of his lord, so did he now fall in love with the Duchess, and she with him. For a long time he had great joy and benefit from her, until she took King Henry of England for a husband. He took her across the English Channel so that Bernart did not see her again, or her messenger either. Wherefore, Bernart became a monk in the abbey of Dordogne for the grief and sadness which he had on her account. He remained there until his death.

Razo C

...E apelava la B(ernart) "Alauzeta", per amor d'un cavalier que l'amava, e ella apelet lui "Rai". E un jorn venc lo cavaliers a la duguessa e entret en la cambra (de) la dona, que lui leva adonc lo pan del mantel e mes li sobra 'l col, e laissa si cazer e(l) lieg. E B(ernart) vi tot, car una donzela de la domna li ac   5
mostrat cubertamen; e per aquesta razo fes adonc la canso que dis:

Quan vei l'alauzeta mover.

RAZO C

And Bernart called her "Alauzeta" on account of the love of a knight who loved her, and she called him "Rai". Then one day the knight came to the Duchess and entered her chamber. She raised the border of his cloak, tucking it under his collar,* and let herself fall on the bed. Bernart was able to see the whole thing because a maiden of the lady showed it to him secretly. For this occasion he made the song where he says:

When I see the lark beat his wings.

(Canso 43)

Razo D

Bernartz de Ventador si ama una domna gentil e bella e si la servi tant e la honret q'ella fetz so q'el volc en dics et en faichs. E duret longa sason lor jois en leieutat et en plasers. Mas puois cambiet voluntatz a la domna, q'ella volc autr'amador; et el o saup e fo tris e dolens e creset se partir d'ella, car mout l'era 5 greus la compaignia de l'autre. Puois s'enpenset, con hom vencuz d'amor, qe miels li era q'el agues en leis la meitat qe del tot la perdes. Puois, cant era davan lei, lai on era l'autr'amics e l'autra gens, a lui era semblans q'ella gardes lui plus qe tota l'autra gen. E maintas ves descresia so qe avia cresut, si con 10 deven far li fin amador, qe non deven creser so qe vesen dels oills, qe sia faillimens a soa domna. Don Berna(r)tz de Ventador si fez aqesta chanson qe dis:

Ar m'aconseillaz, seignor. 15

RAZO D

Bernart de Ventadorn loved a beautiful gentlewoman, serving her and honoring her so much that she did what he wished both in words and deeds. Their joy endured faithfully and pleasantly for a long while. But the lady's desire changed when she wished another lover. Bernart knew of this and was sadly grieved by it, and thought seriously of leaving her because it was so hard for him to bear the company of the other lover. Then he reflected, like anyone overcome with love, that it would be better to have half of her than to lose her entirely. Later, when he was with her, in the presence of his rival and others, it seemed to him that she looked at him more closely than at anyone else. Yet frequently he did not believe what he had thought, as ought indeed to be the case with all true lovers, who ought not to believe what they see with their own eyes, since in the opinion of their lady this may be considered a flaw. Then Bernart de Ventadorn composed the song where he says:

Now, my lords, give me your advice.

(Canso 6)

1. AB JOI MOU LO VERS E·L COMENS

I. Ab joi mou lo vers e·l comens
et ab joi reman e fenis,
e sol que bona fos la fis,
bos tenh qu'er lo comensamens.
    Per la bona comensansa 5
    mi ve jois et alegransa;
e per so dei la bona fi grazir
car totz bos faihz vei lauzar al fenir.

II. Si m'apodera jois e·m vens,
meravilh' es com o sofris 10
car no dic e non esbrüis
per cui sui tan gais e jauzens.
    Mas greu veiretz fin' amansa
    ses paor e ses doptansa
c'ades tem om vas so c'ama, falhir, 15
per qu'eu no·m aus de parlar enardir.

III. D'una re m'aonda mos sens,
c'anc nulhs om mo joi no·m enquis,
qu'eu volonters no l'en mentis;
car no·m par bos essenhamens 20
    ans es foli' et efansa
    qui d'amor a benanansa
ni·n vol so cor ad autre descobrir,
si no l'en pot o valer o servir.

IV. Non es enois ni falhimens 25
ni vilania, so m'es vis,
mas d'ome can se fai devis
d'autrui amor ni conoissens.
    Enoyos, e que·us enansa,
    si·m faitz enoi ni pesansa? 30

Chascus se vol de so mestier formir;
me cofondetz e vos no·n vei jauzir.

V. Ben estai a domn' ardimens
entr' avols gens e mals vezis,
e s'arditz cors no l'afortis,   35
greu pot esser pros ni valens.
    Per qu'eu prec n'aya membransa
    la bel' en cui ai fiansa
que no·s chamje per paraulas ni·s vir
qu'enemics, c'ai, fatz d'enveya morir.   40

VI. Anc sa bela bocha rizens
non cuidei baizan me träis,
car ab un doutz baizar m'aucis
si ab autre no m'es guirens;
    c'atretal m'es per semblansa   45
    com de Peläus la lansa
que del seu colp no podi' om garir
si autra vetz no s'en fezes ferir.

VII. Bela domna, ·l vostre cors gens
e·lh vostre belh olh m'an conquis   50
e·l doutz esgartz e lo clars vis
e·l vostre bels essenhamens
    que, can be m'en pren esmansa,
    de beautat no·us trob egansa.
La genser etz c'om posc' el mon chauzir,   55
o no i vei clar dels olhs ab que·us remir.

VIII. Bels Vezers, senes doptansa
sai que vostre pretz enansa,
que tantz sabetz de plazers far e dir,
de vos amar no·s pot nuls om sofrir.   60

IX.* Ben dei aver alegransa,
qu'en tal domn' ai m'esperansa,
que, qui·n ditz mal, no pot plus lag mentir
e qui·n ditz be, no pot plus bel ver dir.

1. AB JOI MOU LO VERS E·L COMENS   43

I. With Joy embarking I begin the verse, and with joy concluding it will end. Only when the ending is good, do I find the beginning good. In a good beginning, joy and happiness come to me, and so I shall welcome the good ending for I see all good deeds applauded at their end.

II. If joy overcomes and conquers me, it is a wonder that I endure it, since I keep silence, not disclosing why I am so gay and happy. But you will hardly see a true lover without reserve and shyness,* for a man is always afraid of failing the one he loves; therefore I dare not be bold and speak.

III. My common sense helps me in one thing: no man ever asked about my joy to whom I did not gladly lie about it. For it does not seem to me good manners, rather is it foolish and childish, for one who has good luck in love to be willing to reveal his heart to another, unless it can benefit or serve him.

IV. I hold that there is no vexation, vice, or villainy but that of the man who becomes the spy of other people's love. Say, meddler, what good does it do you to cause me worry? Each man wants to manage his own affairs: you ruin me, yet I do not see you happy about it.

V. Courage serves a lady well amid mean people and evil neighbors; and if a stout heart does not give her strength, she is unlikely to be distinguished or admirable. Therefore, I beg the beautiful woman, in whom I have faith, to be mindful of this and not to change or alter because of rumors. Then I can make my enemies die of envy.

VI. I never thought her beautiful, laughing mouth would betray me with a kiss, yet with a sweet kiss she slays me, unless she revives me with another. Her kiss, I think, is like the lance of Peleus,* from whose thrust a man could not be cured unless he were wounded by it once again.

VII. Beautiful lady, your delicate form and lovely eyes, your soft glance, radiant face and charming ways have conquered me; for, as I judge it, your equal in beauty cannot be found. You are the most beautiful that one could choose in all the world, or else I am not seeing clearly with the eyes that look upon you.

VIII. Bel Vezer, I know without a doubt that your worth increases, for you are so well-versed in saying and doing pleasing things that no man can keep from loving you.

IX.* Indeed, I should have great joy, for I place my hope in such a woman that whoever speaks ill of her cannot tell a more vicious lie, and whoever speaks well of her cannot utter a more beautiful truth.

2. AMICS BERNARTZ DE VENTADORN

I. Amics Bernartz de Ventadorn,
    com vos podetz de chant sofrir
    can aissi auzetz esbaudir
    lo rossinholet noih e jorn?
        Auyatz lo joi que demena. 5
    Tota noih chanta sotz la flor,
    melhs s'enten que vos en amor.

II. Peire, lo dormir e·l sojorn
    am mais que·l rossinhol auvir,
    ni ja tan no·m sabriatz dir 10
    que mais en la folia torn.
        Deu lau fors sui de chadena,
    e vos e tuih l'autr' amador
    etz remazut en la folor.

III. Bernartz, greu er pros ni cortes 15
    qui ab amor no·s sap tener,
    ni ja tan no·us fara doler
    que mais no valha c'autre bes,
        car, si fai mal, pois abena.
    Greu a om gran be ses dolor, 20
    mas ades vens lo jois lo plor.

IV. Peire, si fos dos ans o tres
    lo segles faihz al meu plazer,
    de domnas vos dic eu lo ver,
    non foran mais preyadas ges, 25
        ans sostengran tan greu pena
    qu'elas nos feiran tan d'onor
    c'ans nos prejaran que nos lor.

V. Bernartz, so non es d'avinen
    que domnas preyon. Ans cove   30
    c'om las prec e lor clam merce.
    Et es plus fols, mon escien,
        que cel qui semn' en l'arena,
    qui las blasma ni lor valor,
    e mou de mal ensenhador.   35

VI. Peire, mout ai lo cor dolen
    can d'una faussa me sove
    que m'a mort e no sai per que,
    mas car l'amava finamen.
        Faih ai longa carantena   40
    e sai, si la fezes lonhor,
    ades la trobara pejor.

VII. Bernartz, foudatz vos amena
     car aissi vos partetz d'amor,
     per cui a om pretz e valor.   45

VIII. Peire, qui ama, desena,
      car las trichairitz entre lor
      an tout joi e pretz e valor.

I. Bernart de Ventadorn, my friend, how can you refrain from singing when you hear the nightingale rejoicing day and night? Listen to the joy he expresses. All night he sings under the flower; he understands love better than you do.

II. Peire, I prefer sleep and rest to listening to the nightingale. As a matter of fact, no arguments you could find would persuade me to return to that foolishness. Thank God I am out of irons, while you and all the other lovers have stuck to folly.

III. Bernart, he who does not know how to stay firm in love is hardly worthy or chivalrous. Love will be worth more than any other good, even if it causes you so much grief; for if it causes pain, it compensates later on. A man can seldom have any real good without pain, but the joy always surpasses the weeping.

IV. Peire, if the world were the way I liked it for a couple of years, I'll tell you how it would be with women: they would not be courted at all; instead they would suffer such grief that they would do us the honor of courting us rather than we, them.

V. Bernart, it is not proper for women to court, rather should men court them and beg their grace. Whoever blames them or their virtue is, in my opinion, more foolish than one who sows in sand, and besides, he is prompted by a bad teacher.

VI. Peire, I really have an aching heart when I recall one faithless woman who has killed me. I don't know why, unless it was that I really loved her. I have made a long penance, and I know that if I were to do it any longer, I would find her worse than ever.

VII. Bernart, madness leads you on, since you abandon love by which one wins merit and virtue.

VIII. Peire, whoever loves is driven out of his mind, for the cheaters have stolen joy, worth, and merit.

3. AMORS, ENQUERA·US PREYARA

I. Amors, enquera·us preyara
que·m fossetz plus amoroza,
c'us paucs bes desadolora
gran re de mal, e paregra
s'era n'aguessetz merce. 5
Car de me no·us sove?
Mas e·m pes qu'enaissi·m prenha
com fetz al comensamen,
can me mis al cor la flama
de leis que·m fetz estar len, 10
c'anc no m'en detz jauzimen.

II. Mout viu a gran aliscara
et ab dolor angoissoza
selh cui totz tems assenhora
mala domna. Qu'eu m'estegra 15
jauzens, mas aissi m'ave
que leis cui dezir no cre
qu'eu l'am tan c'a mi covenha
l'onors ni·l bes qu'eu n'aten.
Et a·n tort, c'als no reclama 20
mos cors mas leis solamen
e so c'a leis es plazen.

III. Totz tems de leis me lauzara
s'era·m fos plus volontoza,
c'amors, qui·l cor enamora, 25
m'en det—mais no·m n'escazegra—
non plazers, mas sabetz que,
envey' e dezir ancse.
E s'a leis platz que·m retenha,
far pot de me so talen, 30
melhs no fa·l vens de la rama,

qu'enaissi vau leis seguen
con la folha sec lo ven.

IV. Tant es fresch' e bel' e clara
qu'amors n'es vas me doptoza,   35
car sa beutatz alugora
bel jorn e clarzis noih negra.
... ...
... ...
No·n dic laus, mas mortz mi venha   40
s'eu no l'am de tot mo sen.
Mas domn', Amors m'enliama
que·m fai dir soven e gen
de vos manh ver avinen.

V. Doussa res, conhd' et avara,   45
umils, franch' et orgolhoza,
bel' e genser c'ops no fora,
domna, per merce·us queregra,
car vos am mais c'autra re,
que·us prezes merces de me,   50
car tem que mortz me destrenha,
si pietatz no·us en pren.
E s'eu mor car mos cors ama
vos, vas cui res no·m defen,
tem que i fassatz falhimen.   55

VI. Soven plor tan que la chara
n'ai destrech' e vergonhoza,
e·l vis s'en dezacolora,
car vos, don jauzir me degra,
pert que de me no·us sove.   60
E no·m don Deus de vos be,
s'eu sai ses vos co·m chaptenha,
c'aitan doloirozamen
viu com cel que mor en flama.
E si tot no·m fatz parven,   65
nulhs om menhs de joi no sen.

I. Love, once again I would beg you to be more loving to me, since a little good takes the pain from great misfortune; and so it would be now, if you had compassion. Why do you not remember me? But I think that I may be affected as I was at the beginning, when I set a flame in my heart for the one who made me sad, the one you never let me enjoy.*

II. He who is always in the service of a wicked woman lives in great need and anguish. I would be joyous, but it happens that she whom I desire does not believe that I love her so much that the honor and benefit which I expect should come to me. But she is wrong, for my heart asks for nothing but the lady herself, and whatever pleases her.

III. I would always be satisfied with her if she were now more agreeable towards me; for love, who enamours the heart, gave me not pleasure, but—do you know what?—constant longing and desire (but, then, anything else would not be suitable for me).* And if it pleases her to keep me on, she can have her way with me, more than the wind does with the branch, for I follow her as the leaf follows the wind.

IV. So beautiful, fresh and radiant is she, that my love is timid before her,* for her beauty brightens the beautiful day and illuminates the dark night.

I should not praise her, but may death overtake me if I do not love her with all my heart. But lady, Love binds me and makes me frequently repeat many agreeable truths about you.

V. Sweet creature, charming and miserly, mild, fresh and haughty, more beautiful and fair than would ever be necessary, because I love you more than anything else, I beg you for the sake of pity, Lady, to have mercy on me. If you do not have compassion, I fear that I shall die. And if I die because my heart loves you —from whom I can in no way defend myself—I fear that the fault would be yours.

VI. Often I weep until I have distorted my face and am ashamed. My face pales because I am losing you—in whom I should have joy—since you do not think of me. And may God grant me nothing good from you, if I can get along without you, since I live as painfully as one who dies in fire. And 'though I do not show it, no man feels less joy.

4. AMORS, E QUE·US ES VEJAIRE?

I. Amors, e que·us es vejaire?
   Trobatz mais fol mas can me?
   Cuidatz vos qu'eu si' amaire
   e que ja no trop merce?
   Que que·m comandetz a faire, 5
   farai o c'aissi·s cove,
   mas vos non estai ges be
   que·m fassatz tostems mal traire.

II. Eu am la plus de bon aire
   del mon mais que nula re 10
   et ela no m'ama gaire,
   no sai cossi·s esdeve.
   E can plus m'en cuit estraire,
   eu no posc, c'Amors me te.
   Traitz sui per bona fe, 15
   Amors, be·us o posc retraire.

III. Ab Amor m'er a contendre,
   que no m'en posc estener,
   qu'en tal loc me fai entendre
   don eu nul joi non esper; 20
   anceis me fari' a pendre
   car anc n'aic cor ni voler,
   mas eu non ai ges poder
   que·m posca d'Amor defendre.

IV. Pero Amors sap dissendre 25
   lai on li ven a plazer
   e sap gen guizardo rendre
   del maltraih e del doler.
   Tan no·m pot mertsar ni vendre
   que plus no·m posca valer, 30

sol qu'Ela·m denhes vezer
e mas paraulas entendre.

V. Grans enois es e grans nauza
tot jorn de merce clamar,
mas l'amor qu'es en me clauza   35
no posc cobrir ni celar.
Las, mos cors no dorm ni pauza
ni pot en un loc estar,
ni eu no posc plus durar
si·lh dolors no·m asoauza.   40

VI. Eu sai be razon e chauza
que posc' a midons mostrar,
que nuls om no pot ni auza
enves Amor contrastar,
car Amor vens tota chauza   45
e forsa·m de leis amar;
atretal se pot leis far
en una petita pauza.

VII. Domna, res no vos pot dire
lo bo cor ni·l fin talan   50
qu'e·us ai, can be m'o cossire,
c'anc re mais non amei tan.
Tost m'agran mort li sospire,
domna, passat a un an,
no·m fos per un bel semblan,   55
don si doblan mei dezire.

VIII. No·n fatz mas gabar e rire,
domna, can eu re·us deman.
E si vos amassetz tan,
alres vos n'avengr' a dire.   60

IX. Ma chanson apren a dire,
Alegret; e tu, Ferran,
porta la·m a mo Tristan
que sap be gabar e rire.

4. AMORS, E QUE·US ES VEJAIRE?

I. Love, what do you think? Have you ever found a greater fool than I? Do you believe that I should be a lover even though I find no favor? Whatever you order me to do, I do, as is fitting. But it does not become you to treat me so badly all the time.

II. I love the most beautiful woman in the world more than anything else, and she scarcely loves me at all. I don't know how it comes about. Yet when I think about escaping, I cannot because Love holds me. I am betrayed through good faith, Love; surely I can reproach you for that.

III. I must struggle with Love, since I cannot keep away from it, but he makes me love where I have no hope of joy. It would be better if I should hang myself for ever having had the heart and the desire — but I do not have the strength to defend myself against love.

IV. Love, though, knows how to strike wherever he wants to, and he knows how to reward sadness and pain. So little can he barter or sell me that he is no longer any help to me, except when my lady is pleased to look at me and hear my words.

V. It is a great vexation and disturbance to plead for grace all the time, but I cannot conceal or cover up the love which is locked up within me. Alas, my heart neither sleeps nor rests and cannot even stay in one place. I can't endure much longer if the pain does not lessen.

VI. I know well what reasons and arguments I can show my lady. For no man can, or dares, oppose Love, since Love conquers all creatures and forces me to love her. He could do the same to her in a short time.

VII. Lady, when I think about it, there is nothing that can tell you the good heart and fine desire I have for you, since I have never loved another so much. Lady, sighs would have killed me over a year ago, if it were not for the beautiful sight which doubles my desire.

VIII. You do nothing but mock and laugh, Lady, whenever I beg you for grace. If you loved enough, it might occur to you to speak differently.

IX. Learn to sing my song, Alegret; and you, Ferrau, carry it for me to my Tristan, who well knows how to mock and to laugh.

5. ANC NO GARDEI SAZO NI MES

I. Anc no gardei sazo ni mes
ni can flors par ni can s'escon
ni l'erba nais delonc la fon,
mas en cal c'oras m'avengues
d'amor us rics esjauzimens, 5
tan me fo bels comensamens
qu'eu cre c'aquel tems senhorei.

II. Be l'agra per fol qui·m disses
tro aras qu'en sui tan prion
que ja·m tengues tan deziron 10
amors qu'eu morir en pogues,
mas aras sen e sui sabens
que totz autres mals es niens
vas lo dezir ab pauc d'esplei.

III. A, tan doussetamen me pres 15
la bela qui·m te jauzion
qued eu no·m posc saber vas on
re mais tan ben amar pogues;
car, on plus l'esgar, plus me vens
s'amors, e·m dobla mos talens 20
on eu mais d'autras domnas vei.

IV. Depus anc la vi m'a conques,
per que no l'er gen si·m cofon,
car volh mais perdre·ls olhs del fron
qu'eu ja re fassa c'a leis pes. 25
D'aitan cum poira, 'n essiens
no volh que·m si' adiramens,
que Deus aya faih de mi rei.

5. ANC NO GARDEI SAZO NI MES

V. Tota gens ditz que Vianes
    es la melher terra del mon   30
    e las melhors domnas i son;
    doncs sabon tuih c' aisso vers es
    c'aicestas son la plus valens,
    e midons, que totas la vens,
    es la melher qued el mon sei.   35

I. I never considered the seasons, nor the months, nor the time the flowers appear, nor the time when they hide, nor the grass born at the fountain's edge, but when a rich joy in love came to me, it was so beautiful a beginning that I believe such moments are the most perfect.*

II. Until now that I am so deeply involved, I would have considered anyone a fool who told me that love might keep me so full of longing that I could die. But now I feel that I know all other ills are nothing compared with a desire poorly satisfied.

III. Ah, with such sweetness did the beautiful lady, who keeps me joyful, seize me, and I do not know where I could love anyone else so well; for the more I see her, the more her love overcomes me, and my desire is increased the more I compare her with other women.

IV. Ever since I first saw her, she has overwhelmed me. Therefore it would not be right for her to ruin me, for I would rather lose the eyes from my head, than do anything which would trouble her. I would never wittingly do anything which might anger her, even if God were to make me a king.

V. Everyone says that Vienne is the best country in the world, and that the best women are there. Therefore let everyone know that this is true; and that those women are the worthiest, and that my lady, who surpasses all of them, is the best in the world.

6. ERA·M COSSELHATZ, SENHOR,

I. Era·m cosselhatz, senhor,
    vos, c'avetz saber e sen.
    Una domna·m det s'amor
    c'ai amada lonjamen,
    mas eras sai de vertat 5
    qu'ilh a autr' amic privat,
    ni anc de nul companho
    companha tan greus no·m fo.

II. D'una re sui en error
    e·n estau en pensamen, 10
    que m'alonje ma dolor
    s'eu aquest plaih li cossen.
    E s'aissi·l dic mon pessat,
    vei mo damnatge doblat.
    Cal que·n fassa o cal que no, 15
    re no posc far de mo pro.

III. E s'eu l'am a dezonor,
    esquerns er a tota gen,
    e tenran m'en li pluzor
    per cornut e per sofren. 20
    E s'aissi pert s'amistat,
    be·m tenh per dezeretat
    d'amor e ja Deus no·m do
    mais faire vers ni chanso.

IV. Pois voutz sui en la folor, 25
    be serai fols s'eu no pren
    d'aquestz dos mals lo menor.
    Que mais val mon essien
    qu'eu ay' en leis la meitat
    que·l tot perda per foldat, 30

6. ERA·M COSSELHATZ, SENHOR

   car anc a nul drut felo
   d'amor no vi far son pro.

V. Pois vol autre amador
   ma domn', eu no lo·lh defen.
   E lais m'en mais per paor   35
   que per autre chauzimen.
   E s'anc om dec aver grat
   de nul servizi forsat,
   be dei aver guizerdo
   eu que tan gran tort perdo.   40

VI. Li seu belh olh träidor,
   que m'esgardavon tan gen,
   s'atressi gardon alhor,
   mout i fan gran falhimen.
   Mas d'aitan m'an mout onrat   45
   que s'eron mil ajostat
   plus gardon lai on eu so
   c'a totz aicels d'eviro.

VII. De l'aiga que dels olhs plor
   escriu salutz mais de cen   50
   que tramet a la gensor
   et a la plus avinen.
   Manhtas vetz m'es pois membrat
   de so que·m fetz al comjat,
   qu'e·lh vi cobrir sa faisso   55
   c'anc no·m poc dir oc ni no.

VIII. Domna, a prezen amat
   autrui, e me a celat,
   si qu'eu n'aya tot lo pro
   et el la bela razo.   60

IX. Garsio, ara·m chantat
   ma chanso e la·m portat
   a mo Messager, qu'i fo,
   qu'e·lh quer cosselh qu'el me do.

I. Now, my Lords, give me your advice, you who have wisdom and sense: a woman whom I have loved a long time gave me her love. But I know for certain now that she has another secret lover, and never was the company of any companion so difficult for me.

II. I am troubled and worried about one thing: if I permit this affair, it will prolong my pain; and if I share my concern with her, I shall see my misfortune doubled. Whatever I say or do, I can do myself no good.

III. If I love her dishonorably, everyone will scorn me, and the majority will take me for horned and tolerant. And if I lose her friendship in this way, I shall certainly think myself robbed of love, and then may God no longer let me make verse or song.

IV. Since I have been driven to madness, I shall really be mad if I do not take the lesser of these two evils; in my opinion, it is better to have at least half of her than to lose her entirely through folly. For I have never seen any wicked lover advance his cause in love.

V. Then since my lady wants another lover, I will not forbid him to her, though I permit it more because of fear than anything else. If any man should ever receive thanks for an enforced service, I should certainly have a reward for pardoning such a great wrong.

VI. If her beautiful, treacherous eyes, which glanced at me so gently, look elsewhere in the same way, they commit a great offense. But in one thing they have honored me greatly: if a thousand people were gathered together, her eyes would look more where I am, than at all the others 'round about.

VII. With the water that I weep from my eyes, I inscribe more than a hundred greetings which I send to the most gracious and to the most beautiful lady. Then many times I remember what she did to me at our parting: I saw her cover her face so that she could not tell me yes or no.

VIII. Lady, love another in public, and me in secret, so I may have all the benefits and he the fine talk.

IX. Garsior, sing my song for me now, and carry it for me to my Messager, who was there, and I seek from him the advice that he may give me.

7. ARA NO VEI LUZIR SOLELH

I. Ara no vei luzir solelh,
    tan me son escurzit li rai,
    e ges per aisso no·m esmai,
       c'una clardatz me solelha
       d'amor qu'ins el cor me raya; 5
       e, can autra gens s'esmaya,
    eu melhur enans que sordei,
       per que mos chans no sordeya.

II. Prat me semblon vert e vermelh
    aissi com el doutz tems de mai; 10
    si·m te fin' amors conhd' e gai,
       neus m'es flors blanch' e vermelha
       et iverns calenda maya,
       que·l genser e la plus gaya
    m'a promes que s'amor m'autrei. 15
       S'anquer no la·m desautreya?

III. Paor mi fan malvatz cosselh,
    per que·l segles mor e dechai;
    c'aras s'ajoston li savai
       e l'us ab l'autre cosselha 20
       cossi fin' amors dechaya.
       A, malvaza gens savaya
    qui vos ni vostre cosselh crei
       Domnideu perd' e descreya.

IV. D'aquestz mi rancur e·m corelh 25
    qu'ira me fan dol et esglai
    e pesa lor del joi qu'eu ai.
       E pois chascus s'en corelha
       de l'autrui joi ni s'esglaya,
       ja eu melhor dreih no·n aya, 30

        c'ab sol deport venz' e guerrei
           cel qui plus fort me guerreya.

V. Noih e jorn pes, cossir e velh,
    planh e sospir; e pois m'apai.
    On melhs m'estai, et eu peihz trai.   35
        mas us bos respeihz m'esvelha
        don mos cossirers s'apaya.
        Fols, per que dic que mal traya,
    car aitan rich' amor envei,
        pro n'ai de sola l'enveya.   40

VI. Ja ma domna no·s meravelh
    si·lh quer que·m do s'amor ni·m bai.
    Contra la foudat qu'eu retrai
        fara i genta meravelha
        s'ilh ja m'acola ni·m baya.   45
        Deus s'er ja c'om me retraya
    —a, cal vos vi e cal vos vei—
        per benanansa que·m veya?

VII. Fin' Amor ab vos m'aparelh.
    Pero no·s cove ni s'eschai,   50
    mas car per vostra merce·us plai,
        Deus cuit que m'o aparelha,
        c'aitan fin' amors m'eschaya.
        Ai, domna, per merce·us playa
    c'ayatz de vostr' amic mercei,   55
        pus aitan gen vos merceya.

VIII. Bernartz clama sidons mercei,
        vas cui tan gen se merceya.

IX. E si eu en breu no la vei,
    non crei que lonjas la veya.   60

7. ARA NO VEI LUZIR SOLELH

I. Now I cannot see the sun shining, so hidden are the rays from me; and yet, I am not alarmed by this, because one brightness shining within my heart illuminates me with love. And, when other people are alarmed, I get better rather than worse, because my song does not fail.

II. The meadow seems green and crimson to me, just as in the sweet season of May. Since true love, charming and gay, fills me, snow to me is like red and white flowers, and winter seems like May day, for the prettiest and gayest one has promised to grant me her love. But does she not still deny it to me?

III. Fear gives me bad advice, and thus the world withers and dies. Now the vulgar gather and advise one another how to overthrow true love. Ah, wretched, pig-headed people, may whoever believes you and your advice lose God and become a disbeliever.

IV. I protest and complain about them because they cause me vexation, sadness and fear, and any joy I have pains them. Then each one complains of the joy of the other, and is dismayed. I would like to have no greater justice than, only for my amusement, to attack and conquer whoever attacks me most fiercely.

V. Night and day I think, worry and stay awake, weep and sigh; and then I am appeased. The better off I am, the worse I feel. But one good hope which eases my worry awakens me. Fool, why do I say that I suffer? Since I desire such a rich love, the desire itself is a reward.

VI. Indeed, my lady should not be surprised if I ask her to give me her love and to kiss me. She would perform a real miracle against this madness I speak of, if she embraced and kissed me. God, will people ever speak of the good fortune they see in me? Ah, what good fortune I saw, and see in you!

VII. True Love, I cloak myself with you. Not because it is right or necessary, but because in your grace it pleases you that such true love befalls me — God, I think, prepares it for me. Ah, lady, through grace may it please you to have grace for your friend, since he thanks you so politely.

VIII. Bernart cries out for grace from his lady to whom he gives thanks so politely.

IX. And if I do not see her soon, I think I may not see her for a long while.

8. A, TANTAS BONAS CHANSOS

I. A, tantas bonas chansos
    e tan bo vers aurai faih
    don ja no·m mezer' en plaih
    domna si·m pesses de vos
    que fossetz vas me tan dura.   5
    Aras sai qu'e·us ai perduda,
    mas sivals no m'etz tolguda
    en la mia forfachura.

II. Vers es que manhtas sazos
    m'era be dih e retraih   10
    que m'estara mal e laih
    c'ames et amatz no fos.
    Mas lai on Amors s'atura
    er greu forsa defenduda,
    si so coratge no muda   15
    si c'alors meta sa cura.

III. Mas era sui tan joyos
    que no·m sove del maltraih.
    D'ira e d'esmai m'a traih
    ab sos bels olhs amoros,   20
    de que·m poizon' e·m fachura
    cilh que m'a joya renduda,
    c'anc pois qu'eu l'agui veguda
    non agui sen ni mezura.

IV. Mout i fetz Amors que pros,   25
    car tan ric joi m'a pertraih;
    tot can m'avia forfaih
    val ben aquest guizerdos.
    Aissi·l fenis ma rancura
    que sa valors e s'ayuda   30

m'es a tal cocha venguda;
totz sos tortz i adrechura.

V. Qui ve sas belas faissos
ab que m'a vas se atraih
pot be saber atrazaih   35
que sos cors es bels e bos
e blancs sotz la vestidura
— eu non o dic mas per cuda —
que la neus can ilh es nuda
par vas lei brun' et escura.   40

VI. Domna si'st fals enveyos
que mainh bo jorn m'an estraih
s'i metion en agaih
per saber com es de nos,
per dih d'avol gen tafura   45
non estetz ges esperduda;
ja per me non er saubuda
l'amors, be·n siatz segura.

VII.* Bels Vezers un'aventura
avetz et es ben saubuda   50
qued om que·us aya veguda
de vos no fara rancura.

VIII.* Chanso vai t'en a La Mura,
mo Bel Vezer me saluda;
qui c'aya valor perduda,   55
la sua creis e melhura.

I. Ah, so many good songs and such good verses I would have made, Lady, in which I would not have complained if I might have thought of you, who were so harsh to me. Now I know that I have lost you. But at least you have not been taken from me through my own fault.

II. It is true that often I said to myself that she was mean and spiteful to me, for I loved and was not loved. But where

Love attacks, the fort is held only with great difficulty, unless Love changes his mind and directs his attention elsewhere.

III. But now I am so joyous that I do not remember the mistreatment. She who has restored joy to me has lured me away from anger and dismay with her beautiful loving eyes — those same ones with which she bewitched and enchanted me. For ever since I saw her I have had neither wit nor composure.

IV. Love labored brilliantly there, in preparing such rich joy for me. This reward is fair compensation for all the harm of which Love has been guilty to me. And so ends my rancor, since his strength and succor so come to me in my urgent need that they atone for all his wrongs.

V. Whoever sees the beautiful features with which she has attracted me may truly know that her body is fine and beautiful and white under her clothing (I speak only from imagination) so that the newfallen snow seems brown and dark compared to her.

VI. Lady, even if these false, envious men, who have stolen many good days from me, have been watching to find out how it is with us, you are still not lost through the chatter of base, knavish louts. For our love is not known through me; you may be well assured of that.

VII.* Bel Vezer, one thing about you is well-known: that whoever saw you would not hold it against you.

VIII.* Song, go off to La Mura; greet my Bel Vezer for me. No matter who else has lost worthiness, hers increases and grows better.

9. BEL M'ES CAN EU VEI LA BROLHA

I. Bel m'es can eu vei la brolha
reverdir per mei lo brolh
e·lh ram son cubert de folha
e·l rossinhols sotz lo folh
chanta d'amor, don me dolh. 5
E platz me qued eu m'en dolha,
ab sol qued amar me volha
cela qu'eu dezir e volh.

II. Eu la volh can plus s'orgolha
vas me, mas oncas orgolh 10
n'ac vas lei. Per so m'acolha
ma domna, pois tan l'acolh
c'a totas autras me tolh
per lei, cui Deus no me tolha.
Ans li do cor qu'en grat colha 15
so que totz jorns s'amor colh.

III. S'amor colh, qui m'enpreizona,
per lei que mala preizo
me fai, c'ades m'ochaizona
d'aisso don ai ochaizo. 20
Tort n'a mas eu lo·lh perdo,
e mos cors li reperdona,
car tan la sai bel' e bona
que tuih li mal m'en son bo.

IV. Bo son tuih li mal que·m dona. 25
Mas per Deu li quer un do,
que ma bocha, que jeona,
d'un douz baizar dejeo.
Mas trop quer gran guizardo
celei que tan guizardona. 30

   E can eu l'en arazona,
   ilh me chamja ma razo.

V. Ma razo chamja e vira,
   mas eu ges de lei no·m vir
   mo fi cor, que la dezira   35
   aitan que tuih mei dezir
   son de lei per cui sospir.
   E car ela no sospira,
   sai qu'en lei ma mortz se mira
   can sa gran beutat remir.   40

VI. Ma mort remir que jauzir
   no·n posc ni no·n sui jauzire.
   Mas eu sui tan bos sofrire
   c'atendre cuit per sofrir.

  I. It pleases me when I see the trees become green again throughout the woods, the branches covered with leaves, and, under the foliage, the nightingale singing of love, the cause of my suffering. And it pleases me that I suffer from it, provided that she whom I want and desire will want to love me.

  II. I want her when she is most proud toward me; but I am never proud toward her.* Therefore may my lady welcome me, since I welcome her so much that on her account I deprive myself of all others. May God never deprive me of her. Rather may he give her the desire to accept gracefully my constant devotion to her love.

  III. I embrace her love, which imprisons me, for the sake of her who fashions my dreadful prison; and though she is forever reproaching me, it is I rather who have reason to reproach her. She is wrong, but I forgive her for it; and my heart forgives her again, for I know she is so beautiful and good that all her ills are good in my eyes.

  IV. All the ills she gives me are good; but for God's sake I ask of her one gift, that with a sweet kiss she feed my fasting mouth. But I ask too great a reward of the one who rewards so much; and when I reason with her about it she distorts my reasoning.

V. She distorts and turns my reasoning, but from her I do not turn my faithful heart, which desires her so much that all my desires are for her whom I sigh for; and since she does not sigh, I know that my death is seen in her when I see her great beauty.

VI. I see my death, so that I cannot rejoice or be joyful; but I am so good at enduring that I hope to win through endurance.

10. BEL M'ES QU'EU CHAN EN AQUEL MES

I. Bel m'es qu'eu chan en aquel mes
can flor e folha vei parer
et au lo chan doutz pel defes
del rossinhol matin e ser.
    Adoncs s'eschai qu'eu aya jauzimen 5
    d'un joi verai en que mos cors s'aten,
    car eu sai be que per amor morrai.

II. Amors, e cals onors vos es
ni cals pros vo·n pot eschazer
s'aucizetz celui c'avetz pres,
qu'enves vos no s'auza mover?
    Mal vos estai car dols de me no·us pren
    c'amat aurai en perdos lonjamen
    celei on ja merce no trobarai.

III. Pois vei que preyars ni merces 15
ni servirs no·m pot pro tener,
per amor de Deu me fezes
ma domna cal que bo saber.
    Que gran be fai us paucs de jauzimen
    a cel que trai tan gran mal com eu sen. 20
    e s'aissi mor requisitz li serai.

IV. Garit m'agra si m'aucizes,
c'adoncs n'agra faih son voler;
mas eu no cre qu'ela fezes
re c'a me tornes a plazer. 25
    Agra·n esglai e penedera s'en?
    ja no creirai no m'am cubertamen
    mas cela s'en vas me per plan essai.

10. BEL M'ES QU'EU CHAN EN AQUEL MES

V. Del major tort qu'eu anc lh'agues
vos dirai si·us voletz lo ver:
amara la s'a leis plagues
e servira·lh de mo poder.
    Mas no s'eschai qu'ilh am tan paubramen;
    pero be sai c'assatz for' avinen,
que ges amors segon ricor no vai.

VI. Gran mal m'a faih ma bona fes
que·m degra vas midons valer
e s'eu ai falhit ni mespres
per trop amar ni per temer,
    doncs que farai? Ai las chaitiu dolen
    c'a totz es mai de bel aculhimen,
mas me tot sol azira e dechai.

VII. El mon non es mas una res
per qu'eu joya pogues aver
e d'aquela no·n aurai ges
ni d'autra no·n posc ges voler.
    Pero si ai per leis valor e sen
    e·n sui plus gai e·n tenc mo cors plus gen,
car s'ilh no fos, ja no m'en meir' en plai.

VIII. Messatger vai e porta me corren
ma chanso lai a Mo Frances part Mauren,
e digas li·m que breumen lo verai.

    I. It is my delight to sing in this month when I see flowers and leaves appear and hear the sweet song of the nightingale morning and evening in the groves. Then it is fitting that I take consolation from one true joy — the hope of my heart — for I know that I will surely die of love.

    II. Love, what honor is yours and what advantage can come to you if you should kill the one you have captured, who does not dare stir against you? You do wrong in withholding pity from me, for I have long loved in vain one in whom I shall never find mercy.

III. Since I see that neither supplication nor favor nor service can avail me, for the love of God, let my lady do something to please me. For a little joy does great good for one who suffers the great misfortune I feel; and if I die of it, she will stand condemned.*

IV. She would have cured me if she had killed me, for then she would have accomplished her will. But I do not believe that she would do anything that would bring me pleasure. Would she be afraid and would she repent of it? I shall never believe that she does not secretly love me, but she hides it from me simply to test me.

V. If you wish, I will tell you the truth about the greatest wrong I ever had from her. I would love her, if it pleased her, and serve her to the best of my ability. But it is not right for her to love so poorly; I know rather that it would be very gracious of her to love well, for love is not at all concerned with riches.

VI. My good faith, which should have helped me with my lady, has done me great harm. And if I have made a mistake or am guilty of loving or fearing her too much, then what shall I do? Alas, sad wretch! For everyone else there is always a good welcome; on me alone she vents her hate and punishment.

VII. There is only one person in the world from whom I could have joy; but I shall never have any from her, and I do not want it from anyone else. Yet through her I have virtue and wisdom and I am gayer and feel better, for if it were not for her, I would never strive for these things.

VIII. Messenger, go, and swiftly carry my song to my French friend by Mauren, and tell him that I will see him soon.

11. BELS MONRUELS, AICEL QUE·S PART DE VOS.

Appel attributes this poem to Peire Rogier, rather than to Bernart. It may be found in Appel's edition of Peire Rogier (Berlin, 1882), p. 88ff.

12. BE M'AN PERDUT LAI ENVES VENTADORN

I. Be m'an perdut lai enves Ventadorn
tuih mei amic pois ma domna no m'ama,
et es be dreihz que ja mais lai no torn,
c'ades estai vas me salvatj' e grama.
Ve·us per que·m fai semblan irat e morn, 5
car en s'amor me deleih e·m sojorn
ni de ren als no·s rancura ni·s clama.

II. Aissi co·l peis qui s'eslaiss' el cadorn
e no·n sap mot tro que s'es pres en l'ama
m'eslaissei eu vas trop amar un jorn, 10
c'anc no·m gardei tro fui en mei la flama,
que m'art plus fort no·m feira focs de forn;
e ges per so no·m posc partir un dorn,
aissi·m te pres s'amors e m'aliama.

III. No·m meravilh si s'amors me te pres, 15
que genser cors no crei qu'el mon se mire:
bels e blancs es e frescs e gais e les
e totz aitals com eu volh e dezire.
No posc dir mal de leis que non i es,
qu'e·l n'agra dih de joi s'eu li saubes, 20
mas no li sai per so m'en lais de dire.

IV. Totz tems volrai sa onor e sos bes
e·lh serai om et amics e servire
e l'amarai be li plass' o be·lh pes
c'om no pot cor destrenher ses aucire; 25
no sai domna volgues o no volgues
si·m volia c'amar no la pogues
mas totas res pot om en mal escrire.

12. BE M'AN PERDUT LAI ENVES VENTADORN

V. A las autras sui ...... eschazutz.
    la cals se vol me pot vas se atraire,
    per tal cove que no·m sia vendutz
    l'onors ni·l bes que m'a en cor a faire;
    qu'enoyos es preyars pos er perdutz,
    per me·us o dic que mals m'en es vengutz,
    car träit m'a la bela de mal aire.

VI. En Proensa tramet jois e salutz
    e mais de bes c'om no lor sap retraire,
    e fatz esfortz, miracles e vertutz,
    car eu lor man de so don non ai gaire
    qu'eu non ai joi, mas tan can m'en adutz
    mos Bels Vezers e'n Fachura mos drutz
    e'n Alvernhatz lo senher de Belcaire.

VII. Mos Bels Vezers per vos fai Deus vertutz
     tals c'om no·us ve que no si' ereubutz
     dels bels plazers que sabetz dir e faire.

I. All my friends in Ventadorn have surely lost me because my lady does not love me; and it is quite right that I never return, for she is always harsh and ill-disposed toward me. This is why she shows me an angry and gloomy appearance: because I delight and find pleasure in her love. For no other reason does she complain and protest.

II. Like a fish who rushes to the bait and suspects nothing until he has caught himself on the hook, I let myself go one day and did not take care until I was in the midst of the flame which burns me more fiercely than fire in an oven. And I cannot break away by a hand's breadth, so close does her love hold me and bind me.

III. I do not wonder that her love holds me close, for I believe no more beautiful body is to be seen in the world; it is lovely, white, fresh and smooth, exactly as I want and desire it. I cannot speak evil of her because there is none in her; if I had known any,

I would have spoken of it gladly, but I do not know any, and therefore I say nought of it.

IV. I shall always wish her well both in honor and good fortune, and I shall be her vassal, lover and servant. I shall love her whether it pleases her or grieves her, for one cannot force a heart without killing it. I do not know any woman whom I could not love, if I wanted, whether she liked it or not. But one can put the wrong interpretation on anything.*

V. I have fallen to the others; whoever wishes may draw me to her on condition that the honor and good she has in mind to do me are not sold* for it is annoying to beg in vain. For my part, I say that evil has come to me because the beautiful lady of adverse temperament has deceived me.

VI. To Provence I send joy and greetings and more good than one can recount. I perform deeds, wonders and marvels in that I am sending to them what I do not have myself; for I have no joy other than that brought to me by my Bel Vezer and my friend, Lord Fachura, and Lord Alvernhat of Belcaire.

VII. My Bel Vezer, God does such miracles through you that no one can look at you without being enraptured by the fair and winsome things you know how to say and do.

13. BE·M CUIDEI DE CHANTAR SOFRIR

I.   Be·m cuidei de chantar sofrir
     entro lai el doutz tems suau,
     eras, pus negus no s'esjau
     e pretz e donar vei morir,
     no posc mudar no prenha cura   5
     d'un vers novel a la frejura
     que conortz er als autres entre lor;
     e cove·m be, pois tan be·m vai d'amor,
     c'aya melhor solatz a tota gen.

II. Domna, vas cal que part que·m vir,   10
     ab vos remanh et ab vos vau
     e sapchatz que de vos me lau
     assatz mais que no sai grazir.
     Be conosc que mos pretz melhura
     per la vostra bon' aventura   15
     e car vos plac que·m fezetz tan d'onor
     lo jorn que·m detz en baizan vostr' amor,
     del plus, si·us platz, prendetz esgardamen.

III. Amors, aissi·m faitz trassalhir
     del joi qu'eu ai, no vei ni au   20
     ni no sai que·m dic ni que·m fau.
     Cen vetz trobi, can m'o cossir,
     qu'eu degr' aver sen e mezura
     — si m'ai adoncs mas pauc me dura —
     c'al reduire·m torna·l jois en error;   25
     pero be sai c'uzatges es d'amor
     c'om c'ama be non a gaire de sen.

IV. Greu en sabrai mo melhs chauzir
     si sas belas faissos mentau,
     que res mas lauzars no·m abau   30

    e sas grans beutatz essernir.
    Res mais no m'en dezasegura,
    pois tant es douss' e fin' e pura,
   gran paor ai qu'azesme sa valor,
   e lauzenger volon mo dan d'amor   35
   e diran l'en be leu adiramen.

V. Doncs lor deuri'eu be servir,
    pois vei que re guerra no·m vau,
    que s'ab lauzengers estau mau
    greu·m poiria d'amor jauzir.   40
    Per leis es razos e mezura
    qu'eu serva tota creatura
   neis l'enemic dei apelar senhor
   c'ab gen parlar conquer om melhs d'amor
   tot lo pejor ad ops de be volen.   45

VI. Amors, cil que·us volon delir
    son enoyos e disliau,
    e si·us deschanton, me qu'en cau?
    No·s podon melhs envilanir;
    be conosc a lor parladura   50
    qu'ilh renhon mal contra natura.
   Cist an perdut vergonha e paor
   partit de Deu tot per sordeg d'amor
   et eu sui fols si mais ab lor conten.

VII. Ventadorn er greu mais ses chantador,   55
   que·l plus cortes e que mais sap d'amor
   m'en essenhet aitan com eu n'apren.

  I. I thought I would refrain from singing until the sweet and gentle season. Now since no one rejoices, and I see virtue and generosity dying out, I cannot help but strive in this frost for a new song which will be a comfort to others. This is only proper since I get such good from love that I have the best consolation for everyone.

II. Lady, wherever I turn, I come and go with you. Know that I am happier with you than I can say. I realize that my worth improves through your good influence, and since it pleased you to do me such honor the day you gave me your love with a kiss, please think about giving me the rest.

III. Love, you make me tremble so that, in my excitement, I do not see, hear, or know what I am saying or doing. A hundred times a day I force myself to remember that I should have wit and composure, and then I have it, but it does not last long, for joy finally turns to anguish. But I realize that it is customary in love for one who loves well to have scarcely any joy at all.

IV. When I talk about her beautiful features, I hardly know how to choose my best terms, for nothing is fitting save only for me to praise her great beauties. She is so sweet, charming and pure; this troubles me more than anything else. I am afraid she may realize her own worth and then the slanderers seeking my love's ill may incite her against me.

V. But I ought to work for them, since I see that fighting them does not help me. If the slanderers are not pleased with me, I shall scarcely be able to get any joy from love. It is right and fitting for me to serve all creatures for her sake, and even to call my enemy "Sir". For courteous speech is the best means to persuade even the worst creatures to look benevolently on love.

VI. Love, those who want to destroy you are disloyal boors. But what do I care if they speak evil of you? They cannot but make themselves more base. I can easily tell from their chatter that they behave badly and contrary to nature. By slandering love, they have lost shame and fear and have forsaken God. So it is silly to argue further with them.

VII. Ventadorn will scarcely be without a troubadour any longer, for the most courteous of all, the one who knows most about love, has taught me everything I know about it.

14. BERNART DE VENTADORN, DEL CHAN

I. Bernart de Ventadorn, del chan
vos sui sai vengutz assalhir.
Car vos vei estar en cossir,
no posc mudar que no·us deman
co·us vai d'amor. Avetz-en ges? 5
Be par que no·us en venha bes.

II. Lemozi, no·us posc en chantan
respondre ne i sai avenir,
mos cors me vol de dol partir.
Bels amics, a Deu vos coman 10
que mort m'a una mala res,
c'anc no·n me valc Deus ni merces.

III. Bernart, s'anc no·us fetz bel semblan,
enquera·s pot esdevenir.
No·s tanh c'om ab amor s'azir 15
can la troba de son talan;
pauc gazanha drutz d'ira ples,
car per un dol n'a dos o tres.

IV. Lemozi, mout fetz gran enjan
la bela qui·m pogr' enrequir, 20
que, can mi poc de se aizir,
et ela·m tornet en soan.
No i a conort qui fort no·m pes,
car o ilh es, cosselh no·n pres.

V. Bernart, totz om deu aver dan, 25
s'a la cocha no sap sofrir,
c'amors se vol soven servir,
e si so tenetz ad afan,

tot es perdut, s'anc re·us promes,
si n' eran plevidas mil fes. 30

I. Bernard of Ventadorn, I have come here to assault you with song. Since I see you are in misery, I cannot help asking how your love fares. Do you derive any benefit from it? It surely seems that no good comes to you from it.

II. Lemozi, I cannot answer you in singing; I would not know where to begin. My heart wants to break from grief. Dear friend, God be with you, for an evil thing has killed me, and neither God nor grace ever helped me.

III. Bernard, even if she never appeared friendly to you, there is still a chance. It is not right for one to become angry with love when it does not turn out as his desire fancies it.* An angry lover gains little since instead of one pain he has two or three.

IV. Lemozi, the beauty who could have enriched me practiced very great deceit; for when I might have enjoyed her, she scorned me. There is absolutely no comfort for me, only pain, for where she is concerned, I have no counsel.

V. Bernard, every man must have pain if he cannot endure in time of need; for love wants constant service; and if you consider this a burden, all is lost, even if she once promised you something, and even if a thousand oaths were sworn.

15. CHANTARS NO POT GAIRE VALER

I. Chantars no pot gaire valer
    si d'ins dal cor no mou lo chans,
    ni chans no pot dal cor mover
    si no i es fin' amors coraus.
    Per so es mos chantars cabaus   5
    qu'en joi d'amor ai et enten
    la boch' e·ls olhs e·l cor e·l sen.

II. Ja Deus no·m don aquel poder
    que d'amor no·m prenda talans.
    Si ja re no·n sabi' aver,   10
    mas chascun jorn m'en vengues maus,
    totz tems n'aurai bo cor sivaus,
    e n'ai mout mais de jauzimen
    car n'ai bo cor e m'i aten.

III. Amor blasmen per no-saber   15
     fola gens, mas leis no·n es dans,
     c'amors no·n pot ges dechazer
     si non es amors comunaus.
     Aisso non es amors; aitaus
     no·n a mas lo nom e·l parven   20
     que re non ama si no pren.

IV. S'eu en volgues dire lo ver,
    eu sai be de cui mou l'enjans,
    d'aquelas c'amon per aver
    e son merchandandas venaus.   25
    Messongers en fos eu e faus,
    vertat en dic vilanamen,
    e peza me car eu no·n men.

15. CHANTARS NO POT GAIRE VALER 81

V. En agradar et en voler
es l'amors de dos fis amans. 30
Nula res no i pot pro tener
si·lh voluntatz non es egaus.
E cel es be fols naturaus
que, de so que vol, la repren
e·lh lauza so que no·lh es gen. 35

VI. Mout ai be mes mo bon esper
cant cela·m mostra bels semblans
qu'eu plus dezir e volh vezer,
francha, doussa, fin' e leiaus,
en cui lo reis seria saus, 40
bel' e conhd', ab cors covinen,
m'a faih ric ome de nien.

VII. Re mais no·n am ni sai temer
ni ja res no·m seri' afans,
sol midons vengues a plazer. 45
C'aicel jorns me sembla nadaus
c'ab sos bels olhs espiritaus
m'esgarda, mas so fai tan len
c'us sols dias me dura cen.

VIII. Lo vers es fis e naturaus 50
e bos celui qui be l'enten,
e melher es, qui·l joi aten.

IX. Bernartz de Ventadorn l'enten
e·l di e·l fai e·l joi n'aten.

I. There is no use in singing if the song does not spring from the heart; and the song cannot spring from the heart if there is no true love there. And so my singing is superior because I have joy in love and devote my lips and eyes and heart and mind to it.

II. May God never give me the strength not to desire love. Even if I knew that I would never have anything from it, but that each day would bring me sorrow, at least I would always have a good heart; and I have much more joy because I have a good heart and I strive hard.

III. Foolish people criticize love out of ignorance; but there is no harm done, for love cannot be destroyed as long as it is not vulgar love. That is not love; it has nothing but the name and appearance of it and is not interested in anything it cannot profit from.

IV. If I wanted to tell the truth about it, I know well with whom the deceit began: with those who love for money. They are nothing but whores! I wish I could lie about it and cover it up, but shamefully I speak the truth; and it grieves me that I am not lying.

V. The love of two true lovers lies in accord and assent. Nothing avails if the wills are not equal. And he is a true fool who reproaches love for its desires, and asks it for what is not fitting.

VI. I have great hope whenever she whom I most desire and long to see, the noble, sweet, genuine and loyal one in whom a king would find salvation, shows me a friendly face. Beautiful and graceful, with a lovely body, she has made me into a rich man from nothing.

VII. I love and fear no one more than her; and nothing would ever be a hardship for me if only it pleased my lady. The day when she looks at me with her beautiful, spiritual eyes seems like Christmas to me; and she does it so lingeringly that one single day lasts me a hundred.

VIII. The verse is perfect and well-written and good if one understands it well. And it is better for one who hopes for joy.

IX. Bernard of Ventadorn conceived it, wrote it and hopes for joy from it.

16. CONORTZ, ERA SAI EU BE

I. Conortz, era sai eu be
    que ges de me no pensatz
    pois salutz ni amistatz
    ni messatges no m'en ve.
    Trop cuit que fatz lonc aten,   5
    et er be semblans oimai
    qu'eu chasse so c'autre pren
    pois no m'en ven aventura.

II. Bels Conortz, can me sove
    com gen fui per vos onratz   10
    e can era m'oblidatz,
    per un pauc no·n mor desse.
    Qu'eu eis m'o vauc enqueren
    qui·m met de foudat em plai
    can eu midons sobrepren   15
    de la mia forfaitura.

III. Per ma colpa m'esdeve
    que ja no·n sia privatz,
    car vas leis no sui tornatz
    per foudat que m'en rete.   20
    Tan n'ai estat lonjamen
    que de vergonha qu'eu n'ai
    non aus aver l'ardimen
    que i an, s'ans no m'asegura.

IV. Ilh m'encolpet de tal re   25
    don me degra venir gratz.
    Fe qu'eu dei a l'Alvernhatz,
    tot o fi per bona fe.
    E s'eu en amar mespren,
    tort a qui colpa m'en fai   30

84 THE SONGS OF BERNART DE VENTADORN

      car, qui en amor quer sen,
      cel non a sen ni mezura.

V.   Tan er gen servitz per me
      sos fers cors, durs et iratz,
      tro del tot si'adoussatz   35
      ab bels dihz et ab merce.
      Qu'eu ai be trobat legen
      que gota d'aiga que chai
      fer en un loc tan soven
      tro chava la peira dura.   40

VI.   Qui be remira ni ve
      olhs e gola, fron e faz,
      aissi son finas beutatz
      que mais ni menhs no i cove,
      cors lonc, dreih e covinen,   45
      gen afliban, conhd' e gai.
      Om no·l pot lauzar tan gen
      com la saup formar Natura.

VII. Chansoneta, ar t'en vai
      a Mo Frances, l'avinen,   50
      cui pretz enans' e melhura.

VIII. E digas li que be·m vai,
      car de Mo Conort aten
      enquera bon' aventura.

    I. Conort, now I know for sure that you are not thinking of me at all, since no greeting, no token of friendship, no message comes from you. Too long, I think, I have been waiting and now it seems certain that I am forever hunting what another catches, since no good fortune comes to me.

    II. Bel Conort, when I remember how fairly I was honored by you, and how you now forget me, I could die on the spot. I have only myself to blame* if anyone accuses me of folly, because I reproach my lady for my own crime.

III. It is my own fault that I can never be intimate with her, since I have not returned to her because of the folly which holds me back. I am so ashamed to have been away from her for so long that I do not dare be so bold as to go to her, unless she first encourages me.

IV. She blames me for something for which I should receive thanks. By the faith I owe to Alvernhat, I did it all in good faith. And if I err in love, one is wrong to blame me for it, because whoever looks for sense in love has himself no sense or reason.

V. Her cruel heart, hard and embittered, will be well-served by me until it is completely softened with beautiful words and compassion; for I have learned in my reading that a drop of water continually falling and striking the same spot may pierce the hard stone.

VI. If one looks closely and sees her eyes and throat, forehead and face, then he will see that her beauty is so perfectly proportioned that to add or take away anything would impair it: her slender body, straight and graceful, finely clothed, comely and gay. No one can praise her so finely as nature knew how to create her.

VII. Little song, go now to my French friend the handsome one, whose good fame spreads and grows.

VIII. And tell him that I am well, for I still expect good fortune from my Conort.

17. EN COSSIRER ET EN ESMAI

I. En cossirer et en esmai
sui d'un' amor que·m lass' e·m te,
que tan no vau ni sai ni lai
qu'ilh ades no·m tenh' en so fre,
c'aras m'a dat cor e talen 5
    qu'eu enqueses si podia
    tal que si·l reis l'enqueria
auria faih gran ardimen.

II. Ai las, chaitius, e que·m farai
ni cal cosselh penrai de me? 10
Qu'ela no sap lo mal qu'eu trai
ni eu no·lh aus clamar merce.
Fol nesci, ben as pauc de sen,
    qu'ela nonca t'amaria
    per nom que per drudaria, 15
c'ans no·t laisses levar al ven.

III. E doncs pois atressi·m morrai
dirai li l'afan que m'en ve?
Vers es c'ades lo li dirai —
no farai a la mia fe 20
si sabia c'a un tenen
    en fos tot' Espanha mia;
    mais volh morir de feunia
car anc me venc en pessamen.

IV. Ja per me no sabra qu'eu m'ai 25
ni autre no l'en dira re.
Amic no volh ad aquest plai,
ans perda Deu qui pro m'en te,
qu'eu no·n volh cozi ni paren;

17. EN COSSIRER ET EN ESMAI

  que mout m'es grans cortezia   30
  c'amors per midons m'aucia,
mais a leis non estara gen.

V. E doncs ela cal tort m'i fai
  qu'ilh no sap, per que s'esdeve?
  Deus devinar degra oimai   35
  qu'eu mor per s'amor, et a que?
  Al meu nesci chaptenemen
   et a la gran vilania
   per que·lh lenga m'entrelia
can eu denan leis me prezen.   40

VI. Negus jois al meu no s'eschai
  can ma domna·m garda ni·m ve,
  que·l seus bels douz semblans me vai
  al cor, que m'adous' e·m reve.
  E si·m durava lonjamen   45
   sobre sainhz li juraria
   qu'el mon mais nulhs jois no sia.
Mais al partir art et encen.

VII. Pois messatger no·lh trametrai
  ni a me dire no·s cove,
  negu cosselh de me no sai.
  Mais d'una re me conort be:
  ela sap letras et enten
   et agrada·m qu'eu escria
   los motz, e s'a leis plazia   55
legis los al meu sauvamen.

VIII. E s'a leis autre dols no·n pren,
   per Deu e per merce·lh sia
   que·l bel solatz que m'avia
no·m tolha ni·l seu parlar gen.   60

I. I am perplexed and confused about a love which binds and confines me so that there is no place I can go where it does not hold me in its reins. For now love has given me the heart and the desire to court, if I might, such a one that courting her, even if the king himself were her suitor, would be an act of great daring.

II. Alas, wretch, what shall I do; and what counsel shall I take for myself, since she does not know the pain I bear, and I dare not cry out for her mercy? Ignorant fool, you have little sense, if you have not hanged yourself before now, for she will never love you in name or in fact.*

III. And so, since I shall die anyway, shall I tell her of the suffering I undergo? Yes, I shall tell her at once. No, I shall not do it, by my faith, even if I knew all Spain would forthwith be mine for the telling. Indeed, I could die of chagrin for having allowed such a thought to cross my mind.

IV. She will never learn from me what is wrong, nor will another tell her anything about it. I want no friend, cousin or kinsman in this affair. May whoever helps me be forever damned. It would seem a very honorable act for love to kill me for my lady's sake, but for her to do it would not be seemly.

V. And since she does not know what wrong she does me, why does it happen? God, she should realize now that I am dying for her love; and why? Because of my foolish behavior and great cowardice which bind my tongue when I am with her.

VI. No joy matches mine when my lady looks at me or sees me. Then her fair sweet image enters my heart and sweetens and refreshes me. And if she stayed with me a long time, I would swear by the saints that there would be no greater joy in the world. But at parting, I take fire and burn.

VII. Since I will not send a messenger to her, and since for me to speak is not fitting, I see no help for myself. But I console myself with one thing: she knows and understands letters. It pleases me to write the words, and if it pleases her, let her read them for my deliverance.

VIII. If no other ill may befall her on that account,* for God's sake let her not take away the kindness nor the beautiful words she had for me.

18. E MAINH GENH SE VOLV E·S VIRA

I.   E mainh genh se volv e·s vira
    mos talans, e ven e vai,
    lai on mos volers s'atrai.
    Lo cors no·n pauza ni fina,
        si·m te conhd' e gai   5
    fin' amors, ab cui m'apai,
        no sai com me contenha.

II.   Ges amors no·s franh per ira
    ni se fenh per dih savai
    can es de bo pretz verai.   10
    Qui la te en dissiplina
        re no sap que·s fai,
    que no cove ni s'eschai
        que nuls om la destrenha.

III.   Eu·m sui cel qu'e re no tira.   15
    Si tot ma domna·m sostrai,
    ja de re no·m clamarai,
    car es tan pur' e tan fina
        que ja no creirai,
    si de so tort li quer plai,   20
        que merces no l'en prenha.

IV.   Per mo grat eu m'en jauzira
    e pel bo talan qu'eu n'ai
    m'es vejaire que be·m vai.
    Gardatz, s'ela·m fos vezina,   25
        s'eu n'agra re mai?
    Eu oc, c'aissi m'o aurai,
        s'a lei platz que·m retenha.

V. Messatger, mot me täina
   car tost non est lai.   30
Viatz ven e viatz vai,
   mas la chanso lh'ensenha.

I. In many forms my desire turns and twists, comes and goes toward where my will is drawn. My heart does not pause or rest. So true love, in which I find peace, keeps me lively and gay. I do not know how to contain myself.

II. Love, when it is truly worthy, is not shattered by anger, nor diminished by harsh words. Whoever keeps it in check does not know what he is doing. It is not fitting or proper for anyone to compel it.

III. Nothing disturbs me. Even though my lady slanders me, I shall never complain, for she is so pure and fine that I shall never believe that she would not have mercy if I sought justice for her wrongs.

IV. I shall rejoice for the pleasures and the good desire I have. It seems to me that all goes well. Look, would I have anything more if she were close to me? Certainly! Then I shall have it so, if it pleases her to keep me.

V. Messenger, I wait with great impatience because you are so slow. Go quickly and come quickly, but teach her the song.

19. ESTAT AI COM OM ESPERDUTZ

I. Estat ai com om esperdutz
    per amor un lonc estatge,
mas era·m sui reconogutz
    qu'eu avia faih folatge.
    C'a totz era de salvatge,   5
car m'era de chan recrezutz,
et on eu plus estera mutz,
    mais feira de mon damnatge.

II. A tal domna m'era rendutz
    c'anc no·m amet de coratge,   10
e sui m'en tart aperceubutz,
    que trop ai faih lonc badatge.
    Oi mais segrai son uzatge;
de cui que·m volha serai drutz
e trametrai per tot salutz   15
    et aurai mais cor volatge.

III. Truans volh esser per s'amor
    e cove c'ab leis aprenda;
pero no vei domneyador
    que menhs de me s'i entenda.   20
    Mas bel m'es c'ab leis contenda,
c' altra n'am, plus bel' e melhor,
que·m val e m'ayud' e·m socor
    e·m fai de s'amor esmenda.

IV. Aquesta m'a faih tan d'onor   25
    que platz li c'a merce·m prenda.
E prec la del seu amador
    que·l be que·m fara, no·m venda
    ni·m fassa far lonj' atenda,

que lonc termini·m fai paor, 30
car no vei malvatz donador
    c'ab lonc respeih no·s defenda.

V. Ma domna fo al comensar
        franch' e de bela companha,
    per so la dei mais amar
        que si·m fos fer' et estranha;
    Que dreihz es que domna s'afranha
    vas celui qui a cor d'amar.
    Qui trop fai son amic preyar,
        dreihz es c'amics li sofranha. 40

VI. Domna, pensem del enjanar
        lauzengers, cui Deus contranha,
    que tan com om lor pot emblar
        de joi, aitan s'en gazanha,
        e que ja us no s'en planha. 45
    Loncs tems pot nostr' amors durar,
    sol can locs er, volham parlar,
        e can locs non er, remanha.

VII. Deu lau qu'era sai chantar,
     mal grat n'aya na Dous-Esgar 50
        e cil a cui s'accompanha.

VIII. Fis-Jois, ges no·us posc oblidar,
      ans vos am e·us volh e·us tenh char,
        car m'etz de bela companha.

I. I have been like one distracted by love for a long time, but now I realize that I have acted foolishly; for everything has been unpleasant since I gave up singing, and the longer I remain mute, the more I contribute to my own undoing.

II. I gave myself to a woman who never loved me in her heart,* and I realize too late how much time I have lost. I shall no longer follow her ways. I shall be the lover of anyone who wants me; I shall send greetings to everyone, and I shall have a fickle heart.

III. Because of her love, I want to be a deceiver, and it is appropriate that I learn it from her. And yet I see no lover who understands less than I how to be such; however, I am pleased to contend with her, since I love another woman, better and more beautiful, who helps me, aids and comforts me, and rewards me with her love.

IV. That woman has done me great honor and is pleased to receive me graciously; and I beg her not to make me pay dearly for the good she may do me,* her lover, or make me wait a long time or keep me too long in suspense. A long wait frightens me, since I have never seen a bad giver who did not put up a long resistance.

V. My lady was generous, open-hearted and pleasant to be with at first. Therefore I ought to love her more than if she had been cruel and hostile. It is only proper for a lady to be accommodating to one who loves her. And, likewise, it is only proper for her lover to desert the woman who makes him beg too long.

VI. Lady, let us plan to cheat the scandal-mongers — God cripple them — for one may get only as much joy for himself as he can steal from them; and let none of them complain! Our love can last a long time. So let us speak only when the opportunity arises, and contain ourselves when there is none.

VII. I praise God that now I can sing in spite of lady Dous-Esgar and the one who keeps her company.

VIII. Fis-Jois, I cannot forget you; rather, I love you, want you, and cherish you because you are good company to me.

20. GENT ESTERA QUE CHANTES

I. Gent estera que chantes,
    s'a Mon Conort abelis,
    mas eu no cre que·m grazis
    re que·lh disses ni·lh mandes,
    car trop n'ai faih lonc estatge   5
    de vezer lo seu cors gen
    avinen e d'agradatge;
    e lais m'en, si Deus be·m do,
    pel meu dan e pel seu pro.

II. Mas fals lauzenger engres   10
    m'an lunhat de so päis,
    que tals s'en fai esdevis
    qu'eu cuidera que·ns celes
    si·ns saubes ams d'un coratge.
    E car me don espaven,   15
    vau queren cubert viatge
    per on vengues a lairo
    denan leis ses mal resso.

III. Car no parria ames
    nulhs om que d'amor s'aizis,   20
    car per celar es om fis,
    e·n estai de joi plus pres.
    Donc, s'eu en pren bon uzatge,
    midons, c'a valor e sen,
    prec m'esmen dins son ostatge   25
    l'afan can veira sazo
    e no i gart dreih ni razo.

IV. E si·l plazia, ·m tornes
    al seu onrat paradis,
    ja no·s cuit qu'eu m'en partis,   30

ans mor can no i son ades.
Deus, can aurai vassalatge
que denan leis me prezen?
Trop m'aten en voupilhatge,
car no sap s'ai tort o no,   35
per c'a dreih que·m ochaizo.

V. Domna, ·l genzer c'anc nasques
    e la melher qu'eu anc vis,
    mas jonchas estau aclis,
    a genolhos et en pes,   40
    el vostre franc senhoratge,
    e car me detz per prezen
    franchamen un cortes gatge,
    mas no·us aus dire cal fo,
    c'adoutz me vostra preizo.   45

VI. Domna, vos am finamen,
    franchamen, de bo coratge,
    e per vostr' om me razo
    qui·m demanda de cui so.

I. Well would it become me to sing, if it might please my Conort. But I do not think that she would be grateful for anything I may say or send to her because for too long I have refrained from seeing her fair, comely and pleasing person. And so I give up this idea of singing, * as God send me good, to her advantage and my ill.

II. The false, violent slanderers have banished me from her country. Then such a one becomes a spy whom I should think would hide it from us, if he knew us both of one mind. And because I am fearful, I am trying to find a secret way to come furtively to her without harming her reputation.

III. It would not appear that a man really loves, if he can be calm about it, because through secrecy one is true and closer to joy. Then if I follow good custom, I beg my lady, who has worth and wit, to reward my suffering with her hospitality, when she sees the chance, without considering right or reason.

IV. And if it pleased her to return me to her honored paradise, I do not think I would ever leave it. On the contrary, it is death to me that I am not always there. God, when shall I have the courage to be with her? I vacillate too long in cowardice * wondering whether I am wrong or not; therefore she is right to reproach me;

V. Lady, the most beautiful ever born and the best I have ever seen, with hands clasped, kneeling or standing, I submit to your noble rule. For you generously gave me a courtly pledge as a gift — but I don't dare say what it was — which sweetens your imprisonment of me.

VI. Lady, I love you truly, fairly, and with good heart; and I confess myself your vassal to anyone who asks me whose man I am.

21. GES DE CHANTAR NO·M PREN TALANS

I. Ges de chantar no·m pren talans
    tan me peza de so que vei,
    que metre·s soli' om en grans
    com agues pretz, onor e lau
    mas era no vei ni non au 5
        c'om parle de drudaria,
        per que pretz e cortezia
    e solatz torn' en no-chaler.

II. Dels baros comensa l'enjans
    c'us no·n ama per bona fei. 10
    Per so·n sec als autres lo dans
    e negus om de lor no·s jau.
    Ez amors no rema per au,
        car be leu tals amaria
        qui s'en te car no·s sabria 15
    a guiza d'amor chaptener.

III. De tal amor sui fis amans
    don duc ni comte non envei
    e non es reis ni amirans
    el mon que, s'el n'avi' aitau, 20
    no s'en fezes rics com eu fau.
        E si lauzar la volia,
        ges tan dire no·n poiria
    de be que mais no·n sia ver.

IV. Per re non es om tan prezans 25
    com per amor e per domnei,
    que d'aqui mou deportz e chans
    e tot can a proez' abau.
    Nuls om ses amor re no vau
        per qu'eu no volh, sia mia 30

del mon tota·lh senhoria,
si ja joi no·n sabi' aver.

V. De midons me lau cent aitans
qu'eu no sai dir. Et ai be drei
que, can pot, me fai bels semblans 35
e sona me gent e suau.
E mandet me per qu'eu m'esjau
que per paor remania,
car ela plus no·m fazia
per qu'eu n'estau en bon esper. 40

VI. Bona domna, conhd' e prezans,
per Deu ayatz de me mercei
e ja no vos anetz doptans
ves vostr' amic fin e corau.
Far me podetz e ben e mau, 45
en la vostra merce sia,
qu'eu sui garnitz tota via
com fassa tot vostre plazer.

VII. Fons Salada, mos drogomans
me siatz mosenhor al rei, 50
digatz li·m que Mos-Azimans
mi te, car eu ves lui no vau.
Si com a Toren' e Peitau
e Anjau e Normandia,
volgra car li covenria, 55
agues tot lo mon en poder.

VIII.* Lo vers aissi com om plus l'au
vai melhuran tota via.
E i aprendon per la via
cil c'al Poi lo volran saber. 60

I. I am so saddened by what I see that I do not feel like singing. Men used to strive hard to win worth, honor, and praise, but now I do not see or hear anyone speak of love, and, as a result, reputation, nobility and joy become matters of indifference.

II. Deceit begins with the barons, for not one of them loves in good faith. Therefore, harm befalls the others and no man has joy from them. Love declines for no other reason but that anyone inclined to love abstains from it because he does not know how to act in the manner of love.

III. I have such a love that I do not envy duke or count; * and there is no king or emir in the world, who, if he had such a one, could not enrich himself as I have. If I wanted to praise her, no matter how much I talked, some of the truth would still remain to be told.

IV. Man can only achieve worthiness in the love and service of ladies, for sport and song, and all that pertains to nobility, begin there. No man is worth anything without love, and therefore I would not want to rule the whole world if I could not have joy.

V. I am a hundred times more content with my lady than I can say. And rightly so, for when she can, she smiles on me and speaks gently and softly. She let me know (for which I rejoice) that it was only out of fear that she stopped her favors and was unwilling to do more for me, * and therefore I dwell in good hope.

VI. Beautiful lady, charming and worthy, have mercy upon me for God's sake, and never doubt * your true and sincere friend. You can do me both good and evil, depending on your compassion, but I am always prepared to do your pleasure.

VII. Fons Salada, be my interpreter to my lord the king. Tell him that my Aziman holds me, and so I do not go to him. But I wish, since it is worthy of him, that he have all the world in his power, just as he has Touraine, Poitou, Anjou, and Normandy.

VIII.* The verse improves continually the more one hears it. Those in Puy who want to know it, will learn it on the way. *

22 JA MOS CHANTARS NO M'ER ONORS

I.
    Ja mos chantars no m'er onors
    encontral gran joi c'ai conques,
    c'ades m'agr' ops si tot s'es bos
    mos chans fos melher que non es.
    Aissi com es l'amors sobrana   5
     per que mos cors melhur' e sana,
deuri' esser sobras lo vers qu'eu fatz
sobre totz chans e volgutz e chantatz.

II.
    Ai Deus, can bona for' amors
    de dos amics s'esser pogues   10
    que ja us d'aquestz enveyos
    lor amistat no conogues.
    Cortezia, mout etz vilana
     c'az aquesta fausa gen vana
fatz conoisser semblans ni amistatz   15
c'ar' es cortes lo plus mal essenhatz.

III.
    Per merce prec als amadors
    chascus per se cossir e pes
    del segle com es enoyos
    e can pauc n'i a de cortes,   20
    c'amors, pois om per tot s'en vana
     non es amors mas es ufana
et es enois, vilani' e foudatz
qui no gara cui deu esser privatz.

IV.*
    Si tot m'es vergonh' e paors,   25
    blasmat m'er d'Amor, mas be·m pes
    car aquest lauzars no m'es pros
    e pois mos conortz no·n es res
    qu'eu vei que de nien m'apana
     cilh que no·m vol esser umana.   30

e car no·n posc aver joi ni solatz,
chan per conort cen vetz que sui iratz.

V. Chauzit ai entre las melhors
la melhor qued anc Deus fezes,
mas tan a va cor e doptos 35
qu'er' ai leis, era no·n ai ges.
Que val aitals amors aurana
can ges no pot una setmana
us bos amics ab l'autr' estar en patz
ses grans enois e ses enemistatz? 40

VI. Tostems sec joi ir' e dolors
e tostems ira jois e bes,
et eu no cre si jois no fos
c'om ja saubes d'ira que·s es.
Que'eu pert per falsa laus umana 45
tal joi de fin' amor certana
que, qui·m mezes tot lo mon ad un latz,
eu preira·l joi per cui sui enjanatz.

VII. Bela domna, vostre socors
m'auria mester se·us plagues 50
que molt m'es mal' aquist preizos
en c'Amors m'a lassat e pres.
A Deus, can malamen m'afana
can so que·m träis e m'enjana
m'aven amar si tot me pez' o·m platz. 55
Era sai eu qu'eu sui apoderatz.

VIII. ... ...
... ...
car de l'afan no me val amistatz
tan qu'eu disses que sui melhs sos privatz. 60

IX. Messatgers, vai t'en via plana
a mon Romeu lai vas Viana
e digas li qu'eu lai fora tornatz
si mos De-Cor m'agues salutz mandatz.

I. Never will my song be an honor worthy of the great joy I have won. For I always need to make my song better than it is, although it is good. Just as the love in which my heart is improved and cured is superior, so the verse I make should be superior to all songs either intended or sung.

II. Ah God, how good would be the love of two lovers if it were possible that not one of those envious louts knew of their love. Courtesy, you are very base since you have made these false, vain people acquainted with style and friendship, for now the worst-mannered is courtly.

III. For the sake of grace I pray that each lover reflect and consider how vexing the world is and how little courtesy there is. The love which men boast about everywhere is not love, but pretense, and he who does not respect what should be secret is base, villainous, and foolish.

IV. Although shame and fear come to me from it, nevertheless, I complain of love. Then I reflect that praise (or love) does not help me anyway, since there is no consolation for me in it. * And since I see that she who does not wish to be kind does not sustain me and that I cannot have joy or solace, I shall sing for consolation a hundred times in my grief.

V. Among the best women God ever made, I have chosen the finest. But she has such an unreliable and timid heart that now I have her, now I do not. What worth is there in such a vain love, when one good lover cannot be at peace with the other for a week without great trouble and hostility?

VI. Sorrow and grief always follow joy, and joy and good follow grief. And if there were no joy, I do not believe that one would know what grief is. Through false human praise I lose the joy of a love so true and certain that, if all the world were weighed against it, I would rather choose that joy, in which I am now deceived.

VII. Good lady, if it pleases you, I need your help, since the prison in which Love has bound and held me is my great misfortune. Oh God, how badly I am troubled when, whether it pleases me or not, I am fated to love one who betrays and cheats me. Now I know that I am conquered.

22. JA MOS CHANTARS NO M'ER ONORS 103

VIII. ... since Love does not help me in my trouble, I would say that I am better without friends.

IX. Messenger, go straight to my Romeu near Vienne and tell him that I would have returned there if my De-Cor had sent me greetings.

23. LA DOUSA VOTZ AI AUZIDA

I. La dousa votz ai auzida
    del rosinholet sauvatge
    et es m'ins el cor salhida
    si que tot lo cosirer
    e·ls mal traihz qu'amors me dona, 5
    m'adousa e m'asazona.
    Et auria·m be mester
    l'autrui jois al meu damnatge.

II. Ben es totz om d'avol vida
    c'ab joi non a son estatge 10
    e qui vas amor no guida
    so cor e so dezirer,
    car tot can es s'abandona
    vas joi e refrim' e sona,
    prat e deves e verger, 15
    landas e pla e boschatge.

III. Eu las, cui Amors oblida
    que sui fors del dreih viatge,
    agra de joi ma partida
    mas ira·m fai destorber, 20
    e no sai on me repona
    pus mo joi me desazona.
    E no·m tenhatz per leuger
    s'eu dic alcu vilanatge.

IV. Una fausa deschauzida 25
    träiritz de mal linhatge
    m'a träit et es träida,
    e colh lo ram ab que·s fer,
    e can autre l'arazona,
    d'eus lo seu tort m'ochaizona. 30

23. LA DOUSA VOTZ AI AUZIDA

  Et an ne mais li derrer
  qu'eu qui n'ai faih lonc badatge.
V. Mout l'avia gen servida
  tro ac vas mi cor volatge,
  e pus ilh no m'es cobida,   35
  mout sui fols si mais la ser.
  Servirs c'om no gazardona
  et esperansa bretona
  fai de senhor escuder
  per costum e per uzatge.   40

VI. Pois tan es vas me falhida,
  aisi lais so senhoratge
  e no volh que·m si' aizida
  ni ja mais parlar no·n quer,
  mas pero qui m'en razona,   45
  la paraula m'en es bona
  e m'en esjau volonter
  e·m n'alegre mo coratge.

VII. Deus li do mal' escharida
  qui porta mauvais mesatge   50
  qu'eu agra amor jauzida
  si no foso lauzenger.
  Fols es qui ab sidons tensona,
  qu'e·lh perdo s'ela·m perdona
  e tuih cilh son mesonger   55
  que·m n'an faih dire folatge.

VIII. Lo vers mi porta, Corona,
  lai a midons a Narbona
  que tuih sei faih son enter
  c'om no·n pot dire folatge.   60

  I. I have heard the shy nightingale's sweet voice, which has leapt into my heart so that it sweetens and lightens all the worry and mistreatment which love gives me. Still I need the joy of another in my sorrow.

II. Whoever does not dwell with joy nor guide his heart and desire toward love is a man of mean life; for all that is abandons itself to joy, sings out and resounds: meadow, pasture, garden, field and forest.

III. Alas, I whom love forgets because I am out of the right path, would have my share of joy, but bitterness troubles me. I do not know where to hide myself when it spoils my joy for me. So do not consider me frivolous if I say some insulting things.

IV. A false, coarse, treacherous woman of bad blood has betrayed me, yet she is deceived and picks the switch with which she wounds herself. And when another addresses her, she accuses me of those wrongs which are rightly hers. The worst get more from her than I, who have suffered a long delay.

V. I have served her very nobly, but she has a heart too fleeting toward me, and, since she will have no part of me, I am a great fool if I serve her longer. Service which is not rewarded and Breton hope * make, by custom and habit, a squire of a lord.

VI. Since she has failed me, I forsake her rule and do not want her to be near me, nor do I seek any longer to speak of her. But if someone speaks to me about her, his words will seem good to me; I rejoice eagerly and my spirit is happy.

VII. May God grant misfortune to him who bears evil tales, for I would have enjoyed love if there had been no slanderers. He is a fool who quarrels with his lady, and so I forgive her if she forgives me. They are all liars who have made me speak madness of her.

VIII. Carry the verse for me, Corona, to my lady in Narbonne. Since all her acts are perfect, one cannot speak madness of her.

24. LANCAN FOLHON BOSC E JARRIC

I. Lancan folhon bosc e jarric
    e·lh flors pareis e·lh verdura
      pels vergers e pels pratz,
e·lh auzel, c'an estat enic,
    son gai desotz los folhatz,   5
autresi·m chant e m'esbaudei
e reflorisc e reverdei
    e folh segon ma natura.

II. Ges d'un' amor no·m tolh ni·m gic
    don sui en bon' aventura   10
      segon mon esper entratz,
car sui tengutz per fin amic
    lai on es ma volontatz,
que re mais sotz cel no·n envei
ni ves autra part no soplei   15
    ni d'autra no sui en cura.

III. Ben a mauvais cor e mendic
    qui ama e no·s melhura,
      qu'eu sui d'aitan melhuratz
c'ome de me no vei plus ric,   20
    car sai c'am e sui amatz
per la gensor qued anc Deus fei
ni que sia el mon, so crei,
    tan can te terra ni dura.

IV. Anc no fetz semblan vair ni pic   25
    la bela ni forfachura,
      ni fui per leis galiatz,
ni no·m crei c'om tan la chastic,
    tan es fina s'amistatz,
qu'ela ja·s biais ni·s vairei   30

ni per autre guerpisca mei
segon que mos cors s'augura.

V. Midons prec no·m lais per chastic
ni per gelos folatura
que no·m sent' entre sos bratz   35
car eu sui seus plus qu'eu no dic
e serai tostems, si·lh platz.
Que per leis m'es bel tot can vei,
e port el cor on que m'estei
sa beutat e sa fachura.   40

VI.* Anc no vitz ome tan antic,
si a bon' amor ni pura
e per sidons si' amatz,
no sia gais, neis sers e bric,
si's de joi pres e liatz.   45
Que de fol cove que folei
e de savi que chabalei,
que pretz li·n creis e·lh melhura.

I. When woods and thickets shoot forth their leaves, and the flowers and greenery appear throughout the gardens and meadows, and the birds, who have been sulking, are gay beneath the foliage, then I too sing, rejoice and blossom. I am renewed and put forth leaves acording to my nature.

II. I do not at all forsake or abandon a love in which I have good fortune, or the hope of it. For where my desire is I am considered a true lover, since I do not desire anything more beneath the sky, and I do not plead elsewhere or keep any other woman in mind.

III. He who loves and does not better himself certainly has a wicked and wretched heart. I am so improved that I see no man richer than I, because I know that I love and am loved by the most beautiful woman whom God ever made or who may ever be in the world, I believe, so long as the earth remains and endures.

IV. The beautiful lady never showed a fickle and glittering appearance or any deceit, nor was I cheated by her. So true is her love, that I do not think anyone would reprove her so much that she would turn away or change or leave me for another, as my heart prophesies.

V. I pray that my lady may not, out of fear of reproach or jealous folly, so turn from me that I may not again feel her arms about me. For I am hers even more than I say and I shall always be, if it pleases her. On her account everything I see is beautiful to me, and I carry in my heart, wherever I may be, her beauty and her grace.

VI.* You never saw a man so old that, if he has a good and pure love and is loved by his lady, he will not be gay, even servile and foolish, or seized and bound by joy. For it befits the fool to do something foolish and the wise man to act wisely, so that his worth increases and improves.

25. LANCAN VEI LA FOLHA

I.   Lancan vei la folha
jos dels albres chazer,
    cui que pes ni dolha,
a me deu bo saber.
    No crezatz qu'eu volha   5
flor ni folha vezer,
    car vas me s'orgolha
so qu'eu plus volh aver.
    Cor ai que m'en tolha,
mas no·n ai ges poder,   10
    c'ades cuit m'acolha
on plus m'en dezesper.

II.   Estranha novela
podetz de me auzir,
    que can vei la bela   15
que·m soli' acolhir,
    ara no m'apela
ni·m fai vas se venir.
    Lo cor sotz l'aissela
m'en vol de dol partir.   20
    Deus, que·l mon chapdela,
si·lh platz, m'en lais jauzir,
    que s'aissi·m revela
no·i a mas del morir.

III.   Non ai mais fiansa   25
en agur ni en sort,
    que bon' esperansa
m'a cofundut e mort,
    que tan lonh me lansa
la bela cui am fort,   30
    can li quer s'amansa,

com s'eu l'agues gran tort.
   Tan n'ai de pezansa
que totz m'en desconort,
   mas no·n fatz semblansa
c'ades chant e deport.

IV.   Als no·n sai que dire
mas mout fatz gran folor
   car am ni dezire
del mon la belazor.
   Be deuri' aucire
qui anc fetz mirador,
   can be m'o cossire,
no·n ai guerrer peyor.
   Ja·l jorn qu'ela·s mire
ni pens de sa valor,
   no serai jauzire
de leis ni de s'amor.

V.   Ja per drudaria
no m'am, que no·s cove.
   Pero si·lh plazia
que·m fezes cal que be,
   eu li juraria
per leis e per ma fe
   que·l bes que·m faria
no fos saubutz per me.
   En son plazer sia,
qu'eu sui en sa merce.
   Si·lh platz que m'aucia,
qu'eu no m'en clam de re.

VI.   Ben es dreihz qu'eu planha
s'eu pert per mon orgolh
   la bona companha
e·l solatz c'aver solh.
   Petit me gazanha
lo fols arditz qu'eu colh,
   car vas me s'estranha

  so qu'eu plus am e volh.
   Orgolhs, Deus vos franha,
c'ara·n ploron mei olh.   70
   Dreihz es que·m sofranha
totz jois, qu'eu eis lo·m tolh.

VII.   Encontra·l damnatge
e la pena qu'eu trai,
  ai mo bon usatge,   75
c'ades consir de lai.
  orgolh e folatge
e vilania fai
  qui·n mou mo coratge
ni d'alre·m met en plai,   80
  car melhor messatge
en tot lo mon no·n ai
  e man lo·lh ostatge
entro qu'eu torn de sai.

VIII.   Domna, mo coratge,   85
·l melhor amic qu'eu ai,
  vos man en ostatge
entro qu'eu torn de sai.

  I. It should please *me* to see the leaves fall from the trees, whomever else it may pain or grieve. Do not believe that *I* am interested in seeing flowers or leaves: the one I want most to have is haughty to me. I have a mind to leave her, but I don't have the strength because even in the depths of despair, I always think she is about to accept me.
  II. You may hear strange news of me, for now when I see the beautiful lady who used to welcome me, she no longer calls me or bids me come to her. My very heart wants to break from sorrow. If it pleases God, who rules the world, may he let me have joy from her, for she is so obstinate to me that there is nothing to do but die.
  III. I no longer trust in augury or fortune, becanse hoping in good faith has been my ruin, since the beautiful lady, whom I love so

much, rebuffs me when I seek her love, as though I had done her great wrong. I have such pain that I am completely discouraged; but I do not look it, because I am always singing and playing.

IV. I can say nothing but this: I act with very great folly in loving and desiring the most beautiful lady in the world. I should certainly kill whoever contrived the mirror. In fact, when I think about it, I have no worse enemy. Surely, on the day when she looks at herself and thinks of her worth, I shall enjoy neither her nor her love.

V. Indeed, she does not love me with fleshly love, for it would not be fitting. However, if it pleased her to do something good for me, I would swear to her, by her and by my faith, that I would not make known any good that she might do me. Let it be as she will, for I am at her mercy. She may even kill me if she pleases; I shall not complain.

VI. It is right for me to complain though, if I lose the good company and comfort I used to have on account of my own pride. The foolish boldness which I show gains little for me, when what I most love and want is estranged from me. Pride, may God crush you, for now my eyes weep. It is only right if all joy fails me, for I deprive myself of it.

VII. Against the loss and pain which I suffer, I have my good habit: that I always think about that place where she is. Whoever diverts my heart and involves me with something else acts with pride, madness and villainy; for I have no better messenger in all the world than my heart, and I send it to her as a hostage until I return from here.

VIII. Lady, my heart, the best friend I have, I send you as hostage until I return from here.

26. LANCAN VEI PER MEI LA LANDA

I.
Lancan vei per mei la landa
dels arbres chazer la folha,
ans que·lh frejura s'espanda
ni·l gens termini s'esconda,
m'es bel que si' auzitz mos chans,
qu'estat n'aurai mais de dos ans,
e cove que·n fass' esmenda.

II.
Mout m'es greu que ja reblanda
celeis que vas me s'orgolha,
car si mos cors re·lh demanda,
no·lh platz que mot m'i responda.
Be m'auci mos nescis talans,
car sec d'amor los bels semblans
e no ve c'amors lh'atenda.

III.
Tan sap d'engenh e de ganda
c'ades cuit c'amar mi volha.
Be doussamen me truanda,
c'ab bel semblan me cofonda.
Domna, so no·us es nuls enans,
que be cre qu'es vostres lo dans,
cossi que vostr'om mal prenda.

IV.
Deus, que tot lo mon garanda,
li met' en cor que m'acolha,
c'a me no te pro vianda
ni negus bes no·m aonda.
Tan sui vas la bela doptans,
per qu'e·m ren a leis merceyans,
si·lh platz que·m don o que·m venda.

26. LANCAN VEI PER MEI LA LANDA 115

V. Mal o fara si no·m manda
venir lai on se despolha, 30
qu'eu sia per sa comanda
pres del leih, josta l'esponda,
e·lh traga·ls sotlars be chaussans,
a genolhs et umilians,
si·lh platz que sos pes me tenda. 35

VI. Faihz es lo vers tot a randa
si que motz no·i descapdolha
outra la terra normanda
part la fera mar prionda.
E si·m sui de midons lonhans, 40
vas se·m tira com azimans
la bela cui Deus defenda.

VII. Si·l reis engles e·l ducs normans
o vol, eu la veirai abans
que l'iverns nos sobreprenda. 45

VIII. Pel rei sui engles e normans,
e si no fos Mos Azimans,
restera tro part calenda.

I. When, throughout the plain, I see the leaves fall from the trees, just before the cold spreads abroad and the gentle season disappears, I like my song to be heard; for I have abstained * from singing for more than two years, and it is proper for me to make amends.

II. It is very hard for me to serve her who is so haughty to me, because whenever I ask her for anything, she does not see fit even to answer. My foolish desire kills me, for it pursues the fair semblance of love, and does not notice whether love is really paying any attention to it. *

III. She is so well-versed in deception and subterfuge that I am always being persuaded to think she really wants to love me. She deceives * me so gently that she destroys me with a winsome look.

Lady, it is of no advantage to you — in fact, I believe it hurts you — that your vassal fares so ill.

IV. May God, who embraces all the world, give her the heart to welcome me. It is useless for me to eat and nothing does me any good, because I am so fearful of her. Therefore, I surrender myself, a suppliant, to her. If it pleases her, let her give me away or sell me. *

V. She will do ill if she does not bid me come to her boudoir, where, at her command, I may be near the bed, or at the edge of it, so that, humbly kneeling, I may remove her well-fitted shoes, if she pleases to offer me her foot.

VI. This poem has been completed — and with no word out of place * — far from the Norman land, across the wild, deep sea. And though I am far from my lady, she draws me to her like a magnet, her, the beautiful one — God protect her!

VII. If the English king and the Norman duke allow, I will see her before winter overtakes us.

VIII. For the king's sake, I am both English and Norman, and, if it were not for my Aziman, I would stay until Christmas is over.

27. LONC TEMS A QU'EU NO CHANTEI MAI

I. Lonc tems a qu'eu no chantei mai
ni saubi far chaptenemen.
Ara no tem ploya ni ven,
   tan sui entratz en cossire
   com pogues bos motz assire   5
   en est so, c'ai ... ... *
   si tot no·m vei flor ni folha,
   melhs me vai c'al tems florit,
car l'amors qu'eu plus volh, me vol.

II. Totz me desconosc, tan be·m vai,   10
e s'om saubes en cui m'enten,
ni auzes far mo joi parven.
   Del melhs del mon sui jauzire,
   e s'eu anc fui bos sofrire,
   ara m'en tenh per garit,   15
   qu'e re no sen mal que·m dolha.
   Si m'a jois pres e sazit,
no sai si·m sui aquel que sol.

III. El mon tan bon amic non ai,
fraire ni cozi ni paren,   20
que si·m vai mo joi enqueren,
   qu'ins e mo cor no·l n'azire.
   E s'eu m'en volh escondire,
   no s'en tenha per träit.
   No volh lauzengers me tolha
   s'amor ni·m leve tal crit
per qu'eu me lais morir de dol.

IV. C'ab sol lo bel semblan que·m fai
can pot ni aizes lo·lh cossen,
ai tan de joi que sol no·m sen,   30

c'aissi·m torn e·m volv' e·m vire.
E sai be, can la remire,
c'anc om belazor no·n vit,
e no·m pot re far que·m dolha
 Amors can n'ai lo chauzit   35
d'aitan cum mars clau ni revol.

V. Lo cors a fresc, sotil e gai,
et anc no·n vi tan avinen.
Pretz e beutat, valor e sen
 a plus qu'eu no vos sai dire.   40
 Res de be non es a dire,
ab sol c'aya tan d'ardit
c'una noih lai o·s despolha,
me mezes, en loc aizit,
e·m fezes del bratz latz al col.   45

VI. Si no·m aizis lai on ilh jai
si qu'eu remir son bel cors gen,
doncs per que m'a faih de nien?
 Ai las, com mor de dezire.
 Vol me doncs midons aucire   50
car l'am o que lh'ai falhit?
Ara·n fassa so que·s volha
ma domna, al seu chauzit,
qu'eu no m'en planh, si tot me dol.

VII. Tan l'am que re dire no·lh sai,   55
mas ilh s'en prend' esgardamen
qu'eu non ai d'alre pessamen
 mas com li fos bos servire.
 E s'eu sai chantar ni rire,
tot m'es per leis escharit.   60
 Ma domna prec que m'acolha,
e pois tan m'a enriquit,
no sia qui dona, qui tol.

27. LONC TEMS A QU'EU NO CHANTEI MAI 119

VIII.   De cor m'a coras se volha.
        Ve·us me del chantar garnit,   65
pois sa fin'amors m'o assol.

I. For a long time I have not sung nor known how to act. Now I fear neither rain nor wind, so preoccupied am I with composing this song that I have ... * Although no flowers or leaves are to be seen, I am even better off than in summer-time, for the love I most desire, desires me.

II. I do not recognize myself at all, so well off am I. If anyone knew whom I love, or if I dared make known the source of my joy, it would be seen that I rejoice in the best love in the world. If I was ever a good patient, I now consider myself cured, for I feel no pain hurting me. Joy has so taken and seized me that I do not know whether I am the same person I used to be.

III. I do not have, in the whole world, such a good friend, brother, cousin, or relative that, if he goes prying into my joy, I will not hate him deeply for it. And if I want to defend myself in this matter, let him not feel betrayed. I do not want a scandalmonger to rob me of her love or to raise such a cry about me that I shall be forced to die of sorrow.

IV. Just from the fair glance alone, which she gives me when she can or when the opportunity allows, I get such joy that I am not even aware of myself as I turn, spin, and whirl for sheer delight. I know very well, when I look at her, that no one ever saw a more beautiful woman. Love cannot do anything that would grieve me since I have the choice of the best that the sea encloses and surrounds.

V. She has a fresh, delicate and gay personality, and I never saw such a gracious lady. She has more of esteem and beauty, virtue and wisdom than I know how to tell you. Nothing good is lacking, * provided that she be daring enough to place me, for one night, in a suitable place in her boudoir, and to make a necklace of her arms.

VI. If she does not bring me to where she lies so that I see her beautiful, fair person, then why has she created me? * Alas, how I die of desire. Does my lady then want to kill me because I love her? How have I failed her? Now let my lady do what she wants, at her discretion, for I do not complain even though it grieves me.

VII. I love her so much that I do not know how to say anything to her; but let her take notice that I am concerned with nothing else than to be a good servant to her. And if I can sing and laugh, it has all come to me through her. I beseech my lady to welcome me, and since she has so enriched me, let her not be one who gives only to take away.

VIII. She has all my heart whenever she wishes. See how I am prepared to sing since her love allows me to.

28. LE GENS TEMS DE PASCOR

I. Le gens tems de pascor
 ab la frescha verdor
 nos adui folh' e flor
 de diversa color,
 per que tuih amador 5
 son gai e chantador
 mas eu, que planh e plor,
 cui jois non a sabor.

II. A totz me clam, senhor,
 de midons e d'Amor, 10
 c'aicist dui träidor,
 car me fiav'en lor,
 me fan viur' a dolor
 per ben e per onor
 c'ai faih a la gensor, 15
 que no·m val ni·m acor.

III. Pen' e dolor e dan
 n'ai agut e n'ai gran,
 mas sofert o ai tan.
 No m'o tenh ad afan, 20
 c'anc no vitz nulh aman
 melhs ames ses enjan,
 qu'eu no·m vau ges chamjan
 si com las domnas fan.

IV. Pois fom amdui efan, 25
 l'am ades e la blan,
 e·s vai mos jois doblan
 a chascu jorn del an.
 E si no·m fai enan
 amor e bel semblan, 30

cant er velha, ·m deman
que l'aya bo talan.

V. Las, e viure que·m val
    s'eu no vei a jornal
    mo fi joi natural   35
    en leih, sotz fenestral
    cors blanc tot atretal
    com la neus a nadal,
    si c'amdui cominal
    mezuressem egal?   40

VI. Anc no vitz drut leyal
    sordeis o aya sal;
    qu'eu l'am d'amor coral,
    ela·m ditz "no m'en chal,"
    enans ditz que per al   45
    no m'a ira mortal.
    E si d'aisso·m vol mal,
    pechat n'a criminal.

VII. Be for' oimais sazos,
     bela domna e pros,   50
     que·m fos datz a rescos
     en baizan guizardos,
     si ja per als no fos
     mas car sui enveyos,
     c'us bes val d'autres dos   55
     can per fors' es faihz dos.

VIII. Can vei vostras faissos
      e·ls bels olhs amoros,
      be·m meravilh de vos
      com etz de mal respos.   60
      E sembla·m trassios
      can om par francs e bos
      e pois es orgolhos
      lai on es poderos.

IX.   Bel Vezer, si no fos
      mos Denan-totz e vos,
      laissat agra chansos
      per mal dels enoyos.

I. The gentle season of spring with its fresh greenery brings us leaves and flowers of various colors; therefore all lovers and singers are gay except me, who lament and weep, for joy has not delighted me.

II. To everyone I complain, my lords, of my lady and of Love. Because I trusted in them, these two traitors make me live in sorrow for the good and the honor I have done the most beautiful lady, who does me no good and gives me no help.

III. I have had pain and sorrow and misery, and I now have them in abundance, but I have endured them well. I do not consider it a hardship, for you have never seen any man who loved better without deceit; I am not at all inconstant as women are.

IV. Since we were both children, I have loved her and wooed her constantly; and my joy doubles each day of the year. Yet if she does not grant me her love and her welcome sooner, when she is old she will beg me to feel desire for her.

V. Alas! What good is life to me if I do not daily see my fine, true joy in bed, her white body beneath the window just like the snow at Christmas, so that we may lie together breast to breast. *

VI. You never saw a true lover have worse luck for his pains. Because I love her with sincere love, she tells me: "It doesn't concern me;" on the contrary, she says that for that very reason she has a deadly anger for me. And if on that account she wishes me ill, she commits a heinous sin.

VII. Surely, beautiful and good lady, there would sometime be an occasion when a rewarding kiss might secretly be given to me, even if it were for no other reason but that I am desirous. For one good is worth two others when the two are done under constraint.

VIII. When I see your face and your beautiful, affectionate eyes, I wonder that you give a bad answer. And it seems to me treason for someone to appear noble and good and then be haughty when he is powerful.

IX. Bel Vezer, if all my well being did not lie in you, I would abandon singing because of evil vexations.

29. LO ROSSINHOLS S'ESBAUDEYA

I.
    Lo rossinhols s'esbaudeya
    josta la flor el verjan,
    e pren m'en tan grans enveya
    qu'eu no posc mudar no chan.
Mas no sai de que ni de cui 5
car eu non am me ni autrui
    e fatz esfortz car sai faire
    bo vers, pois no sui amaire.

II.
    Mais a d'Amor qui domneya
    ab orgolh et ab enjan 10
    que cel que tot jorn merceya
    ni·s vai trop umilian.
C'a penas vol Amors celui
qu'es francs e fis si com eu sui.
    So m'a tout tot mon afaire 15
    c'anc no fui faus ni trichaire.

III.
    C'aissi com lo rams si pleya
    lai o·l vens lo vai menan,
    era vas lei que·m guerreya
    aclis per far so coman. 20
Per aisso m'afol' e·m destrui,
don a mal linhatge redui,
    c'ams los olhs li don a traire
    s'autre tort me pot retraire.

IV.
    Soven me rept' e·m plaideya 25
    e·m vai ochaisos troban,
    e can ilh en re feuneya,
    vas me versa tot lo dan.
Gen joga de me e·s desdui,
que d'eus lo seu tort me conclui. 30

Mas ben es vertatz que laire
cuida tuih sion sei fraire.

V. Om no la ve que no creya
sos bels olhs e so semblan
e no cre qu'ilh aver deya   35
felo cor ni mal talan,
mas l'aiga que soau s'adui
es peyer que cela que brui.
Enjan fai qui de bon aire
sembla e non o es gaire.   40

VI. De tot loc on ilh esteya
me destolh e·m vau lonhan,
e per so que no la veya
pas li mos olhs claus denan.
Car cel sec Amors que·s n'esdui   45
e cel l'enchaussa qu'ela fui.
Ben ai en cor del estraire
tro que vas midons repaire.

VII. Ja non er, si tot me greya
qu'enquer fin e plaih no·lh man, 50
que greu m'es c'aissi·m recreya
ni perda tan lonc afan.
A sos ops me gart e·m estui,
e si non em amic amdui,
d'autr' amor no m'es vejaire,   55
que ja mais mos cors s'esclaire.

VIII. Enaissi fos pres com eu sui
Mos Alvernhatz, e foram dui,
que plus no·s pogues estraire
d'en Bel Vezer de Belcaire.   60

IX. Tristan, si no·us es veyaire,
mais vos am que no solh faire.

29. LO ROSSINHOLS S'ESBAUDEYA

I. The nightingale rejoices beside the blossom on the branch, and I have such great envy of him that I cannot keep from singing, though I do not know of what or of whom, for I do not love myself or any other. Yet I force myself to write * good verse even though I am no lover.

II. Whoever courts with arrogance and deceit gets more from love than one who pleads every day and goes about most humbly; for Love hardly wants one so honest and true as I am. Thus he has spoiled everything for me, since I was never a deceiver or cheater.

III. Just as the branch bends wherever the wind takes it, so I was bent to do the command of her who wars with me. For thus she ruins and destroys me, and thus stoops to bad behavior. * I offer her both eyes to pluck out if she can reproach me with any other fault.

IV. Often she blames me and argues with me and finds complaints against me, and when she does anything wrong, she turns all the injury toward me. She acts nobly indeed when she tricks me and amuses herself condemning *me* for *her* own wrongs! But then it is true that a thief thinks all men are his brothers.

V. No one sees her who would not believe her beautiful eyes and her appearance, nor think that she should have an evil heart or wicked desire. But the water which flows quietly is worse than that which roars. Whoever seems gracious and is not so at all practices deceit.

VI. From every place where she may be I turn and go far away, and in order that I may not see her, I pass by her with my eyes closed. For love follows the one who flees and shuns the one who pursues it. Indeed I have a mind to escape from it until it returns to my lady.

VII. In truth I will not do anything about it, even though it grieves me to seek peace and to offer her no quarrel; for it is hard for me thus to renounce and lose such long suffering. I regard her needs and dedicate myself to her, and, even if we two are not friends, it does not seem to me that my heart glows more from any other love.

VIII. May my Alvernhat be taken just as I am, and we would be two, and he would no longer be able to withdraw from the Bel Vezer of Beauclaire.

IX. Tristan, even if it does not seem so to you, I love you more than I used to.

30. LO TEMS VAI E VEN E VIRE

I. Lo tems vai e ven e vire
per jorns, per mes e per ans,
et eu, las, no·n sai que dire,
c'ades es us mos talans.
Ades es us e no·s muda, 5
c'una·n volh e·n ai volguda
don anc non aic jauzimen.

II. Pois ela no·n pert lo rire,
a me·n ven e dols e dans,
c'a tal joc m'a faih assire 10
don ai lo peyor dos tans,
c'aitals amors es perduda
qu'es d'una part mantenguda,
tro que fai acordamen.

III. Be deuri' esser blasmaire 15
de me mezeis a razo,
c'anc no nasquet cel de maire
que tan servis en perdo.
E s'ela no m'en chastia,
ades doblara·lh folia, 20
que fols no tem tro que pren.

IV. Ja mais no serai chantaire
ni de l'escola n'Eblo,
que mos chantars no val gaire
ni mas voutas ni mei so. 25
Ni res qu'eu fassa ni dia
no conosc que pros me sia
ni no·i vei melhuramen.

V. Si tot fatz de joi parvensa,
mout ai dins lo cor irat. 30

Qui vid anc mais penedensa
faire denan lo pechat?
On plus la prec, plus m'es dura,
mas si'n breu tems no·s melhura,
vengut er al partimen.   35

VI.   Pero ben es qu'ela·m vensa
      a tota sa volontat,
      que s'el' a tort o bistensa,
      ades n'aura pietat;
      que so mostra l'escriptura,   40
      causa de bon'aventura
      val us sols jorns mais de cen.

VII. Ja no·m partrai a ma vida
      tan com sia sals ni sas,
      que pois l'arma n'es issida,   45
      balaya lonc tems lo gras.
      E si tot no s'es cochada,
      ja per me no·n er blasmada,
      sol d'eus adenan s'emen.

VIII. Ai, bon' amors encobida,   50
      cors be faihz, delgatz e plas,
      frescha chara colorida,
      cui Deus formet ab sas mas,
      totz tems vos ai dezirada,
      que res autra no m'agrada.   55
      Autr' amor no volh nien.

IX.   Dousa res ben ensenhada,
      cel que·us a tan gen formada
      me·n do cel joi qu'eu n'aten.

I. Time comes and goes returning through days, through months, and through years, and I, alas, know not what to say, for my long-

30. LO TEMPS VAI E VEN E VIRE

ing is ever one. It is ever one and does not change, for I want and have wanted one woman, from whom I have never had joy.

II. Since she does not lose a chance to mock, grief and pain come to me; she has made me sit at such a game that I have the worst two to one until she makes peace. But that love is lost which is maintained by one side only.

III. In fact I should be the accuser of myself, since there was never a man born of woman who served so long in vain; and if she does not chastise me for it, I will forever double my madness towards her, for a fool does not fear until he experiences.

IV. I will no longer be a singer or of the school of Lord Eble, for neither my singing, my voice, nor my melodies do me any good; and no matter what I may do or say, I do not know how it may profit me and I see no improvement.

V. Although I make a show of joy, I have great sadness in my heart. Who ever saw more penance done before the sin? The more I implore her, the crueller she is to me, but if she does not improve in a short time, there will be a parting.

VI. However, it is well that she subjects me utterly to her will, for, though she unjustly delays things, she will soon have pity. For so the Scriptures show: a single day of good fortune outweighs more than a hundred others.

VII. Indeed I will not part with my life so long as I am safe and sound, just as after the kernel is gone, the straw flutters a long time. And although she has shown no haste, she will certainly not be blamed by me, if only she improves by herself from now on.

VIII. Oh good and desirable love; body well-formed, slender and smooth; fresh and fine-hued flesh which God has fashioned with his hands; I have always desired you, for no other creature pleases me. I want no other love at all.

IX. Sweet, noble creature, may the one who has so finely formed you give me the joy I hope for.

31. NON ES MERAVELHA S'EU CHAN

I. Non es meravelha s'eu chan
melhs de nul autre chantador,
que plus me tra·l cors vas amor
e melhs sui faihz a so coman.
Cor e cors e saber e sen   5
e fors' e poder i ai mes.
Si·m tira vas amor lo fres
que vas autra part no·m aten.

II. Ben es mortz qui d'amor no sen
al cor cal que dousa sabor.   10
E que val viure ses valor
mas per enoi far a la gen?
Ja Domnedeus no·m azir tan
qu'eu ja pois viva jorn ni mes
pois que d'enoi serai mespres   15
ni d'amor non aurai talan.

III. Per bona fe e ses enjan
am la plus bel' e la melhor.
Del cor sospir e dels olhs plor
car tan l'am eu, per que i ai dan. 20
Eu que·n posc mais s'Amors me pren,
e les charcers en que m'a mes
no pot claus obrir mas merces,
e de merce no·i trop nien?

IV. Aquest' amors me fer tan gen   25
al cor d'una dousa sabor;
cen vetz mor lo jorn de dolor
e reviu de joi autras cen.
Ben es mos mals de bel semblan,
que mais val mos mals qu'autre bes. 30

E pois mos mals aitan bos m'es,
bos er lo bes apres l'afan.

V. Ai Deus, car se fosson trian
d'entrels faus li fin amador
e·lh lauzenger e·lh trichador   35
portesson corns el fron denan.
Tot l'aur del mon e tot l'argen
i volgr'aver dat, s'eu l'agues,
sol que ma domna conogues
aissi com eu l'am finamen.   40

VI. Cant eu la vei, be m'es parven
als olhs, al vis, a la color,
car aissi tremble de paor
com fa la folha contra·l ven.
Non ai de sen per un efan,   45
aissi sui d'amor entrepres,
e d'ome qu'es aissi conques
pot domn' aver almorna gran.

VII. Bona domna, re no·us deman
mas que·m prendatz per servidor,   50
qu'e·us servirai com bo senhor,
cossi que del gazardo m'an.
Ve·us m'al vostre comandamen,
francs cors umils, gais e cortes.
Ors ni leos non etz vos ges   55
que·m aucizatz s'a vos me ren.

VIII. A Mo Cortes, lai on ilh es,
tramet lo vers, e ja no·lh pes
car n'ai estat tan lonjamen.

I. It is no wonder that I sing better than any other singer, for my heart draws me more toward love and I am better suited to its command. In it I have placed my heart and body, my knowledge and mind, my force and power. The rein so draws me toward love that I turn my attention nowhere else.

II. He is surely dead who does not feel the sweet taste of love in his heart, and what purpose has life without virtue except to cause people annoyance? May God never hate me so much that I may live a day or a month longer, once I become a nuisance to others and lose all desire of love.

III. In good faith and without deceit I love the best and the most beautiful lady. I sigh from my heart and weep from my eyes because I love her so much that I am in pain. What more can I do if Love captures me and if no key but pity can open the prison into which he puts me, and I find no pity there?

IV. This love wounds me in the heart gently with a sweet savor; a hundred times a day I die of sorrow, and I revive with joy another hundred. My ill is entirely from a fair semblance, and my ill is better than any other good. And since my ill is this good to me, good will be my reward after the suffering.

V. Oh God, that true lovers might be distinguishable from the false and scandal-mongers and deceivers might wear horns on their foreheads! I would have given all the gold and all the silver in the world, if I had it, if only my lady might know just how truly I love her.

VI. When I see her, it is surely apparent in me, in my eyes, in my face, in my color, for I tremble with fear just as the leaf does against the wind. I am so seized by love that I have not the sense of a child. For a man who is so vanquished, a lady may have great pity.

VII. Good lady, I ask nothing of you but that you take me as a servant, for I will serve you as a good lord, whatever my reward. Behold me at your command, noble creature, humble, gay, and courtly. You are not at all a bear or lion, that you should kill me if I give myself up to you.

VIII. I send the verse to my Cortes, where she is, and may it not grieve her that I have been away so long.

32. PEIROL, COM AVETZ TAN ESTAT*

I. Peirol, com avetz tan estat
que no fezetz vers ni chanso?
Respondetz me, per cal razo
reman que non avetz chantat,
s'o laissatz per mal o per be, 5
per ir' o per joi o per que,
que saber en volh la vertat.

II. Bernart, chantars no·m ven a grat
ni gaire no·m platz ni·m sap bo,
mas car voletz nostra tenso, 10
n'ai era mon talan forsat.
Pauc val chans que dal cor no ve;
e pois jois d'amor laisse me,
eu ai chan e deport laissat.

III. Peirol, mout i faitz gran foudat, 15
s'o laissatz per tal ochaizo.
S'eu agues agut cor felo,
mortz fora, un an a passat,
qu'enquer no posc trobar merce.
Ges per tan de chan no·m recre, 20
car doas perdas no m'an at.

IV. Bernart, ben ai mon cor mudat,
que totz es autres c'anc no fo.
No chanterai mais en perdo
… … … … … … … 25
mas de vos volh, chantetz jasse
de celei qu'en grat no·us o te,
e que perdatz vostr' amistat.

V. Peirol, manh bo mot n'ai trobat
    de leis, c'anc us no m'en tenc pro.   30
    E s'ilh serva cor de leo,
    no m'a ges tot lo mon serrat,
    qu'e·n sai tal una, per ma fe,
    c'am mais s'un baizar me cove,
    que de leis si·l m'agues donat.   35

VI. Bernart, ben es acostumat,
    qui mais no·n pot, c'aissi perdo.
    E la volps al sirieir dis o
    can l'ac de totas partz cerchat
    las sirieias vi lonh de se,   40
    e dis que no valion re.
    Atressi m'avetz vos gabat.

VII. Peirol, sirieias son o be,
     mas mal aya eu si ja cre
     que la volps no·n aya tastat.   45

VIII. Bernart, no·m n'entramet de re,
      mas peza·m de ma bona fe,
      car no·n i ai re gazanhat.

I. Peirol, why have you gone so long without writing poetry or songs? Tell me, for what reason haven't you sung? Are you giving it up because of bad luck or good, because of sorrow or joy or what? I want to know the truth of the matter.

II. Bernart, singing does not agree with me, and it does not please me or amuse me, but since you desire our tenso, I have now forced my will. A song which doesn't come from the heart is of little value; and since the joy of love forsakes me, I have forsaken song and amusement.

III. Peirol, you act very foolishly if you give it up on such a pretext. If I had had such a wicked heart, I would have been dead a year ago; even now I can find no favor. But in spite of that I do not renounce song, since two losses are no use to me.

32. PEIROL, COM AVETZ TAN ESTAT*

IV. Bernart, I have indeed changed my mind, for it is completely different from what it used to be. No longer will I sing in vain... but I want you always to sing of her who does not favor you and of how you are losing your love.

V. Peirol, I have composed many words about her, but not a one ever does me any good. And even though she is furnished with the heart of a lion, she has by no means closed the whole world to me, for, by my faith, I know a certain lady whom I love more if she but promise me a kiss, than I would the other if she had given me one.

VI. Bernart, it is quite usual for one who cannot do anything else to pass it off as the fox did with the cherry tree. After he had looked it over on all sides and saw that the cherries were far away from him, he said that they were worthless. You have fooled yourself in the same way.

VII. Peirol, so it is with cherries, but I'll be damned if I don't still believe the fox enjoyed them.

VIII. Bernart, I don't press the point, but I suffer on account of my good faith, because I have gained nothing by it.

33. PEL DOUTZ CHAN QUE·L ROSSINHOLS FAI

I. Pel doutz chan que·l rossinhols fai
    la noih can me sui adormitz
    revelh de joi totz esbäitz
    d'amor pensius e cossirans;
    c'aisso es mos melhers mesters 5
    que tostems ai joi volunters
    et ab joi comensa mos chans.

II. Qui sabia lo joi qu'eu ai
    que jois fos vezutz ni auzitz
    totz autre jois fora petitz 10
    vas qu'eu tenc que·l meus jois es grans.
    Tals se fai conhdes e parlers
    que·n cuid' esser rics e sobrers
    de fin' amor, que'eu n'ai dos tans.

III. Can eu remire so cors gai 15
     com es be faihz a totz chauzitz
     sa cortezi' e sos bels ditz,
     ja mos lauzars no m'er avans,
     c'obs m'i auri' us ans enters,
     si·n voli' esser vertaders 20
     tan es cortez' e ben estans.

IV. Cil que cuidon qu' eu sia sai
    no sabon ges com l'esperitz
    es de leis privatz et aizitz
    si tot lo cors s'en es lonhans. 25
    Sapchatz, lo melher messatgers
    c'ai de leis es mos cossirers
    que·m recorda sos bels semblans.

33. PEL DOUTZ CHAN QUE·L ROSSINHOLS FAI

V. Domna vostre sui e serai
    del vostre servizi garnitz.   30
    Vostr' om sui juratz e plevitz
    e vostre m'era des abans.
    E vos etz lo meus jois primers
    e si seretz vos lo derrers
    tan com la vida m'er durans.   35

VI. No sai coras mais vos veirai,
    mas vau m'en iratz e maritz.
    Per vos me sui del rei partitz
    e prec vos que no·m sia dans
    qu'e·us serai en cort prezenters   40
    entre domnas e chavalers
    francs e doutz et umilians.

VII. Huguet mos cortes messatgers
     chantatz ma chanso volonters
     a la rëina dels Normans.   45

I. During the night when I am asleep, I wake with joy at the nightingale's sweet song, all confused, troubled and pensive in love; for this is my best pastime, in which I always gladly take joy; and with joy my song begins.

II. If someone knew the joy I have, and this joy were seen and heard, all other joys would be slight next to the one I have, so great is my joy. A man becomes genial and eloquent when he feels rich and great in true love. And I have twice my share!

III. When I gaze at her lively beauty — how well she is endowed with everything desirable, with courtly manner and beautiful speech — then my praise is worthless, * for it would take me an entire year if I wished to be truthful, so courtly and excellent is she.

IV. Those who think that I am here do not know how close and intimate with her my soul is, even though my body is far away from her. Know then that the best messenger I have from her is my memory, which recalls her fair semblance to me.

V. Lady, I am yours and will be, ready for your service. I am your man, sworn and pledged, and yours I was before. You are my first joy and will be my last, so long as my life endures.

VI. I do not know when I shall see you again, but I depart bitter and grieved. For your sake I have left the king, and I pray that there may be no trouble for me when I, frank, gentle and humble, am ready to do your service in court among ladies and knights.

VII. Hugh, my courtly messenger, sing my song eagerly to the Queen of the Normans.

34. PER DIEU, AMOR, EN GENTIL LOC CORTES

Appel attributes this poem to Guillem de Saint-Didier. It may be found in the new edition of Guillem by Aimo Sakari, *Poésies du troubadour Guillem de Saint-Didier* (Helsinki, 1956), pp. 146-152.

35. PER MELHS COBRIR LO MAL PES E·L COSSIRE

I. Per melhs cobrir lo mal pes e·l cossire
chan e deport et ai joi e solatz,
e fatz esfortz car sai chantar ni rire,
car eu me mor e nul semblan no·n fatz,
e per Amor sui si apoderatz, 5
tot m'a vencut a forsa ses batalha.

II. Anc Deus no fetz trebalha ni martire
ses mal d'amor qu'eu no sofris en patz;
mas d'aquel sui, si be·m peza, sofrire,
c'Amors mi fai amar lai on li platz. 10
E dic vos be que s'eu no sui amatz,
ges no reman en la mia nualha.

III. Midons sui om et amics e servire
e no·lh en quer mais autras amistatz
mas c'a celat los seus bels olhs me vire, 15
que gran be·m fan ades can sui iratz,
e ren lor en laus e merces e gratz,
qu'el mon non ai amic que tan me valha.

IV. Molt me sap bo lo jorn qu'eu la remire,
la boch' e·ls olhs e·l fron e·ls mas e·ls bratz 20
e l'autre cors, que res no·n es a dire
que no sia belamen faissonatz.
Gensor de leis no poc faire Beltatz,
per qu'eu m'en ai gran pen' e gran trebalha.

V. A mo talen volh mal, tan la dezire, 25
e pretz m'en mais, car eu fui tan auzatz
qu'en tan aut loc auzei m'amor assire,
per qu'eu m'en sui conhdes et ensenhatz.

35. PER MELHS COBRIR LO MAL PES E·L COSSIRE 143

E can la vei, sui tan fort envezatz;
vejaire m'es que·l cors al cel me salha. 30

VI.   Dins en mo cor me corrotz e·m azire,
car eu sec tan las mias volontatz.
Mas negus om no deu aital re dire,
c'om no sap ges com s'es aventuratz.
Que farai doncs dels bels semblans privatz?   35
Falhirai lor? Mais volh que·l mons me falha.

VII. Ab lauzengiers non ai ren a devire,
car anc per lor no fo rics jois celatz.
E dic vos tan que per mon escondire
et ab mentir lor ai chamjatz los datz.   40
Ben es totz jois a perdre destinatz
quez es perdutz per la lor devinalha.

VIII. Corona, man salutz et amistatz
e prec midons que m'ayut e me valha.

IX.   E que·m volha, sia sens o foudatz,   45
no·m pot esser ni afans ni trebalha.

I. To conceal better my painful thought and grief, I sing and play, and have joy and comfort. I force myself to sing and laugh,* for I am dying, though I do not let it show at all. I am completely overcome by Love, who conquered me by force without a struggle.

II. Never did God create any torment or agony which I do not suffer in peace, save the pain of love. But I endure it, though it is difficult for me, since Love makes me love where it pleases him. I assure you that if I am not loved, it is not the fault of my indolence.

III. To my lady I am vassal, lover and servant. I seek no other friendship but the secret one shown me by her beautiful eyes, which always do me so much good when I am unhappy. Therefore, I offer them praise, thanks, and gratitude because I have no friend in the world who is worth so much to me.

IV. I am greatly pleased on the day when I behold her, and her mouth, her eyes, her brow, her hands and her arms, and the rest of the body, for there is nothing to speak about which is not beautifully fashioned. Beauty cannot create a finer woman than she for whom I have great trouble and torment.

V. I am annoyed with my desire, so much do I want her. I prize myself more because I was bold enough to dare to place my love so high; therefore I am genial and wise. And when I see her, I am so happy it seems to me that my heart will vault to heaven.

VI. I am annoyed and provoked in my heart because I so readily follow my desires. But no one should say anything of that, for no one knows what is ventured. What shall I do then with her beautiful secret glances? Shall I fail them? I would rather the world failed me.

VII. I have nothing to do with flattering louts, for never was noble joy kept secret by them. So I assure you that to defend myself and to give them the lie I have loaded the dice.* All joy lost through their spying is destined to be lost.

VIII. Corona, I send health and friendship, and I pray that my lady may help and avail me.

IX. And, be it wise or foolish, may she wish neither to trouble nor torment me.

36. POIS PREYATZ ME, SENHOR,

I. Pois preyatz me, senhor,
    qu'eu chan, eu chantarai,
    e can cuit chantar, plor
    a l'ora c'o essai.
    Greu veiretz chantador   5
    be chan si mal li vai.
    Vai me doncs mal d'amor?
    Ans melhs que no fetz mai.
    E doncs, per que m'esmai?

II. Gran ben e gran onor,   10
    conosc que Deus me fai,
    qu'eu am la belazor
    et ilh me, qu'eu o sai.
    Mas eu sui sai, alhor,
    e no sai com l'estai.   15
    So m'auci de dolor,
    car ochaizo non ai
    de soven venir lai.

III. Empero tan me plai
    can de leis me sove   20
    que qui·m crida ni·m brai
    eu no·n au nula re.
    Tan dousamen me trai
    la bela·l cor de se
    que tals ditz qu'eu sui sai   25
    et o cuid et o cre
    que de sos olhs no·m ve.

IV. Amors, e que·m farai?
    Si guerrai ja ab te?
    Ara cuit qu'e·n morrai   30

del dezirer que·m ve
si·lh bela lai on jai
no m'aizis pres de se,
qu'eu la manei e bai
et estrenha vas me 35
so cors blanc, gras e le.

V. Ges d'amar no·m recre
per mal ni per afan,
e can Deus m'i fai be,
no·l refut ni·l soan. 40
E can bes no m'ave,
sai be sofrir lo dan,
c'a las oras cove
c'om s'an entrelonhan
per melhs salhir enan. 45

VI. Bona domna, merce
del vostre fin aman.
Qu'e·us pliu per bona fe
c'anc re non amei tan.
Mas jonchas, ab col cle, 50
vos m'autrei e·m coman.
E si locs s'esdeve,
vos me fatz bel semblan,
que molt n'ai gran talan.

VII. Mon Escuder e me 55
don Deus cor e talan
c'amdui n'anem truan.

VIII. Et el en men ab se
so don a plus talan,
et eu Mon Aziman. 60

I. My lords, since you ask me to sing, I shall sing. But when I think of singing, I bemoan the hour that I tried it. Rarely will

36. POIS PREYATZ ME, SENHOR 147

you see a singer sing well if things are going badly for him. Are things bad for me in love then? No, better than before. Then why am I dismayed?

II. I know that God does me great honor and good, since I love the most beautiful woman and she, me, as I well know. But I am here, not there, and I do not know how she is. And so I am dying of grief, for I seldom have a chance to go there.

III. However, I am so pleased when I think of her that, no matter who calls or shouts for me, I do not hear a thing. So gently does the beautiful one draw my heart from my breast that many people who do not see me with their eyes say, think, and believe that I am here.

IV. Love, what shall I do? Shall I wage war with you? I think now I shall die of the desire I have if the beautiful one does not bring me close to her, where she lies, so that I may caress and kiss her and take to me her white body, round and smooth.

V. I do not renounce love because of either pain or trouble. When God is good to me, I neither reject nor refuse my lot; and when good does not come to me, I can well endure the trouble at the hour when it is best for people to separate in order to make progress.

VI. Good lady, thank you for your noble love. I pledge you, in good faith, that I never loved anyone so much. With hands clasped and neck bowed, I yield and commend myself to you. And if the chance comes, give me that beautiful look for which I have great longing.

VII. May God give heart and desire to my Escudor and me, for we both wander in misery.*

VIII. He brings with him what he desires most; and I, my Aziman.

37. CAN LA FREJ' AURA VENTA

I. Can la frej' aura venta
deves vostre päis,
vejaire m'es qu'eu senta
un ven de paradis
per amor de la genta 5
vas cui eu sui aclis,
on ai meza m'ententa
e mo coratg' assis,
car de totas partis
per leis, tan m'atalenta. 10

II. Sol lo be que·m prezenta
sos bels olhs e·l francs vis,
que ja plus no·m cossenta,
me deu aver conquis.
No sai per que·us en menta, 15
car de re no·n sui fis,
mas greu m'es que·m repenta,
qued una vetz me dis
que pros om s'afortis
e malvatz s'espaventa. 20

III. De domnas m'es vejaire
que gran falhimen fan
per so car no son gaire
amat li fin aman.
Eu no·n dei ges retraire 25
mas so qu'elas volran,
mas greu m'es c'us trichaire
a d'amor ab enjan
o plus o atretan
com cel qu'es fis amaire. 30

IV. Domna, que cujatz faire
de me que vos am tan,
c'aissi·m vezetz mal traire
e morir de talan?
Ai, francha de bon aire, 35
fezetz m'un bel semblan,
tal don mos cors s'esclaire.
Que mout trac gran afan,
e no·i dei aver dan,
car no m'en posc estraire. 40

V. Si no fos gens vilana
e lauzenger savai,
eu agr' amor certana,
mas so en reire·m trai.
De solatz m'es umana 45
can locs es ni s'eschai,
per qu'eu sai c'a sotzmana
n'aurai encara mai,
c' astrucs sojorn' e jai
e malastrucs s'afana. 50

VI. Cel sui que no soana
lo be que Deus li fai,
qu'en aquella setmana
can eu parti de lai
me dis en razo plana 55
que mos chantars li plai.
Tot' arma crestiana
volgra agues tal jai
com eu agui et ai,
car sol d'aitan se vana. 60

VII. Si d'aisso m'essertana
d'autra vetz la·n creirai,
o si que no, ja mai
no creirai crestiana.

I. When the cold wind blows from your land, I seem to feel a wind from paradise because of love for a gentle lady, toward whom I am drawn and in whom I have placed both my understanding and my feeling. I break with all women on her account, so greatly does she please me.

II. That good alone, which her beautiful eyes and pure face offer me, must have conquered me even if she allowed me nothing else. I do not know why I should lie to you about it, for I am not sure of anything. But it would be difficult for me to repent it,* since she said to me one time that a good man strengthens himself, while a wretch languishes in fear.

III. It seems too that women make a great error in hardly ever loving true lovers. I ought not to report anything about them except what the women like, but it is painful for me when, by trickery, a cheater gets more love or at least as much as one who is a true lover.

IV. Lady, what do you plan to do with me, who love you so much, when you see me suffer thus, dying of desire? Alas, noble and gracious lady, give me a pleasing look, one which will light up my heart! For I endure great pain, and I ought not to suffer harm, because I cannot escape it.

V. If it were not for peasants and scandal-mongers, I know I would have a constant love; but these pull me back. She is human enough to comfort me when there is occasion or when the opportunity arises; therefore, I know that I shall have still more in secret, because the lucky find joy and pleasure, while the unlucky have grief.

VI. I am one who does not scorn the good God does him; for, the week when I parted from her, she told me in plain words that my songs please her. I wish every Christian soul might have such joy as I had and have, for only of this may one boast.

VII. If she assures me of this, I will believe her another time;* but if not, certainly I will never again believe a Christian woman.

38. CAN LA VERZ FOLHA S'ESPAN*

I. Can la verz folha s'espan
    e par flors blanch' el ramel,
    per lo douz chan del auzel
    se vai mos cors alegran.
    Lancan ve·ls arbres florir   5
    et au·l rossinhol chantar,
    adonc deu·s ben alegrar
    qui bon' amor saup chauzir.
    Mas eu n'ai una chauzida
    per qu'eu sui coindes e gais.   10

II. E se tuih el mon garan
    desoz la chapa del cel
    eron en un sol tropel,
    for d'una non ai talan.
    Mai d'aquesta no·m cossir,   15
    que·l jorn me fai sospirar
    e la noih no posc pauzar
    ni·m pren talans de dormir,
    tan es grail' et eschafida,
    ab cor franc e dihz verais.   20

III. S'eu fos a lei destinan,
     e for' eu dinz d'un chastel
     que·l jorn manges un morsel,
     lai viuria sens afan,
     se·m don' aisso qu'eu dezir.   25
     De be far se deu penar,
     car se·m ten en lonc pensar,
     no posc viure ni morir.
     Ar eslonh en breu ma vida,
     si com ja de mort me trais.   30

I. When the green leaf unfolds, and the white flower blossoms forth on the branch, my heart goes rejoicing with the sweet song of the bird. When one sees the trees flower, and hears the nightingale sing, then he who knew how to choose a good love ought to rejoice. And I have chosen one for whose sake I am bright and gay.

II. And if all the people in the world's circle,* under the spread of the sky, were in a single flock, I would have no desire except for one lady. I concern myself only with that woman who makes me sigh all day, while at night I cannot rest and have no desire to sleep, so delicate and slender is she, with noble heart and true speech.

III. If I were destined by her to stay in a castle and eat only one mouthful a day, I would live there without suffering if she gave me what I desire. She ought to strive to do rightly (by me), for if she holds me in suspense for long, I can neither live nor die. Now let her prolong* my life soon, as before she delivered me from death.

39. CAN L'ERBA FRESCH' E·LH FOLHA PAR

I. Can l'erba fresch' e·lh folha par
    e la flors boton' el verjan
    e·l rossinhols autet e clar
    leva sa votz e mou so chan,
    joi ai de lui e joi ai de la flor   5
    e joi de me e de midons major.
    Daus totas partz sui de joi claus e sens,
    mas sel es jois que totz autres jois vens.

II. Ai las, com mor de cossirar,
    que manhtas vetz en cossir tan,   10
    lairo m'en poirian portar
    que re no sabria que·s fan.
    Per Deu, Amors, be·m trobas vensedor,
    ab paucs d'amics e ses autre senhor.
    Car una vetz tan midons no destrens   15
    abans qu'eu fos del dezirer estens?

III. Meravilh me com posc durar
    que no·lh demostre mo talan.
    Can eu vei midons ni l'esgar,
    li seu bel olh tan be l'estan   20
    per pauc me tenh car eu vas leis no cor.
    Si feira eu si no fos per paor,
    c'anc no vi cors melhs talhatz ni depens
    ad ops d'amar sia tan greus ni lens.

IV. Tan am midons e la tenh car   25
    e tan la dopt' e la reblan
    c'anc de me no·lh auzei parlar
    ni re no·lh quer ni re no·lh man.
    Pero ilh sap mo mal e ma dolor,
    e can li plai, mi fai ben et onor,   30

    e can li plai, eu m'en sofert ab mens,
    per so c'a leis no·n avenha blastens.

V. S'eu saubes la gen enchantar,
    mei enemic foran efan
    que ja us no saubra triar   35
    ni dir re que·ns tornes a dan.
  Adoncs sai eu que vira la gensor
  e sos bels olhs e sa frescha color
  e baizera·lh la bocha en totz sens
  si que d'un mes i paregra lo sens.   40

VI. Be la volgra sola trobar,
    que dormis, o·n fezes semblan,
    per qu'e·lh embles un doutz baizar,
    pus no valh tan qu'eu lo·lh deman.
  Per Deu, domna, pauc esplecham d'amor; 45
  vai s'en lo tems, e perdem lo melhor.
  Parlar degram ab cubertz entresens
  e pus no·ns val arditz, valgues nos gens.

VII. Be deuri'om domna blasmar
    can trop vai son amic tarzan,   50
    que lonja paraula d'amar
    es grans enois e par d'enjan,
  c'amar pot om e far semblan alhor
  e gen mentir lai on non a autor.
  Bona domna, ab sol c'amar mi dens,   55
  ja per mentir eu no serai atens.

VIII. Messatger, vai e no m'en prezes mens
  s'eu del anar vas midons sui temens.

  I. When the fresh grass and the leaf appear and the flower buds on the branch, and when the nightingale lifts his voice high and clear and sings his song, I rejoice in him, I rejoice in the flower, and I rejoice in myself, but even more in my lady. I am surrounded and bound with joy, but this is a joy which conquers all others.

II. Alas, I am dying of confusion. Often I worry so intensely that thieves could carry me off and I would not even know what they were doing. For God's sake, Love, you find me indefensible — with few friends and no other lord. Why didn't you once afflict my lady thus before I was perishing of desire?

III. I marvel that I can endure without revealing to her my longing. When I see my lady and gaze upon her, her beautiful eyes so become her that I can scarcely keep from running to her. And I would do it, if it were not for fear, since I never saw a body better formed and fashioned for the service of love, and yet so slow and reluctant.

IV. I love and cherish my lady so much, and I fear and serve her so passionately, that I have never dared speak to her of myself. Neither do I seek or demand anything of her. However, she knows my pain and grief, and so, when it pleases her, she treats me well and honorably; and when it pleases her, I get along with less, so that blame will not fall upon her.

V. If I could bewitch people, my enemies would be children, so that not one would be able to discover or tell anything which might bring harm to us. Then I would see the most beautiful one, her lovely eyes and her fresh color. I would kiss her mouth on all sides, and the marks would show for a month.

VI. I would like to find her alone, either sleeping or feigning sleep, so that I might steal a sweet kiss, since I am not worthy enough to ask her for one. My God, lady! How little we achieve in love. The time flies and we lose the best part of it. We should speak by secret signs. Since boldness does us little good, perhaps trickery might be of some worth.

VII. One ought to blame a woman when she puts off her lover too long. Talking a long time about love is a great annoyance and seems a trick, for one can love in one place and only pretend elsewhere; and people permit lies when there is no witness. Good lady, if only you might deign to love me, then I would not be affected by lying.

VIII. Messenger, go, and do not think less of me if I am afraid to go to my lady.

40. CAN LO BOSCHATGES ES FLORITZ

I. Can lo boschatges es floritz
  e vei lo tems renovelar
  e chascus auzels quer sa par
  e·l rossinhols fai chans e critz,
  d'un gran joi me creis tals oblitz   5
  que ves re mais no·m posc virar.
  Noih e jorn me fai sospirar,
  si·m lassa del cor la razitz.

II. Per midons m'esjau no-jauzitz,
  don m'es l'afans greus a portar,   10
  qu'e·m perdrai per leis gazanhar,
  et er li crims mout deschauzitz.
  Las, que farai? Com sui träitz
  si s'amor no·m vol autreyar.
  Qu'eu no posc viure ses amar,   15
  que d'amor sui engenöitz.

III. Ar sui de leis trop eissernitz.
  Lenga, per que potz tan parlar?
  Que de menhs me sol acuzar
  sí que·m sui per las dens feritz,   20
  que·m n'es si fer s'eu sui delitz,
  ja no trobara, li m'ampar.
  Mas ab doutz sentir d'un baizar
  for'eu tost d'est mal resperitz.

IV. En greu pantais sui feblezitz   25
  per leis cui Beutatz volc formar,
  que com Natura poc triar,
  del melhs es sos cors establitz,
  los flancs grailes et escafitz,
  sa fatz frescha com roza par   30

40. CAN LO BOSCHATGES ES FLORITZ

don me pot leu mort revivar.
Dirai com? No sui tan arditz.

V. De tal dousor sui replenitz
can de prop la posc remirar,
c'a totz jorns vei lo meu sobrar   35
ta fort sui de s'amor techitz.
E·l freis es tals qu'e·n sui marritz
can la vei de me deslonhar,
que·l focs que m'en sol eschalfar
fug, e remanh escoloritz.   40

VI. Lo bes e·l mals sia·lh grazitz,
pos de me denha sol preyar.
Ara folei de trop gabar
et es dreihs qu'en fos desmentitz.
Domna, no·us pes si·lh lenga ditz   45
so c'anc mos cors no poc pessar,
tatz, bocha. Nems potz lengueyar
et es t'en grans mals aramitz.

VII. Autz es lo pretz qu'es cossentitz,
car sol me denhet saludar.   50
Moutas merces. Deus la·n ampar.
Del plazer me sui engrevitz,
totz l'uctre bes m'es si frezitz
que no·m valgra·n merce clamar.
Clama·l cors que no pot cessar   55
et apres m'es parlars falhitz.

VIII. Domna, s'eu fos de vos auzitz
si charamen com volh mostrar,
al prim de nostr' enamorar
feiram chambis dels esperitz,   60
azautz sens m'i fora cobitz,
c'adonc saubr' eu lo vostr' afar
e vos lo meu, tot par a par,
e foram de dos cors unitz.

IX. Ai can brus sui, mal escharnitz. 65
 Qu'eu no posc la pena durar
 de tal dolor me fai pasmar,
 car tan s'amistat m'esconditz.
 Ab bel semblan sui eu träitz.
 Que·m val? Res no·m pot chastiar. 70
 Mortz venh' a sel qui·m vol blasmar
 qu'eu no l'am mortz e sebelitz.

X. Car forsatz m'en part e marritz,
 leu m'auci, mas greu fui noiritz.
 Tal ira·m sen al cor trenchar, 75
 car me mor e volh trespassar,
 mas ses leis no serai gueritz.

I. When the wood is in flower and I see the spring reborn, and each bird seeks its mate, while the nightingale sings and cries, I grow so distracted with great joy that I cannot care about anything else. Night and day it makes me sigh and binds the very root* of my heart.

II. For my lady I rejoice without joy* and it is difficult to bear the suffering. I shall ruin myself to win her, and this will indeed be for her a base crime. Alas, what shall I do? How I am betrayed if she does not wish to grant me her love! I cannot live without love, for I was engendered by love.

III. Now I am too picayune* for her! Tongue, why do you talk so much? She usually accuses me for less, so that now I have hurt my case by my own mouth, which is so harsh to me that I am ruined.* Indeed, I shall not find anyone who may protect me from it. But with the sweet touch of a kiss, I would soon be cured of this evil.

IV. I have been weakened by a great distress for the sake of her whom beauty chose to create. Her body is formed of the best which Nature can select: her hips are slim and slender while her face appears fresh as a rose. With these, she could easily revive me from death. Shall I say how? I am not so bold.

V. I am filled with such sweetness when I can look at her closely, that I see my good fortune continually surpassing itself, so much have I gained* from her love. And when I see her leave me, I am so cold that I am stricken, because the fire that used to warm me flees and I remain pale.

VI. Let her be thanked for good and ill alike when she deigns to demand a favor from me alone. But now I play the fool with too much bragging, and it is proper that I should be rejected. Lady, do not be upset if my tongue says what my heart could never think. Quiet, mouth! You chatter far too much, and there is much harm in you.

VII. High honor is granted me, for she deigned to greet me alone. Many thanks, may God protect her for it. I am burdened* with pleasure, and all other good is so indifferent for me that I cannot cry out for mercy, but my heart cries out for it and cannot help it; then words fail me.

VIII. Lady, if you were to listen to me as seriously as I wish to speak, at the beginning of our love we would exchange souls. An agreeable knowledge would be mine since I would know how it is with you, and you would know how it is with me. Everything equal, we would unite two hearts.

IX. Ah, how melancholy I am, and badly fated. I cannot endure the pain of this grief which makes me faint when she denies me her love so often. I am betrayed by a fair semblance. What can help me? Nothing can teach me. May death come to anyone who wants to say that I will not love her even when I am dead and buried.

X. Grieved and against my will, I leave her. She kills me easily, since I had so little to keep me alive.* I feel such pain slash my heart that I am dying and wish to pass on. But without her, I shall not be cured.

41. CAN PAR LA FLORS JOSTA·L VERT FOLH

I. Can par la flors josta·l vert folh
    e vei lo tems clar e sere
    e·l doutz chans dels auzels pel brolh
    m'adousa lo cor e·m reve,
    pos l'auzel chanton a lor for, 5
    eu, c'ai mais de joi en mo cor,
    dei be chantar pois tuih li mei jornal
    son joi e chan, qu'eu no pes de ren al.

II. Cela del mon qued eu plus volh
    e mais l'am de cor e de fe 10
    au de joi mos dihz e·ls acolh
    e mos precs escout' e rete.
    E s'om ja per ben amar mor,
    eu en morrai, qu'ins en mo cor
    li port amor tan fin' e natural 15
    que tuih son faus vas me li plus leyal.

III. Be sai la noih, can me despolh,
     el leih qu'eu no dormirai re.
     Lo dormir pert, car eu lo·m tolh
     per vos, domna, don me sove, 20
     que lai on om a so tezor
     vol om ades tener so cor.
     S'eu no vos vei, domna, don plus me cal,
     negus vezers mo bel pesar no val.

IV. Can me membra com amar solh 25
    la fausa de mala merce,
    sapchatz c'a tal ira m'o colh
    per pauc vius de joi no·m recre.
    Domna, per cui chan e demor,
    per la bocha·m feretz al cor 30

41. CAN PAR LA FLORS JOSTA·L VERT FOLH 161

   d'un doutz baizar de fin' amor coral
   que·m torn en joi e·m get d'ira mortal.

V. Tals n'i a qued an mais d'orgolh
   can grans jois ni grans bes lor ve,
   mas eu sui de melhor escolh   35
   e plus francs can Deus me fai be.
   C'ora qu'eu fos d'amor a l'or,
   er sui de l'or vengutz al cor.
   Merce, domna, non ai par ni engal;
   res no·m sofranh, sol que Deus vos me sal.   40

VI. Domna, si no·us vezon mei olh,
   be sapchatz que mos cors vos ve,
   e no·us dolhatz plus qu'eu me dolh,
   qu'eu sai c'om vos destrenh per me.
   Mas si·l gelos vos bat de for   45
   gardatz qu'el no vos bat' al cor.
   Si·us fai enoi, e vos lui atretal,
   e ja ab vos no gazanh be per mal.

VII. Mo Bel-Vezer gart Deus d'ir' e de mal,
   s'eu sui de lonh e de pres atretal.   50

VIII. Sol Deus midons e mo Bel-Vezer sal,
   tot ai can volh, qu'eu no deman ren al.

  I. When the flower appears by the green leaves, and I find the season clear and quiet, and soft songs of the birds in the grove sweeten my heart and refresh me, then the birds sing in their fashion; and I, who have more joy in my heart, must also sing well, for every day's work is mirth and melody; I think of nothing else.
  II. She, whom I desire most in the world and whom I most love with all my heart and faith, hears my words with pleasure, welcomes them, listens to my pleas and remembers them. And if a man ever dies of great love, I will die of it, since within my heart I carry a love so true and real that, compared with me, the most sincere are all false.

III. I know full well that when I undress at night, I will not sleep at all in bed. I lose sleep because I deprive myself of it for your sake, lady, whom I call to mind. For where one has his treasure, there too he wants ever to keep his heart. Lady, if I do not see you who are most dear to me, no other sight is worth as much as my beautiful thought.

IV. When I recall how I used to love the false, unmerciful woman, know that I get so angry that I almost give up this vibrant joy.* Lady, for whom I sing and rejoice, wound me through the mouth to the heart with a sweet kiss of true, sincere love, so returning me to joy and casting fatal sorrow from me.

V. There are those who become puffed up with pride when great joy and fortune come to them. But I am of a better school and am more noble when God grants me good fortune. For then I was on the brink of love; now I have come from the brink to the heart. Mercy, lady; I have neither peer nor equal. I would lack nothing, if only God saved you for me.

VI. Lady, know well that even if my eyes do not look on you, my heart sees you. You do not suffer more than I do, though I know you are oppressed for my sake. But if your jealous husband beats your body, take care that he does not strike your heart. If he inflicts harm on you, do likewise to him, and he will never gain good things from you by wickedness.

VII. My Bel-Vezer, may God keep you from grief and evil, whether I am far from you or near.

VIII. If only God protect my lady and Bel-Vezer, I have all I want; I ask nothing else.

42. CAN VEI LA FLOR, L'ERBA VERT E LA FOLHA

I. Can vei la flor, l'erba vert e la folha
    et au lo chan dels auzels pel boschatge,
    ab l'autre joi qu'eu ai en mo coratge
    dobla mos jois* e nais e creis e brolha.
    E no m'es vis c'om re poscha valer   5
    s'eras no vol amor et joi aver,
    pus tot can es s'alegr' e s'esbaudeya.

II. Ja no crezatz qu'eu de joi me recreya
    ni·m lais d'amar per dan c'aver en solha,
    qu'eu non ai ges en poder que m'en tolha,   10
    c'amors m'asalh que·m sobresenhoreya
    e·m fai amar cal que·lh plass' e voler.
    E s'eu am so que no·m deu eschazer,
    forsa d'amor m'i fai far vassalatge.

III. Mas en amor non a om senhoratge,   15
    e qui l'i quer vilanamen domneya,
    que re no vol amors qu'esser no deya.
    Paubres e rics fai amdos d'un paratge;
    can l'us amics vol l'autre vil tener,
    pauc pot amors ab ergolh remaner,   20
    qu'ergolhs dechai e fin' amors capdolha.

IV. Eu sec cela que plus vas me s'ergolha
    e cela fuih que·m fo de bel estatge,
    c'anc pois no vi ni me ni mo messatge,
    per qu'es mal sal que ja domna m'acolha,   25
    mas dreih l'en fatz qu'eu m'en fatz fol parer,
    car per cela que·m torn' en no-chaler
    estauc aitan de leis que no la veya.

V. Mas costum' es tostems que fols foleya,
    e ja non er qu'el eis lo ram no colha   30

    que·l bat e·l fer, per c'ai razo que·m dolha,
    car anc me pres d'autrui amor enveya.
    Mas fe qu'eu dei leis e mo Bel-Vezer,
    si de s'amor me torn' en bon esper,
    ja mais vas leis no farai vilanatge.   35

VI. Ja no m'aya cor felo ni sauvatge,
    ni contra me mauvatz cosselh no creya,
    qu'eu sui sos om liges on que m'esteya
    si que de sus del chap li ren mo gatge;
    mas mas jonchas li venh a so plazer   40
    e ja no·m volh mais d'a sos pes mover
    tro per merce·m meta lai o·s despolha.

VII. L'aiga del cor c'amdos los olhs me molha
    m'es be guirens qu'eu penet mo folatge
    e conosc be midons en pren damnatge   45
    s'ela tan fai que perdonar no·m volha.
    Pois meus no sui et ilh m'a en poder,
    mais pert s'ela qu'eu el meu dechazer,
    per so l'er gen s'ab son ome plaideya.

VIII. Mo messatger man a mo Bel-Vezer,   50
    que cilh que·m tolc lo sen e lo saber,
    me tol midons e leis que no la veya.

IX.* Amics Tristans, car eu no·us posc vezer,
    a Deu vos do cal que part que m'esteya.

I. When I see flowers, green grass and leaves, and hear the song of the birds through the wood, my joy, blended with the other joy that I have in my heart, is doubled,* reborn, flourishes and blossoms. And it does not seem to me that a man may be at all worthy if he does not want to have love and joy now, when everything that lives is happy and rejoices.

II. Never believe that I renounce joy or that I abstain from love because of the grief I am wont to suffer for it, for I do not have the strength to cut myself off from it, since love assails me and lords it over me, making me love and desire whomever he pleases. If I love one who should not be mine, love's power makes me act like a knight.*

III. But man does not have mastery in matters of love, and whoever seeks it courts basely, since love wants nothing which is not proper. He makes both poor and rich the same rank. And when one lover wants to consider the other base, love and pride remain together only a short time, for pride collapses and true love reigns.

IV. I follow the woman who is most arrogant towards me, while fleeing the lady who was full of goodness. Never since her kindness to me, has she seen me or my messenger — whence it is a mistake for any woman to be kind to me. But I make amends to her when I let myself look like a fool by remaining away where I cannot see her; all on account of the other woman who is indifferent to me.*

V. It is ever the habit of a fool to act foolishly, and it will always be he himself who chooses the rod that beats and wounds him; therefore I have cause to grieve that I ever desired the love of another woman. But by the faith which I owe her and my Bel Vezer, I will never again act basely to her, if she gives me good reason to hope for her love.

VI. She should never have a cruel and villainous heart toward me, nor believe any bad rumors against me. I am her liegeman wherever I may be, and I give her my pledge from the crown of my head.* With hands clasped I present myself to her at her pleasure, and I never wish to move from her feet until, through her compassion, she takes me to her boudoir.

VII. The tears from my heart that moisten my eyes are surely a pledge that I repent my folly. I know for sure that my lady will regret it if she goes so far as to refuse to pardon me. Since I am not my own master, and since she has me in her power, she has more to lose from my downfall than I do. Therefore, it would be good for her to negotiate with her vassal.

VIII. I send my messenger to my Bel Vezer, for the one who robbed me of my wit and intelligence takes away my lady and her, so that I may not see her.

IX.* Friend Tristan, because I cannot see you, I give you over to God wherever I may be.

43. CAN VEI LA LAUZETA MOVER

I. Can vei la lauzeta mover
de joi sas alas contral rai
que s'oblid' e·s laissa chazer
per la doussor c'al cor li vai,
ai, tan grans enveya m'en ve
de cui qu'eu veya jauzion,
meravilhas ai, car desse
lo cor de dezirer no·m fon.

II. Ai, las, tan cuidava saber
d'amor e tan petit en sai,
car eu d'amar no·m posc tener
celeis don ja pro non aurai.
Tout m'a mo cor e tout m'a me
e se mezeis e tot lo mon,
e can se·m tolc, no·m laisset re
mas dezirer e cor volon.

III. Anc non agui de me poder
ni no fui meus de l'or' en sai
que·m laisset en sos olhs vezer
en un miralh que mout me plai.
Miralhs, pus me mirei en te,
m'an mort li sospir de preon
c'aissi·m perdei com perdet se
lo bels Narcisus en la fon.

IV. De las domnas me dezesper.
Ja mais en lor no·m fiarai,
c'aissi com las solh chaptener,
enaissi las deschaptenrai.
Pois vei c'una pro no m'en te
va leis que·m destrui e·m cofon,

totas las dopt' e las mescre,
car be sai c'atretals se son.

V. D'aisso·s fa be femna parer
ma domna, per qu'e·lh o retrai,
car no vol so c'om deu voler 35
e so c'om li deveda fai.
Chazutz sui en mala merce
et ai be faih co·l fols en pon,
e no sai per que m'esdeve
mas car trop puyei contra mon. 40

VI. Merces es perduda per ver,
et eu non o saubi anc mai,
car cilh qui plus en degr'aver
no·n a ges, et on la querrai?
A, can mal sembla, qui la ve, 45
qued aquest chaitiu deziron
que ja ses leis non aura be
laisse morir, que no l'aon.

VII. Pus ab midons no·m pot valer
precs ni merces ni·l dreihz qu'eu ai, 50
ni a leis no ven a plazer
qu'eu l'am, je mais no·lh o dirai.
Aissi·m part de leis e·m recre.
Mort m'a e per mort li respon,
e vau m'en pus ilh no·m rete, 55
chaitius, en issilh, no sai on.

VIII. Tristans, ges no·n auretz de me,
qu'eu m'en vau, chaitius, no sai on.
De chantar me gic e·m recre,
e de joi e d'amor m'escon. 60

I. When I see the lark beat his wings for joy against the sun's ray, until, for the sheer delight which goes to his heart, he forgets to fly and plummets down, then great envy of those whom I see filled with happiness comes to me. I marvel that my heart does not melt at once from desire.

II. Alas! I thought I knew so much about love, but really, I know so little. For I cannot keep myself from loving her from whom I shall have no favor. She has stolen from me my heart, myself, herself and all the world. When she took herself from me, she left me nothing but desire and a longing heart.

III. Never have I been in control of myself or even belonged to myself from the hour she let me gaze into her eyes: —that mirror which pleases me so greatly. Mirror, since I saw myself reflected in you, deep sighs have been killing me. I have destroyed myself just as the beautiful Narcissus destroyed himself in the fountain.

IV. I despair of women. No more will I trust them; and just as I used to defend them, now I shall denounce them. Since I see that none aids me against her who destroys and confounds me, I fear and distrust all of them, for I know very well that they are all alike.

V. In such things my lady acts like a woman, and for this I reproach her. She does not want to do what she should, and she does what is forbidden to her. I have fallen into ill-favor, and I have acted like the fool on the bridge;* yet I do not know how it happens to me, unless it is that I tried to climb too high.

VI. Mercy is lost for good — although I never knew it anyway — for she, who ought most to have it, has none at all. Yet where shall I seek it? How sorry it must appear, when one considers it,* that she lets this miserable, longing creature, who has no good without her, perish without helping him.

VII. Since neither prayers, pity, nor the justice of my cause help me with my lady, and since my loving her brings her no pleasure, I will say no more to her. I leave her and renounce her. She has slain me and with death* I shall answer her. Since she does not retain me, I depart, wretched, into exile, I know not whither.

VIII. Tristan, you shall have nothing more from me,* for I depart, wretched, I know not whither. I forsake and renounce singing, and I seek shelter from joy and love.

44. TANT AI MO COR PLE DE JOYA,

I. Tant ai mo cor ple de joya,
    tot me desnatura.
Flor blancha, vermelh' e groya
    me par la frejura,
c'ab lo ven et ab la ploya   5
    me creis l'aventura,
per que mos pretz mont' e poya
    e mos chans melhura.
    Tan ai al cor d'amor,
    de joi e de doussor,   10
per que·l gels me sembla flor
    e la neus verdura.

II. Anar posc ses vestidura,
    nutz en ma chamiza,
car fin' amors m'asegura   15
    de la freja biza.
Mas es fols qui·s desmezura
    e no·s te de guiza.
Per qu'eu ai pres de me cura,
    deis c'agui enquiza   20
    la plus bela d'amor
    don aten tan d'onor,
car en loc de sa ricor
    no volh aver Piza.

III. De s'amistat me reciza,   25
    mas be n'ai fiansa
que sivals eu n'ai conquiza
    la bela semblansa.
Et ai ne a ma deviza
    tan de benanansa   30
que ja·l jorn que l'aurai viza,

    non aurai pezansa.
  Mo cor ai pres d'Amor,
  que l'esperitz lai cor,
  mas lo cors es sai, alhor,   35
    lonh de leis en Fransa.

IV. Eu n'ai la bon' esperansa.
    Mas petit m'aonda,
  c'atressi·m ten en balansa
    com la naus en l'onda.   40
  Del mal pes que·m desenansa,
    no sai on m'esconda.
  Tota noih me vir' e·m lansa
    desobre l'esponda,
    plus trac pena d'amor   45
    de Tristan l'amador,
    que·n sofri manhta dolor
      per Izeut la blonda.

V. Ai Deus, car no sui ironda
    que voles per l'aire   50
  e vengues de noih prionda
    lai dins so repaire?
  Bona domna jauzionda,
    mor se·l vostr' amaire.
  Paor ai que·l cors me fonda   55
    s'aissi·m dura gaire.
    Domna, per vostr' amor
    jonh las mas et ador.
  Gens cors ab frescha color,
    gran mal me faitz traire.   60

VI. Qu'el mon non a nul afaire
    don eu tan cossire
  can de leis au re retraire,
    que mo cor no i vire
  e mo semblan no·m n'esclaire.   65
    Que que·m n'aujatz dire,
  si c'ades vos er vejaire

44. TANT AI MO COR PLE DE JOYA

   c'ai talan de rire.
  Tan l'am de bon' amor
  que manhtas vetz en plor   70
 per o que melhor sabor
   m'en an li sospire.

VII. Messatgers, vai e cor
  e di·m a la gensor
 la pena e la dolor   75
   que·n trac e·l martire.

 I. My heart is so full of joy that everything seems changed* to me: the frost seems like white, red, and yellow flowers. With the wind and rain my good fortune prospers, so that my fame increases and rises, and my songs improve. My heart is so full of love, of joy, and of sweetness that ice seems like flowers to me, and snow like greenery.

 II. I can go without clothing, naked beneath my shirt, for true love protects me from the freezing north wind. But he is a fool who overreaches himself, and does not act as he should. Therefore, I have been very careful while courting the most beautiful lady, from whom I hope for so much honor. I would not trade all of Pisa for her rich favor.

 III. Let her cut me off from her friendship. I would still have great confidence that at least I had won its fair semblance. For my part,* I have enough happiness to sustain me from now until I can see her again.* My heart is close to Love, and my soul hastens there too; but my body is elsewhere: here in France, far from her.

 IV. I have great hope from her. But it does me little good, because she keeps me poised like a ship on a wave. I do not know how to escape from the sorrowful thought that afflicts me. All night, I toss and turn on the edge of the bed. I endure more love-pain than Tristan, the lover, who suffered so much for the sake of Iseut the blonde.

 V. Ah, God, why am I not a swallow who might fly through the air to come, in the dead of night, into her room? Good Lady, full of joy, your lover is dying. I fear my heart will melt if it goes on much longer like this. Lady, for your love, I clasp my hands and worship you. Fair form, with fresh color, you make me suffer great wrong.

VI. There is nothing in the world about which I worry so much. When I hear anything said about her, my heart turns toward her, and my face brightens. Whatever you may hear me say about it, you will always think I feel like smiling. I love her with such true love that many times I weep, whence my sighs become the sweeter.

VII. Go, messenger, run. Speak for me; tell the fairest lady of the pain, the grief, and the torment which I suffer for her.

45. TUIH CIL QUE·M PREYON QU'EU CHAN,

I. Tuih cil que·m preyon qu'eu chan,
    volgra saubesson lo ver,
    s'eu n'ai aize ni lezer.
    Chantes qui chantar volria,
    qu'eu no·n saup ni chap ni via, 5
    pois perdei ma benanansa
    per ma mala destinansa.

II. Ai las, com mor de talan.
    Qu'eu no dorm mati ni ser,
    que la noih can vau jazer 10
    lo rossinhols chant' e cria,
    et eu que chantar solia
    mor d'enoi e de pezansa,
    can au joi ni alegransa.

III. D'amor vos dirai aitan, 15
    qui be la saubes tener
    res plus no·n pogra valer.
    Per Deu mout fo bona·lh mia.
    Mas no·m duret mas un dia,
    per qu'es fols qui ses fermansa 20
    met en amor s'esperansa.

IV. Amors m'a mes en soan
    e tornat a no-chaler.
    E s'eu l'agues en poder,
    dic vos qu'e·n feira feunia. 25
    Mas Deus no vol c'Amors sia
    res don om prenda venjansa
    ab coup d'espa' o de lansa.

V. Amors, e·us prec de mon dan,
    c'autre pro no i posc aver. 30

Ja mais blandir ni temer
no·us quer, c'adoncs vos perdria.
Ben es fols qui'n vos se fia,
c'ab vostra fausa semblansa
m'avetz träit en fiansa. 35

VI. Pero per un bel semblan
sui enquer en bon esper.
Mon Conort dei grat saber,
c'ades vol qu'eu chan e ria.
E dic vos que, s'ilh podia, 40
eu seria reis de Fransa,
car al plus qu'ilh pot, m'enansa.

VII. Lemozi, a Deu coman
leis que no·m vol retener,
qu'era pot ilh be saber 45
s'es vers aco que·lh dizia,
qu'en terr' estranha·m n'iria,
pois Deus ni fes ni fiansa
no m'i poc far acordansa.

VIII. No m'o tenh a vilania 50
s'eu m'ai sai bon' esperansa,
pois ilh lai re no m'enansa.

IX. Romeu man que per m'amia
e per lui farai semblansa
qu'eu ai sai bon' esperansa. 55

I. I want all those who ask me to sing to know the truth, if I have occasion or leisure for it. Let him sing who wants to. I have not been able to do it since I lost my happiness through my dark destiny.

II. Alas, how I die of desire! I do not sleep day or night, for at night when I go to lie down, the nightingale sings and cries, and I who used to sing, die from distress and chagrin, whenever I hear joy or exultation.

45. TUIH CIL QUE·M PREYON QU'EU CHAN 175

III. I will tell you this much about Love: no one could be more worthy of it than the man who knows well how to hold on to it. By God, my love was fine and good, but it did not last more than a day. For that reason, anyone is a fool to put his hope in love without a guarantee.

IV. Love has scorned me and become indifferent to me. But if I had him in my power, I tell you that I would treat him cruelly! Yet God does not want Love to be someone on whom one may take vengeance with the blow of a sword or a lance.

V. Love, I plead with you about my pain, since I can have no other help. No longer will I seek to fawn on you or fear you, for that would be the surest way to lose you. Anyone would be a fool to trust you, because with your false pretense you have betrayed my trust.

VI. However, because of her beautiful semblance, I am still full of good hope. I ought to be grateful to my Conort, because she always wants me to sing and laugh. And I tell you that if it were in her power, I would be king of France, for she advances me as much as she can.

VII. Lemozi, to God I commend her who does not want to keep me. Now she may know for sure whether what I told her is true: that I would go into a foreign land since God cannot grant me either faith or fidelity in this affair.

VIII. I do not count it shameful of me to have good hope here, even though she advances me in nothing.

IX. I tell Romeu that for the sake of my lady and for his own sake, I shall give the impression that I have good hope here.

NOTES

Vidas. The texts of *vida* B and the *razos* are taken from Boutière (Jean) et Schutz (A. H.). *Biographies des troubadours* (Toulouse, 1950), pp. 26-9. The text of *vida* A is from Hill and Bergin, p. 30, and the text of the stanza by Peire d'Alverhne which is cited in *vida* B is also taken from Hill and Bergin, p. 72.

Razo C *que lui leva adonc lo pan del mantel,* etc. The abundance of pronouns without clear reference in this sentence makes it difficult to ascertain whose coat is actually being raised and tucked under whose collar. It seems difficult to believe that the relative pronoun *que,* following *dona,* should refer as far back as *cavaliers.* Under the circumstances, it seems better to read the *que* as referring to the *dona.* Then the indirect object *lui* should refer to the *cavaliers.* One would expect a reflexive as in *laissa si cazer,* if the *lui leva* and the *mes li* were referring to actions the woman was doing to herself.

1,14 *ses paor e ses doptansa.* There has been no general agreement on the precise meaning of *doptansa.* Levy (*Supp.-Wörter.* ii, 286a) lists 'Gefahr' as the meaning of *doptansa.* Appel translates *paor,* in this line, by 'Furcht' and *doptansa* by 'Sorge'. Lewent ("Weitere textkritische Bemerkungen zu den Liedern B. von V.," p. 657) attempts to refine the definition of these words with particular regard for the love situation. He feels that *paor* means 'Zurückhaltung' in this case, and *doptansa* 'Scheu'.

1,46 *com de Pelaus la lansa.* This idea goes back to Ovid, *Remedium Amoris,* 47-8:

> Vulnus in Herculeo quae quondam fecerat hoste,
> Vulneris auxilium Pelias hasta tulit.

Pelias hasta was translated "the spear of Pelius," instead of "the spear of Mt. Pelion" where the centaur Cheiron, who gave the spear to Peleus, lived. See Paget Toynbee, *Modern Language Quarterly,* (London), I (1897), p. 58.

1,61-64 This *tornada* is found only in ms. C.

3,11 *C'anc no m'en detz jauzimen.* Kurt Lewent (p. 659) thinks it improbable that *detz,* second person plural going all the way back to the first and fifth lines, would be used here. He thinks that the reading for *detz* should be *des* (following mss. MDHSa), and that the third person is therefore intended. He would then translate, "Ohne dass sie (die Liebe) mir je eine Freude von ihr (der Dame) gegeben hätte."

3,26   *mais no·m n'escazegra.* Lewent (p. 659) remarks that this is a usual parataxis which we must render today by a complete sentence. He suggests, "Amor gab mir in Bezug auf sie mehr als mir zustehen würde."

3,35   *qu'amors n'es vas me doptoza.* Appel remarks that it seems incredible that *Amors* should be afraid of the poet, and this would seem to be true. He wonders if it would be possible to read *vas leis* for *vas me.* One might explain it without a ms. change, though, by seeing an impersonal construction here which actually does not refer to the external force, love, but to the love in the poet, i. e. that part of himself which dares to love the *domna.* It is this love in himself which is shy before the dazzling beauty of the woman. Appel seems to be thinking of *amors* the state of being, in terms of *Amors,* the ruling divinity.

5,7   *qu'eu cre c'aquel tems senhorei.* Appel expresses some doubt as to whether *senhorei* is first or third person. Schultz-Gora ("Zum texte des Bernart von Ventadorn," p. 352) sees no reason to doubt that it is the third person singular. Lewent (p. 660) translates, "dass diese Zeit die schönste sei", defending this absolute sense of *senoreiar* by reference to a *tenso* of Guilh. de Saint-Leidier.

8,49-56   The *tornadas* are found only ms. C.

9,10-11   *mas oncas orgolh/n'ac vas lei.* Appel punctuates this sentence with a question mark, and translates: "denn, gab es je deshalb Hochmut ihr gegenüber?" Schultz-Gora (p. 353) objects to Appel's translation of *mas* by 'denn'. This is unnecessary he says, denying Appel's assertion that *n'* seldom is *no,* if one reads the *n'* in *n'ac* as the negative *no* belonging to the construction *oncas ... n!* Schultz-Gora then translates: "aber ich bezeigte nie Hochmut ihr gegenüber." In any case, Appel's use of a question mark to indicate a halfmusing reflection of the poet seems unfounded. The line is a perfectly straight-forward assertion on which he bases the following wish which begins (1,11), *per so ...*

10,21   *e s'aissi mor, requisitz li serai.* Appel (p. 65) ascribes the variety of readings offered by the ms. tradition to a basic misunderstanding of the line on the part of the copyists. He points out that the poet is evidently saying that the lady will be guilty if she lets her lover die. His state will then become an indictment of her action: "I shall be her indictment". A *requisitoire* is even today the accusation delivered by the state's office of prosecution: "acte du ministère public énumérant les charges qui pèsent sur l'accusé et requérant contre lui". Salvatore Battaglia (*Jaufre Rudel e Bernardo di Ventadorn,* p. 171), who follows Appel's stanza re-ordering (1, 2,

NOTES 179

5, 6, 4, 3, 7, 8), also concurs with Appel's opinion on 1.21. He translates: "e se così muoio, a lei ne sarà fatta colpa".

12,28 *mas totas res pot om en mal escrire.* i. e. the poet intends his love as a good thing, but the lady, twisting his words, views it as an evil.

12,31 *que no·m sia vendutz.* This may be a reference to a proverb such as "vendre ou donner," or "Qui ben fai non es dreg qel car vendra". The poet would be saying that he has left one woman because she had not offered her love willingly. Hence the natural stipulation to be laid down for the next woman would be that she give her love freely and willingly as the first woman did not. The following line (1.33, *qu' enoyos es preyars, pos er perdutz*) would then be a concise warning as well as an aphorism. 19,28-9 (*e prec ... / que · l be que·m fara no·m venda*) is to be compared to the expression under consideration. Both examples seem to have a proverb as their base. Appel's translations of both lines are: "... nicht teuer verkauft werde (12,31); ... mir nicht (teuer) verkaufte" (19,29). These translations (especially the inclusion of "teuer") would seem to indicate that Appel, too, understood a proverbial expression, perhaps something like the second one quoted above. 26,28 (*si·lh platz, que·m don o que·m venda*) seems to be an example of the first proverb quoted above used in the sense of: "let her do whatever she pleases with me". For a list of troubadour proverbs see Eugen Cnyrim, "Sprichwörter bei den provenzal Lyrikern". E. Stengel, *Ausgaben und Abhanglungen*, LXXI, 1888.

14,16 *can la troba de son talan.* As Appel points out (p. 83), one expects a negation, something like: "no one ought to despise love just because it does *not* suit his desire." There is no such negation in line 16, however, and the ms. tradition offers none. In attempting to explain the affirmative statement the line makes, Appel and Lewent have concentrated their attention on the latter part of the line, *de son talan,* accepting *trobar* simply in its literal sense of 'to find'. The general message of the poem, however, as with *canso* 2 (also a *tenso*), suggests that the line might better be explained by the figurative sense of *trobar*. The point made by Bernart's partner in each *tenso* is that things are not really as bad as they are represented to be in the individual's own mind (cf. *mas totas res pot om en mal escrire* — 12,28). It does not seem impossible, then, that *trobar* be taken in its figurative sense 'to create, invent, imagine, fancy'. The lines would say, in that case, something like: "it is not right for anyone to become angry with love (i. e. the real love situation) when he imagines it according to his own desire". Lemozi is thereby underlining the difference between love as it is imagined in the mind of the lover, and love as it actually turns out in reality.

16,13-16 *qu'eu eis m'o vauc enqueren,* etc. Appel, p. 96) understands the *o* (1.13) to refer back to *oblidatz* (1.11) and translates: "ich selbst suche es mir, ich selbst bin Schuld daran, dass Ihr mir vergesst." Lewent (p. 664) takes 1.14 as a relative clause without antecedent and thinks *o* refers to *qui* (1.14). Accordingly, he translates: "denn ich selbst habe es mir zuzuschreiben, wenn mich einer der Torheit anklagt, die darin besteht, dass ich ... " Lewent's explanation seems better than Appel's for two reasons. First, there is a clear syntactical break dividing the stanza into two halves at the end of line 12. Secondly, there is a switch from the direct address (*vos, oblidatz*) to the impersonal *midons*. Translating after Appel one would find himself in the awkward position of translating a personal 'you' and an impersonal 'my lady' in the same sentence.

17,16   *c'ans no·t laisses levar al ven*. Appel's note (p. 102) offers the following translation for lines 14-15: "Sie wird Dich nimmer lieben; derart, dass Du Dich eher vom Wind hinwegführen liessest (als dass sie Dich liebte)." Lewent (pp. 664-6) has a very long and interesting note on the history of *levar* in Old Provençal. The note is too long to reproduce here, but we can cite one of the main conclusions supporting his reading of *levar* and the translation of lines 14-16. Lewent first cites from Raynouard and Levy examples of the use of *levar* which seem to indicate that *levar* had the meaning 'to raise, elevate, as on the gallows or on the cross' (... *el crotz on Jhesus pres dolor E mort ... e·y fo per nos levatz* Aim. Bel. gr. 9,10). He then states: "*levar* ist also dasselbe wie *pendre* und *levar al ven* bei Bernart gleichbedeutend mit *pendre al*(s) *ven*(z) 'hangen'." He continues by citing examples where hanging and being unlucky in love are associated (as in Bernart 4,21 ... *anceis me fari'a pendre* ...), finally translating lines 14-16: "Tor! du hast wahrlich wenig Verstand, dass du dich nicht vorher hängen liessest, denn nimmer würde sie dir zugetan sein, weder dem Namen (äusseren Schein) nach noch in wirklicher Liebe."

17,57   *e s'a leis autre dols no·n pren*. Appel's note (p. 102) asks "Ist *autre dol* 'eines Anderen (in diessem Fall: mein) Schmerz?, ... oder bezeichnet es den vorgestellten, aber nicht angesprochenen, Gegensatz zur gewöhnlichen, gluchgiltigen, Stimmung der Dame: 'wenn nicht (etwas Anderes, nämlich) Schmerz sie ergreift ... ?' Die letzte Auffassung trifft wohl hier zu." Appel then translates: "Und wenn Schmerz sie nicht darob ergreift, so möge um Gottes und der Gnade willen (wenigstens) geschehen..." Schultz-Gora (pp. 355-6): "Die erste Deutung (given by Appel in his note) des *autre* ist die richtige und die zweite ist abzulehnen, s. Prov. Stud. S. 112 zu 32-3."

19,10   *de coratge*. Levy's *Petit dictionnaire* gives 'volontiers' as the meaning for *de coratge*; Apel translates 'von Herzen'. Should this expression be translated 'willingly' or 'sincerely'? Both would fit in the context.

19,29   *que·l be que·m fara no·m venda*. See note on 12,31 where expressions dealing with *vendre* are discussed.

20,8   *e lais m'en*. This refers to the first four lines of the stanza, "it would be fine if I were to sing ... but I do not think she is grateful ... and so I give up the idea of singing, etc."

20,34   *trop m'aten en voupilhatge*. In conjunction with the note referred to in our note on 1,14, Lewent (p. 657, n. 2) cites the line presently

NOTES 181

under consideration, giving 'Zurückhaltung' as a translation for *voupilhatge*: "Allzu sehr säume ich in vorsichtiger Zurückhaltung."

21,18 *don duc ni comte non envei*. Lewent (p. 666) feels that *don* has a causal meaning here, saying: "Bernart würde jeden, also auch einen Herzog oder Grafen, um die Dame beneiden! *Don* steht hier Kausal: 'um deren Willen (weil ich sie besitze) ich weder Herzog noch Grafen beneide'."

21,38 *que per paor remania*. *Remania* recalls the qualification *can pot* (1.35), which warned the reader that the lady was not free to indulge her benevolence all the time. The situation is similar to 20,15-18 (*e car me don espaven*, etc.). The basic fear of discovery underlies the psychology in both passages.

21,43 *e ja no vos anetz doptans*. Lewent (p. 666) refers the reader to his note which we discuss in our note on 1,14. Apparently, he would translate *doptans* here, the same way he translates *doptansa* in 1,14: "shy". But there it is the lover who is *doptansa* while it is a question of the *domna* here. It is difficult to see how the roles of shy poet-lover and imperious *domna* could become so reversed that *he* should be telling *her* not to be bashful. Raynouard translates *ja no i anetz doptans* as "jamais n'y allez doutant," and 'douter' would seem to be correct in this case.

21,57-60 This *tornada* is found only in ms. G. It has been added to ms. N by a later hand. See Appel (pp. 122-5) for a discussion of the establishment of lines 49-60.

21,59 *e i aprendon per la via*. Appel translates this line: "und die ... lernen ihm fürs leben." Defending his translation, in a note (p. 124), he states that, despite the lack of corroboration in Bernart's language for taking *via* as *vita* ("die sprachliche Einleitung führt aus, dass diese Form allerdings sonst Bernart fremd ..."), *via* must, nevertheless, be translated 'life'. It must be read in this way, he says, because he does not see how "for the road" — the natural translation — would fit into the context ("Und wie passt 'auf den Wege' in den Zusammenhang?"). Yet Bernart speaks twice of the propagation of his song (11.49-51 and 57-58) and in light of the peripatetic nature of the circulation of songs by the *jongleurs*, not to mention the frequent allusions to messengers by Bernart himself, it would seem that our translation ("and those in Puy who want to know it will learn it on the way") would fit the context more readily than Appel's ("will learn it for life"). The people in Puy will presumably learn the song from the messenger on his way to the king, if one takes the *tornada* literally.

22,25-32 This stanza is not in ms. C. Vossler ("Der Minnesang des B. von V.", pp. 18-19) rejects it altogether.

22,25-8 *Si tot m'es vergonh'e paors* etc. Appel (p. 131) believes that this stanza, though lacking in ms. C, originally followed the first stanza. Schultz-Gora (pp. 356-7) and Lewent (pp. 666-7) deny this assertion, but, more cogently, they attack Appel's reading *blasmatz* (l. 26) for the mss. *blasmat*. S.-G. points out that: "Allein *blasmat* kann sehr wohl ein neutrales Partizip sein." Lewent translates *blasmat m'er d'Amor*: "ich habe mich über die Liebe beklagt." Denying the assertion made both by Appel and Schultz-Gora that *lauzar* (l. 27) goes back to stanza one, Lewent translates the wholepassage: "Wenngleich mir Scham und Furcht daraus erwächst, so habe ich mich doch über die Liebe beklagt; denn es bedünkt mich, dass mir jenes Leben nichts nüzt und es dann auch mit meinem Trost daraus nichts ist." Lewent is right in saying that *lauzar* does not go back to the first stanza. It refers to the *blasmat* in l. 26: "I am afraid when I blame love, but then I reflect that praising him would not do me any good either." The whole passage, however, is certainly related to the thought developed in stanza one.

23,38   *et esperansa bretona.* People say of the Bretons that they are still waiting for King Arthur's return. This vain hope became proverbial; cf. Eugen Cynrim (*op. cit.* note 1,14) p. 53.

24,41-8   Appel (p. 142) calls this stanza a *cobla esparsa* written by another hand than Bernart's in conjunction with the third stanza of this poem.

26,6   *qu'estat n'aurai mais de dos ans.* We take *estar de*, here, in the sense given by Levy (*Petit dictionnaire*; cf. also *Supp.—Wörter.* iii, 307 b): "*estar de* 'etre eloigné de, s'abstenir' ".

26,14   *e no ve c'amors lh'atenda.* Lewent (pp. 667-8), citing a precedent for the intransitive use of *atendre ad alcu* 'jemanden Beachtung schenken' from Boethius and an Old French example *prêter attention* (Godefroy, viii, 226), suggests the following translation for line 14: "...dass die Liebe ihm Beachtung schenke."

26,17   *...me truanda.* There is an unclear ms. tradition: DIKN hav *me truanda*, C G *matruanda*. Appel (p. 153-4) accepts the first, proposing the translation 'betrügen', because the translations of Levy and Raynouard, 'traiter en truand' and 'mendier, gueuser,' do not make good sense in this context.

26,28   *si'lh platz que·m don o que·m venda.* See note for 12,31.

26,37   *descapdolha.* Levy (*Supp.-Wörter.*, ii, 119) gives 'emporragen' as the definition of *capdolhar*, offering (with a question mark) 'mangelhaft sein' as the definition of *descapdolhar*. Appel (p. 154) proposes 'unter das Mass hinabgehen, minderwertig sein.'

27,6   *en est so, c'ai...* The ms. tradition offers a variety of rhyme-words for this line (see Appel pp. 160-1 for a list and discussion of them). The word with the most ms. support (AIKMN) is *apedit*, past participle of *apedir*. Whether this word should be understood in a technical sense ("die Singweise die ich *in pedes* gebracht habe,"— Appel) or in a more general sense of 'demander, convoiter' (Levy, *Petit dictionnaire*) is impossible to say. Appel offers: "in dieser Singweise, die ich erstrebt habe," with the comment: "eine bessere und vor allen sicherere Erklärung des Wortes aber vermag ich auch nicht zugeben." Battaglia (p. 199) prints *apedit* in his text, translating freely: "su questa melodia che ho ideata."

27,41 *re de be non es a dire.* In translating this line "Nichts an Guten fehlt an ihr," Appel (p. 162) is guided by the feeling that the repeated rhyme *dire-dire* (11. 40-1) indicates a different meaning for the second *dire.* He also feels that a more literal translation would not be in accord with the meaning of the preceding and following lines. Schultz-Gora (pp. 357-8) points out that there is, in fact, a different meaning for the second *dire,* supporting his opinion with an example from Arnaut Daniel: "...auch bei A. Daniel XV,21 haben wir zu einfachem *dire* (V. 71) ein *si' a dire* 'mangele' im Reime..." Battaglia (p. 201) translates: "Nessuna bonta le manca." Besides the main interpretation of the line, we have also accepted S.-G's reading *non* for *no·n* in the text.

27,48 *per que m'a faih de nien?* Bernart sometimes repeats whole lines or constructions in different songs. Compare this line with 15, 42, and line 27,31 with the similar construction in 30,1.

28,39-40 *si c'amdui cominal / mezuressem egal?* Appel (p. 170) comments: "schwerlich wird an 'sich miteinander messen' (im Liebesspiel) zu denken sein." He does not explain why it would be difficult to accept such an interpretation especially in the light of other references to the physical aspects of love (cf., for example, 9,27-8; 36,32-5; 37,47-8; 39,23-4; 39,47-8). Vossler (p. 49) does accept an erotic reading: "den ganzen hellen Tag lang (*a jornal*) möchte er nackend mit ihr im Bett liegen und unterm Fenster sich an ihr messen, doch wohl nicht anders, als indem er sich vor aller Augen lange streckt auf ihren weissen Körper legt." Lewent (pp. 668-9) rejects the extreme eroticism of Vossler's reading, but, at the same time, he feels Appel was too hasty in rejecting the reading 'sich miteinander messen'. Lewent himself proposes a textual reading *mezurem s'em egal* which he translates: "so dass wir beide gemeinsam messen, ob wir gleich (lang) sind." If this reading is an effort to avoid the more erotic one, it is unsatisfactory because it substitutes a silly action for one which is perfectly understandable and has, moreover, the support of the other references cited above. Finally, Moshé Lazar ("classification des thèmes amoureux de B. de V.," p. 383) classifies the line in question under: "VIII. Les désirs sensuels et érotiques: (c) pour le jeu érotique."

29,7 *e fatz esfortz car sai faire.* Schultz-Gora (pp. 358-9) glosses this line: "ich zwinge mich es fertig zu bringen, einen guten Vers zu dichten." He comments further: "*saber* erscheint hier... als neben der geistigen Fähigkeit das Können bezeichnend, das ein Ausfluss der Willensanstrengung ist." Lewent (p. 670) also comments on this line, but without adding anything pertinent for the problem of translation.

29,22 *don a mal linhatge redui.* Appel translates *linhatge* by 'Geschlecht' which is more literal than our translation, 'behavior'. The context does seem to indicate, though, that it is a question of the action resulting from a *mal linhatge*; hence 'behavior'.

32 *Peirol, com avetz tan estat.* Appel (pp. 277-8) considers the authorship of this poem uncertain not on stylistic grounds — for the style seems consistent with Bernart's — but on the basis of the name of the opponent in the *tenso, Peirol.* The only known troubadour by that name (see the edition by S. C. Aston, Cambridge University Press, 1953) belongs to a later period. Aston (p. 3) places his birth in c. 1164 and the beginning of his creatively active period in 1190. Yet as Aston points out (p. 3): "the name [Peirol] is not uncommon in the contemporary history of the region [Auvergne]." It is possible, therefore, that it is a question of another Peirol in Bernart's *tenso.* Or, perhaps, Bernart wrote the whole poem himself, using the name of a friend as his opponent. Finally, one may believe, as Appel hints, that the Bernart who takes part in the *tenso* is not Bernart de Ventadorn, in spite of the fact that mss. ADIK ascribe it to B. de V.

33,18 *ja mos lauzars no m'er avans. Avans* is not to be found in Raynouard or in either of Levy's dictionaries. Appel suggests giving *avans* the same sense as the *enans* offered bi ms. a, 'Förderung, Vorteil' ('avantage' Levy, *Petit dictionnaire*).

35,3 *e fatz esfortz car sai chantar ni rire.* See note for 29,7. In his note (*op. cit.* 29,7) Schultz-Gora glosses the construction *fatz esfortz car sai* the same way for both examples.

35,40 *...ai chamjatz los datz.* Examples of this expression in Old Provençal poetry may be found in Levy (*Supp.-Wörter*, ii, 11ff.). Appel (p. 203) cites the Italian expression *barattare le carte* (*in mano a uno*). The analogy between the Italian expression and the Provençal is weakened, though, by the different gambling media: the Italian expression refers to cards while the Provençal explicitly mentions dice. It is true that the main intent conveyed by both expressions is to ruin someone's game. In this sense, the American expressions "loaded dice" or "fix the dice" seem closer to the original.

36,57 *c'amdui n'anem truan.* Appel (pp. 209-11) offers a long discussion of the establishment of the text of the *tornadas* (11. 55-60). Part of the discussion centers on the interpretation of *truan.* Appel thinks that the poet wants God to grant him and his friend the good fortune to go wandering "mit dem Freunde... sorglos und glücklich wie die Zigeuner, oder besser wie die Vaganten, durch die Welt zu ziehen, überraschend, aber vor allem weil er uns so romantisch modern anmutet." The romantic picture of happy gypsies is difficult to accord with either the context of this poem (cf. especially stanzas 1, 2, and the wish in 3) or the traditional connotations given by Raynouard (V, 435-6) of *truan* as an adjective 'truand, vilain, misérable, gueux, pauvre, fripon, mendiant, coquin' and as a verb 'truander, mendier, gueuser, coquiner'.

37,17 *mas greu m'es que·m repenta.* "It would be difficult for me to repent it," i.e. "to regret loving her since she offered me the advice..." Comforting words from the *domna,* though they may appear quite void of emotion to us, were considered a mark of the lady's esteem by the troubadours.

37,61-2 *si d'aisso m'essertana / d'autra vetz la·n creirai.* Appel reads: "wenn sie mir darüber Gewissheit gibt, werde ich ihr noch einmal (?) glauben..." Battaglia (p. 225) agrees, translating: "Se adesso mi è verace— un'altra volta le crederò ancora". As Appel's question mark indicates, the lines could be read another way: "If she assures me of this once more, I will believe her..."

38 *Can la verz folha s'espan.* This fragment is ascribed to Bernart in four mss. (DIKN²). It was first edited by Zingarelli, *Studi Medievali* 1.609. Appel (p. 281) states: "bei der Art der Überlieferung ist die Attribution an Bernart natürlich nicht sicher." He advances no stylistic mannerisms which would indicate an authorship other than Bernart's, and it should be remarked that *canso* 9, whose authenticity has not been challenged, has almost the same ms. tradition (DIKN) as *canso* 38. Vossler, Schultz-Gora and Lewent are silent on this poem.

38,11 *e se tuih el mon garan.* The meaning of *garan* is uncertain. Appel (p. 283) concludes his note by saying: "*garan* kann aber auch Form von *garar* sein, zwar nicht 'alle die in der Welt schauen,' aber wie afz. *veant* auch 'sichtbar' heisst (Tobler I², 45), so kann hier übersetzt werden: 'alle in der Welt zu schauenden'."

38,29 *ar eslonh en breu ma vida.* Taking the opposite meaning from that given in our reading, Appel (p. 284) offers: " 'sie entferne mein Leben, töte mich,' nicht 'sie verlängere es mir'." But he does point out in the same note that *eslonh* is subjunctive, not indicative, and it is as a subjunctive wish that we read the line.

40,8 *si·m lassa del cor la razitz.* Schultz-Gora (p. 361) rightly points out the rarity of the expression *del cor la razitz.* His perplexity as to the meaning of *razitz* in this context ("auch vermisst man dort eine genaue Sinnesbetrachtung für den ganzen Vers dessen [Appel's] Übersetzung, 'so bindet sie mir die Wurzel des Herzens' das Verständnis nicht fördet") seems more difficult to understand. Levy (*Supp.-Wörter,* vii, 59) gives 'Wurzel (real); Wurzel (fig.), Ursprung.' Battaglia (p. 230) translates: "sì m'attanaglia la radice del cuore." Roughly paraphrased in American idiom, the expression means something like "joy... reaches to the very bottom of my heart."

40,9 *per midons m'esjau no-jauzitz.* The line is a reference to the paradoxical behavior of love — a frequent theme in the troubadour tradition. Schultz-Gora (p. 361) notes: "dass eine Art Oxymoron vorliegt: 'ich freue mich einerseits, und anderseits bin ich doch mit Bezug auf das Gleiche unfroh'."

40,17 *ar sui de leis trop eissernitz*. There is general disagreement on the meaning of *eissernitz*, no one having really arrived at a clear understanding of the word in this context. Raynouard (III, 21a) gives 'distingué'; Levy (*Supp.-Wörter*, ii, 337b) pleads ignorance; and Appel translates 'klug'. Lewent (pp. 671-2) points out the inconsistency of Appel's translation with the lines which follow it in the stanza. Citing the etymology of *eisernir* from *excernere* 'to single out,' Lewent proposes 'ausgezeichnet' for *eisernit* (which brings us pretty much back to Raynouard's definition). He continues to build upon this foundation by reasoning: "absondern von den anderen tut sich auch, wer kühn ist..." From this, Lewent proposes 'kühn' for the meaning of *eissernit* in this particular example. 'Bold' is certainly the sense of the line, but within the context of the stanza and poem, where Bernart is regretting his loquacity, Lewent's definition may be further refined to give the sense 'making too much of a thing', hence 'picayune'.

40,20-2 *si que·m sui per las dens feritz*, etc. Zingarelli, who first edited this poem (*Mélanges Chabaneau*, 1907, p. 1025ff), and Appel propose different readings for lines 21-2. Zingarelli (who takes *per las dens* — l. 20 — to refer to the lady) breaks l. 21 in half with a question: "che cosa è tanto feroce per me?" and then runs the rest of the line over to l. 22. There he changes the ms. *li* to *ki* and reads, "Se io son distrutto, non troverei già chi abbia cura di me." Appel, rejecting the ms. change in l. 22 (actually unnecessary anyway, since one may assume an elliptical *ki*), takes the entire line 21 as a question and reads the two lines: "Was ist mir denn so arg, wenn ich vernichtet bin? Sie wird nimmer finden, ich schütze mich ihr gegenüber." Both of these interpretations, based on the assumption of an interrogative *que* in l. 21, cause a break in the progression of the stanza by jumping to the effect before the cause has been fully developed. Rather than insisting on an interrogative *que*, it seems more logical to take *que* as a conjunction or as a relative pronoun (with the antecedent *per las dens feritz*). The description of the unhappy effects of the poet's loquaciousness is thus continued for two more lines. This expansion is important, since his garrulous tendency is one of the main causes. whithin the poem, of the poet's grief (cf. the *reprises* ll. 43, 45, 47 — twice, 48). It is also finely ironic since this *canso*, though only his secondlongest (*canso* 25 has 87 lines), contains more words than any other.

40,36 *ta fort sui de s'amor techitz*. We accept the meaning 'to further, promote, advance' of *techit* established by Appel (p. 229): "*techir* ist in erster Linie intrans. 'gedeihen, wachsen.' aber auch afz. kommt es faktitiv vor: 'wachsen machen, gedeihen machen,' und so hier 'fördern'."

40,52 *Del plazer me sui engrevitz*. The ms. gives *engrenitz*, but this has not been accepted by any editor. We accept Appel's reading (p. 229) *engrevitz*: "afz. ist *engrevir* im Sinne von 's'aggraver' belegt (s. Godefroy, *per cascun jor li langors engrevissoit*) und Levy bringt *grevit* 'Nachteil, Schade.' *Se engrevir* würde heissen 'sich belasten, beschweren.' In this sense the line refers to the pendant pain ac-

NOTES 187

companying each joy in love (cf. l. 9). The more favor the lady shows the poet, the greater will be the loss, if she withdraws that favor.

40,74 *leu m'auci, mas greu fui noiritz.* This line is only difficult in its conciseness — a characteristic of Bernart's style. The poet is saying that the lady, having been stingy (cf. 3,45) with her favors, made it difficult for him to stay alive (the pre-condition of the lady's favor to sustain the lover is a frequently developed convention). But, by withdrawing her favor altogether (easy enough for her since she gave it only grudgingly anyway), the lady kills the poet, who has no further source of life in her.

41,28 *per pauc vius de joi no·m recre. Vius* is not the noun object of a preposition as Battaglia (p. 235) translates: "che per poco non rinunzio alla gioia per tutta la vita." It is an adjective modifying *joi* as in the following examples given by Raynouard (V, 555b) from lo Monge de Montaudon (*aissi cum cel*): *Ja per ren vius no m'accossegria* 'jamais pour rien *vivant* il ne m'atteindrait.'

42,4 *dobla mos jois.* Mss. ADIK attest this reading, but V has *poya mos chans.* We accept Appel's reading (p. 245), although Battaglia takes that of V, translating it: "s'alza il mio canto..."

42,14 *forsa d'amor m'i fai far vassalhatge.* The poet is socially beneath the lady he loves, but love's power will raise him to be her equal. Equality before love is a common medieval topos (cf. for example, l. 18).

42,26-8 *mas dreih l'en fatz,* etc. The confused pronominal references make the sense of this passage difficult to follow. The demonstrative *cela* (l. 27) definitely refers to the lady mentioned in l. 22 (the clause *que·m torn'en no-chaler* makes that clear). Whether the *leis* in l. 28 refers to the whoman who is indifferent to the poet, or to the woman he has forsaken is not clear. However, the causal conjunction *car* (l. 27) leads one to expect that these last two lines of the stanza should be the explanation of l. 26. In that case, the poet says he is playing the fool by staying away from the woman who *would* accept him, in order to court the lady who spurns him. This explanation is strengthened by the import of the rest of the poem and, in particular, stanza five where the poet attempts to get back in the good graces of the first lady, to whom he has been faithless. A good excuse for his previous faithlessness would be that he had been a fool to leave her in the first place.

42,39 *de sus del chap.* In the fealty ritual, something from the head (originally hair) was given as a token of submission. Appel (p. 246) discusses the theories on the ritual in some detail.

42,53-4 This *tornada* is found only in ms. P.

43,38 *co·l fols en pon.* This proverb, though the meaning is clear, has yet to be satisfactorily explained. Appel (p. 256) cites an Old French proverb, "sages hon ne chiet au pont," from "sage home ne chara ja au pont, quar il decend". This sheds some light on Bernart's usage perhaps. Schultz-Gora (pp. 364-5) rejects Appel's explanation, but has nothing of his own to offer.

43,45 *a, can mal sembla, qui la ve.* There is a lack of agreement between Appel, Schultz-Gora, and Lewent as regards the construction *mal sembla*. We accept Lewent's reading (p. 674) as being the simplest: "...*mal* ist das Adverb 'schlecht,' und *semblar* bedeutet 'erscheinen, in die Erscheinung treten, zum Ausdruck kommen'. Bernart sagt also: 'wenn man sie ansieht, wie schlecht kommt es da (in ihrem Äusseren) zum Ausdruck, dass sie diesen armen Sehnsuchtsvollen... sterben lässt, ohne ihm zu helfen'."

43,54 *e per mort li respon.* Appel understands *mort* as a substantive, *mortem*. Schultz-Gora (p. 365) thinks it is a conjunction such as is found in Jaufré Rudel's *vida*; qu'ill lo conduisseron a Tripol en un alberc com per mort. In this example, the meaning is clearly 'for dead, like a corpse'. So S.-G. would translate Bernart's *per mort* as 'an Stelle eines Toten'. It should be observed, however, that the example from Jaufré Rudel's *vida* as well as the other examples S.-G. advances in support of his reading invariably have *com* (*com per mort*) or, in the case of the O. F. example, *cum* (*cum pur morte*). These do not, therefore, seem to support S-G's reading of the line in question, and we accept Appel's reading.

43,57 *Tristans, ges no·n auretz de me.* The question in this line is the meaning of *auretz*. Levy gives 'erfahren, lernen' as one of the meanings for *aver*. Appel (p. 256) proposes 'entnehmen' as suitable to the context of the poem. In any case, the meaning is that Tristan will have no more service from the poet, hence no more songs.

44,2 *tot me desnatura.* Appel considers *desnaturar* transitive, defining it 'aus der Natur, aus dem Gleichgewicht bringen'. Accordingly, he translates the line: "sie will mein Wesen ganz verrücken." Lewent (p. 674) proposes that *desnaturar* be considered intransitive "sein Wesen ändern". The subject would then be *tot*, while *me* would be the dative indirect object. He would then translate "so sehr ist mein Herz mit Freude erfüllt, dass alles für mich seine Natur ändert: die Kälte erscheint mir als weisses, rotes und gelbes Blühnen." André Berry (*Florilège des troubadours*, p. 177) reads similarly: "tout me paraît changé dans la nature."

44,29 *a ma deviza.* There is no general agreement as regards the meaning of *deviza*. Levy (*Supp.-Wörter*, ii, 204) gives: 1) 'Teilung' from Raynouard (III,38) 'division, partage', 2) 'Meinung' (?) from Bartsch (who cites Bernart's line). Appel (pp. 265-6) rejects 'Meinung' and 'Anteil', saying "das wort bezeichnet die 'Teilung' die man vornimmt, und so 'Entscheid' und weiter 'Wille, Wunsch'. This last meaning seems too derived. "For my part" is a good English equivalent and has, moreover, the advantage of remaining closer to the sense of the Provençal word.

44,31-2 *que ja·l jorn que l'aurai viza,* etc. One expects *jusca·l jorn* instead of the adverb *ja*. As the lines now read, the statement is almost a tautology: "I have so much happiness that I will not have any sadness on the day when I see her." Since the point of the stanza is to illustrate the self-sufficiency of the inner happiness the poet has gained from the lady's previous manifestations of friendship, it would make more sense to translate, "For my part, I have enough happiness to sustain me from now until I am able to see her again." Berry (*Florilège*, p. 179) offers another possible reading, although it does not seem consistent with the rest of the stanza: "je m'en trouve si parfaitement heureux qu'il me sera désormais impossible d'être triste, pourvu que je l'aie aperçue dans la journée."

GLOSSARY

A

A *before vowel* ad 1,23; 17,27; 22,14,47 *etc.*
  Prep. place: *to* 8,53 *etc.*; (*to a person*) 4,63; 6,51 *etc.*; (gardar ad alcu) 6,48; *in* 3,9 *etc.*; *place where* parven m'es als olhs 31,42 *etc. time*: a nadal *etc.* 28,38; 13,6; 27,8; a chascu jorn 28,28; a jornal *always* 28,34; a ma vida 30,43. *dative*: 3,18,22; 5,25; 6,18; 9, 13; 10,25 *etc. dative and infin.* 6,31; 17,16;
  goal, objective 4,26; 10,25; 15, 45; 17,56; *a and infin.*: 4,17,60; 40,10;
  in accordance with: 2,23; 30,37; 31,4; *characteristic circumstance, form and manner*: 3,12; 6,17,57, 58; 8,31; 20,17; 28,13; 30,38; *related circumstance*, 1,8; 3,8; 6,54; 13,50; 17,36,48; 23,8.
a *interjection* 5,15; 7,22,47; 8,1; 22,53; 43,45.
ab *prep. with, by, beside. spatial concept* 13,11; 23,10; *community* 7,20,49; 18,6; 36,58; 41,48; 42,3; 43,49; *inimical relation* 4, 17; 13,39,54; 19,21; 23,53; 36, 29; *causal situation* 1,1,2; 3,13; 5,14; 28,2,13; 29,10; 36,50; 39, 31; 44,5; *particular* 15,41; ab sol que 9,7; 27,42; 39,55; *device* 1,43,56; 8,20,34; 13,44; 15,47; 23,28; 30,53; 39,47; apenre ab alcu 19,18.

abandonar *v. tr. to leave, abandon, refl.* se a. vas joi 23,13.
abans *adv.* des abans *beforehand* 33, 32; a. que *before* 26,44; 39,16.
abauzir (*3 pres.* abau 13, 30; 21,28), *v. intr. to be fitting, to belong* 13, 30; 21, 28.
abelir *v. intr. to be pleasing to* 20,2; vida A.
abenar *v. intr. to compensate* 2, 19.
aclî *adj. humble, under submission* 20,39; (per far) 29, 20; vas alcu 37,6.
aco *that, this* 45,46.
acolar *v. tr. to hug, embrace*, 7, 45.
acolhimen *s. m. reception, welcome* esser de bel a. 10,41.
acolhir *v. tr. to receive, welcome* (alcu) 9,11; 25,11,16; 26,23; 27, 61; 42,25; a. los dihz 41,11.
acompanhar *v. refl.* se a. ad alcu *to accompany* 19,51.
acordamen *s. m.* far a. *to agree, to come to an agreement* 30,14.
acordansa *s. f. agreement* far a. *to bring about an agreement* 45,49.
acorre *v. intr. to help* 28,16.
acuzar *v. tr. to accuse* (de) 40,19.
ades *adv. immediately* 17,19; 30,39; *always* 1,15; 9,19; 12,4; 17,4; 25,36; 26,16; 28,26; 41,22; 44, 67; 45,39; *still* 2,42; 22,3; a. on 25,11; a can 35,16.
adiramen *s. m. anger, resentment* 5, 27; dire a. *to say what causes displeasure* 13,36.
adoncs *adv. therefore, then* 10,5,23; 13,24; 39,37; 45,32.

adorar v. *to adore, venerate (a lady)* 44,58.
adormir v. *to be asleep* 33,2.
adoussar v .tr. *to sweeten* 20,45; 23, 6; (lo cor) 17,44; 41,4; (alcu) 16,35.
adrech, adreit adj. *skilled, clever.* vida A.
adrechurar v. tr. sos tortz *to make amends for* 8,32.
aduire (3. pr. ind. adutz 12,40; adui 28,3; 29,37;) v. tr. *to bring to* 12,40; 28,3; se a. *to flow* 29,37.
afaire s. m. *business, duty* 44,61; so m'a tout tot mon a. *thus it has spoiled everything for me* 29,15.
afan s. m. *hardship, pain, suffering* 15,44; 17,18; 29,52; 22,59; 20, 26; 31,32; tener ad a. 28,20; traire a. 37,38.
afanar v. tr. *to trouble* 22,53,58; refl. *to have trouble* 37,50.
afar s. m. adoncs saubr'eu lo vostr' afar *how everything is with you* 40,62.
aflibar *to clothe,* puton gen afliban 16,46.
afolar v. tr. (alcu) *to ruin* 29,21.
afortir v. tr. *to strengthen, encourage* 1,35; refl. *to have courage* 37,19.
afranher v. refl. (vas alcu) *to be complaisant toward* 19,37.
agaih s. m. se metre en a. *to lie in wait, be on the watch* 8,43.
agradar v. intr. *to please* 17,54 (que with subj.) 30,55. Inf. *grant, accord* 15,29.
agradatge s. m. *pleasure* d'a. *agreeable, charming* 20,7.
agur s. m. *augury* 25,26.
ai *interjection alas!, ah!* 7,54; 30, 50; 43,5; ai las 10,40; 17,9; 27, 49 etc; ai Deus 22,9; 31,33.
aicel pron. adj. *that* 15,46; totz aicels d'eviro 6,48.
aicest pron. *this* 5,32; 28,11.
aiga s. f. *water* 16,38; 29,37; a. que dels olhz plor 6,49; l'a. del cor 42,43.
aire s. m. *descent, birth, manner, sort* de bon aire 4,9 (la plus de-bon-aire); 29,39; 37,35; de mal aire 12,35.
aire s. m. *air* 44,50.
aissela s. f. *shoulder* 25,19.
aissi adv. *so, as, thus* 4,6; 13,19; 29,51; 31,46; 44,56; *following from what has preceded* 8,29; 23,42; 43,53; *introducing an answer* 18,27; aissi que 3,16; aissi son finas beutatz que 16,43; aissi com *just as* 7,10; 21,57; 22,5; 29,17; aissi co 12,8; aissi com = com 31,40; s'aissi *or* sai si 6,13.
aisso pron. *this, that* 5,32; 15,19; 28,47; 33,5; 37,61; (car) 43,33; per aisso *therefore* 7,3; 29,21.
aital, aitau 21,20 pron. adj. *such* 22, 37; (que) 30,12; (com) 12,18; aital re *such a thing* 35,33; subst *referring to previous idea* 15,19; 21,20.
aitan pron. subst. *so much* 19,44; 37,60; 45,15; (com) 5,26; 13,57; 27,36; d'a. que *in so much as, in so far as* 6,45; 24,19; cen aitans qu'eu no sai dire 21,33; adv. *with adj.* 7,39,53; 31,31; *with adverb* 7,56; (com) 3,63; *with verb, so that* (que) 9,36; 42,28.
aize s. m. *opportunity* 27,29; 45,3.
aizir v. tr. *to bring in a place, a situation* 27,46; 36,33; *to put in possession of* (de) 14,21; se a. *to be at ease, to be quiet* 20,20; aizit *fitting, suitable* 27,44; *close, near* 23,43; 33,24.
ajostar v. tr. *to collect, unite, gather together* 6,46; se a. 7,19.
al 28,45; 41,8,52; au 21,13 *anything else, other things*; no... ren al *nothing else* 41,8,52; no de ren als *for nothing else* 12,7; per al no... *for no other reason* 21,13; 28,45.
ala s. f. *wing* 43,2.
alborn s. m. *laburnum* vida B.
albre, arbre s. m. *tree* 25,2; 26,2.
alcu pron. adj. *some, any* 23,24.
alegransa s. f. *joy, happiness* 1,6; 45,14.
alegrar v. tr. *to make happy* (sé a. so

GLOSSARY

coratge) 23,48; se a. *to rejoice* 42,7.
alhor *adv. elsewhere* 36,14; 44,35; (an other person is meant) 6,43; 39,53; 8,16.
aliamar *v. tr. to bind, chain* 12,14.
aliscara *s. f. need, misery,* 3,12.
almorna *s. f. pity, charity* aver a. d'alcu 31,48.
alonjar *v. tr. to prolong* 6,11.
alre (s) *indet. pron. another* 4,60; 25,80; 27,57.
als. *indef. pron. another* ren als 12, 7; 3,20; 25,37; per als no...-*for no other reason* 28,53.
alugorar *v. tr. to brighten,* 3,36.
ama *s. f. fish-hook* 12,9.
amador *s. m. lover* 2,13; 6,33; 19, 27; 22,17; 28,5; 31,34; (*n. s.* 4,3; 29,8; 37,30; 44,54).
aman *s. m. lover* 15,30; 21,17; 28, 21; 36,47.
amansa *s. f. love* 1,13; 25,31.
amar *v. tr. to love* 1,15,60; 2,39; 3, 18; 4,9; etc.; de bon'amor 44,69; d'amor coral 28,43; per drudaria 25,50; a. vas... 5,17; *without object* 4,59; 21,10; a. lo dormir 2,9.
amdos *pron. both* 42,18; a. los ohhs 42,43; *nom.* amdoi (*we*) *both* 28, 25,39; 29,54; 36,57.
amenar *v. tr. to guide, bring* 2,43.
amia *s. f. friend* 45,53.
amic *s. m. friend* 12,2; 17,27; 27, 19; 39,14; (*as address to Tristan*) 42,53; *said from the heart* 25,86; midons soi hom et amics e servire 35,13; = *lover* 6,6; 7,55; 19,39, 40; 21,44; 24,12 etc.; dos amics = amics et amia 22,10,39.
amiran *s. m. emir* 21,19.
amistat *s. f. friendship, love* 6,21; 24, 29; 40,68; 44,25; *of the lovers themselves* 22,12; *symbol of the friendship* 22,15; 35,14; salutz et a-tz 16,3; 35,43.
amor *s. f.* (*n. s.* amors 22,9) *love* fin' a. 7,11; 15,4; 18,6; 33,14; amar d'a. 28,43; autreyar s'a. 7,15; 40, 14; aver a. certana 37,43; dar, donar s'a. 6,3; 7,42; 13,17; en-

veyar a. 7,39; faire a. az alcu 28, 30; saber d'a. 13,56; per a. de *for the sake of, for the love of* 10,17; 19,17; morir per s'a. 17, 36; *symbol of the beloved* 21,17; 27,9?; 30,50; 44,33; (*Love or the beloved*), (*personified* =) *Love* 3, 35; 4,17; 17,31; 22,26,52; 28,10; 29,45; 31,21; 35,5,10; (*address to Love*) 3,1; 4,1,16; 10,8; 13,19,46; 22,57; 36,28; 39,13; (Fin'a.) 7, 49; (*doubtful personification*) 3, 25; 17,2.
amoros *adj. loving, affectionate* 3,2; olhs a. 8,20; 28,58.
amparar *v. tr. to protect, defend* 40, 22,51.
ams *adj. both* 20,14; ams los olhs 29,23.
an *s. m. year* 2,22; 4,54; 26,6; 28, 28; 30,2; 33,19.
anar *v. intr. 1 Pres. Ind.* vau 13,11; 21,52; *vauc before a vowel* 16, 13; *3 Pres. Ind.* vai 10,35; 16, 52; 18,31; 43,4; *1 Pres. Subj.* an 16,24; *3 Pres. Subj.* 31,52; *Imperative* vai 16,49; 18,31; 43,4;) *to go* 13,11; (vas alcu) 39,58; (*in a particular condition*) a. tuan 36, 57; a. ses vestidura 44,13; *with infinitive* 45,10; *with Pres. Part.* 21,43; *with gerund.* 3,32; 20,16; 21,58; 27,21; 28,23; 29,12; 36, 44; a. al cor 17,43; 43,4; ges amors segon ricor no vai 10,35; be. m vai (d'amor) *etc.* 13,8; 14, 5; 16,52; 18,24; 27,8; 36,6,7; 31,52; *reflexive:* anar s'en 8,53; 43,55; vai s'en lo temps 39,46.
anc *adv.* a. no. *never* 1,18,41; 3,11; 4,52; 5,1; 6,7 *etc.*; non-anc mai *never* 43,42; a. no. *emphatic denial* 6,56; 28,21; 35,7; a. *ever* 4,22; 6,37; 10,29; 17,24; 42,32.
ancar *see* encar.
anceis *adv. rather* 4,21.
ancse *adv. always* 3,28.
angoissos *adj. anguished* 3,13.
ans *adv. before* 16,24; a. que *earlier than, before* 2,28; 26,3; *rather* 1, 21; 2,26; 9,15; 17,16,28; 19,53; 36,8.

antic *adj. old.* 24,41.
aondar *v. intr. to help, aid* 1,17; 26, 25; 43,48; 44,38.
apanar *v. tr. to nourish, support* 22, 29.
aparelhar *v. refl. to array, prepare oneself* (ab) 7,49; *tr. to prepare, array* 7,52.
apayar *v. refl. to be satisfied, find peace* 7,34,37; 18,6.
apedir 27,6 *see Appel's note, pp. 160-61 of his edition.*
apelar *v. tr. to call* 13,43; 25,17.
apenre (*1. Pres. Ind.* apren 13,57; *1. pr. subj.* aprenda 19,18) *v. tr. to learn* 13,57; a. a dire 4,61; *without an object* 21,59; (ab alcu) 19,18.
apercebre *v. tr. to perceive*; *refl.* (de) 19,11; vidas A & B.
apoderar *v. tr. to conquer, overcome* 1,9; 22,56; 35,5.
apres *adv. afterwards* 40,56; *prep. after* 31,32.
aquel *pron. adj. that, that one* 5,7; 10,45; 35,9; (can) 10,1; 37,53; (a. que *such that*) 15,8; *subst.* 15, 24; a. que 27,18.
aquest *pron. adj. this, this one* 6,12; 8,28; 17,27; 22,27; 43,46; *subst.* 7,25; 19,25.
aqui *adv. here, there* 21,27.
ar 16,49; 40,17; ara, era, aras, eras *adv. now* 3,5; 5,12; 6,1,5,61; 7,1, 19; 8,6,17 etc.; tro a. que 5,9.
aramir *v. tr. to fix, set firmly* 40,48.
arazonar *v. tr. to address, speak to* (de) 9,31; 23,29.
ardimen *s. m. courage, boldness* 1,33; 16,23; faire a. 17,8.
ardit *adj. daring, bold* 1,35; 40,32; *s. m. boldness* 25,66 (colhir a.); 27,42; 39,48.
ardre *v. tr. to burn* 12,12; 17,48.
arena *s. f. sand* semnar en l'a. 2,33.
argen *s. m. silver* 31,37.
arma *s. f. soul* 30,45; tot'a. crestiana 37,57.
arnes *s. m. equipage, costume* vida B.
asalhir *v. tr. to attack, assault* 14,2 (del chan); 42,11.

asatz *adv. much, very, enough* 10,34; a. mais 13,13.
asazonar *v. tr. to lighten, alleviate, leaven* 23,6.
asegurar *v. tr. to assure, protect* 16, 24; 44,15.
asenhorar *v. tr. to govern* 3,14.
asire (*Inf.* 27,5; 30,10; *Part.* assis 37,8) *v. tr. to sit, place, to compose poetry* se a. a un joc 30, 10; a. bos motz en un so 27,5; a. son amor en aut loc 35,27; a. so coratge en alcu 37,8.
asoauzar *v. intr. to become alleviated, soothed* 4,40.
asolver *v. tr. to free* 27,66.
astruc *s. m. one who is lucky, fortunate* 37,49.
at *s. m. need, use* 32,21.
atainar *see* tainar.
atalentar *v. intr. to please* 37,10.
aten *s. m. wait* 19,29.
atendre *v. tr. to expect, hope for, await* 3,19; 15,52,54; 16,53; 30, 59; 44,22; *to attain, reach* (a. cuit per sofrir) 9,44; *consider* no ve c'amors lh'atenda 26,14; *refl.* se a. en, a, ves *to strive for* 10,6; 15,14; 20,34; 31,8.
atenher 9,44 (*Pres. Part.* atens 39,56) *v. tr. to attain* 39,56.
atraire *v. tr. to draw, attract* 8,34; 12,30; *refl. to strive for* 18,3.
atrasaih *adv. surely* 8,35.
atressi *adv. likewise* 6,43; 24,6; 44, 39; *any way* 17,17.
atretal *pron. adj. of the same sort* 43,32; *adv. likewise* (com) 1,45; 4,47; 28,37; 41,47,50.
atretan *adv. as much as* 37,29.
atruandar *v. tr.* 26,17. *See Appel's note, pp. 153-4 of his edition.*
aturar *v. refl. to take pains, strive, endeavor* 8,13.
au *see* al.
aucire (auci *3 pres. ind.* 26,12; 40, 74; aucia *3 pres. subj.* 17,31; 25, 59; aucis *3 perf.* 1,43; aucizes *3 imperf. subj.* 10,22) *v. tr. to kill* 10,10; 12,25; 27,50; 31,56; 36, 16.

GLOSSARY

augurar *v. tr. to prophesy*; *refl.* 24,32.
aur *s. m. gold* 31,37.
aura *s. f. wind* 37,1.
aura *adj. airy*; *vain* amors a-na 22, 37.
aut *adj. high* 35,27; 40,49.
autet *adv. aloud* 39,3.
autor *s. m. witness* 39,54.
autre *pron. adj. another* 1,44; 2,13; 5,13; 6,6 *etc.*; autre re 3,49, vas autra part 24,15; 31,8; *standing after the subst.* res autra 30,55, l'autre cors *the rest of the body* 35,21; cen vetz mor... e reviu autres cen 31,28; *more, once again* autra vetz 1,48; *of another* 31,30; 33,10; autra amor *love for another woman* 42,32. — *subst. another* 7,20; 16,7; 17,26; 24,31; 1,23; autra *another woman* 10, 46; 19,22; 24,16; *someone* 23,29; li autre *other people* 13,7; 21,11; las autras, totas autras 9,13; 12, 29. — autrui *another* 6,58; 29, 6; *of another* 1,28; 7,29; 23,8.
autreyar *v. tr. to grant, assure* 7,15; 40,14; *refl. to yield, submit* 36,51.
auvir, auzir (*1. pr. ind.* au 13,20; 21, 5) *v. tr. to hear* 2,9; 10,3; 21, 57; 25,14; 26,5; 33,9 (que); 21, 5; *to listen to* esser auvitz d'alcu 40,57.
auzar *v. tr. to dare, with Inf.* 1,16; 4, 43; 10,11; 16,23; 20,44; 27,12; 39,27; esser auzatz 35,26.
avans *s. m. advantage, gain* 33,18.
avar *adj. avaricious, miserly* 3,45.
avenir *v. intr. to succeed, attain* 14,8; *to come to, happen* 3,16 (que); 5,4; 36,41; 39,32; mortz m'avenha si... 3,40; 22,55; 4,60.
aventura *s. f. fate, adventure* un'a. avetz que 8,49; bon'a. *good fortune, happiness* 13,15; 16,54; 24, 10; 30,41 (chausa de b. a.); a. = bon'a. 16,8; 44,6.
aventurar *v. refl. to venture* 35,34.
aver (*3. Pres. Subj.* aya 7,30; *1. Perf.* aic 4,22; 30,7; agui 8,23,24; 44, 20) *v. tr. to have, possess* 1,40; 6,6,29 *etc.*; er'ai leis, era no·n ai ges 22,36; 13,24; non sabra qu'eu m'ai (*what is wrong with me*) 17,25; a. cor, dreih, esperansa, grat, joi, merce, tort *etc. see these words*; *to get*, 6,39,59; 7,30; 14,5; 15,10; 18,26; ges [no·n] auretz de me 43,57; *with subst. and pred. adj.* 2,36; a. o sal *see sal*; mort m'a. *see mort*; a. per fol 5,8; a *there is* 14,23; no i a mas del morir 25,24; 4,54; 27,1. *s. m. wealth, possession, property* 15,24.
avinen *adj. suitable, charming, attractive, pleasing* 10,34; 3,44; 6,52; 20,7; mo Frances l'av. 16,50.
avol *adj. bad, base* 1,34; 8,45; 23,9.
ayuda *s. f. help* 8,30.
ayudar *v. tr. to help* 19,23; 35,44.
azaut *adj. charming, agreeable* 40,61.
azesmar *v. tr. to estimate, realize* 13, 34.
aziman *s. m. magnet* 26,41; *see Proper Names*.
azirar *v. tr. to hate* 10,42; 27,22; ja Domnedeus no m'azir tan 31,13; *refl. to become angry, be provoked* 35,31.

B

Badatge *s. m. delay, idleness*; faire b. *to wait, lose time* 19,12; 23,32.
baizar, bayar (*3 Pres. Ind.* baya 7,45; *1 Pres. Subj.* bai 36,34; *3 Pres. Subj.* bai 7,42) *v. tr. to kiss* 1,42; 13,17; 28,52; 39,39; *s. m.* 1,43; 9,28; 39,43; 40,23; 41,31.
balansa *s. f. balance, uncertainty* 44, 39.
balayar *v. intr. to flutter, dangle* 30, 46.
baro *s. m. knight, baron* 21,9.
batalha *s. f. battle* 35,6.
batre *v. tr. to beat, strike* 41,45,46; 42,31.
be *before vowel* ben 1,33; 5,18 *etc.* *adv. well* 1,53; 5,18 *etc.*; ben estai 1,33; 4,7; ben es que 30,36; *to affirm a statement: indeed* 1,61; 4,16,33; 8,10; 16,37; 35,11; 39,

196   GLOSSARY

13; be... o be *with. subj. whether... or* 12,24.
be *s. m. good, benefit* 3,3,19; 14,6; 26,25; 31,30; 41,34; dire be 1,64; 21,24; faire ben ad alcu 19,28; 25,52; 35,16; *plur.* voler los bes d'alcu 12,22; mandar bes 12,37.
bel *adj. beautiful* 1,41,50; 3,34; 4, 55; 5,6 *etc.*; bel ver 1,64; bela razo 6,60; bels dihz 16,36; 33,17; bel solatz 17,59; esser de bela companha 19, 34, 54; bel m'es (cant, que) 9,1; 10,1; 19,21; 26, 5; bels amics *vocative* 14,10; bela domna 1,49; 22,49; *subst.* la bela *symbol of the beloved* 24,26; 26,26; la bela qui... 1,38; 5,16; 14,20; 25,15; la plus bela 31,18; 44,21.
belamen *adv. beautifully, nicely* 35,22.
belazor *adj (comparative) more beautiful* 27,33; *s. f.* la b. *the most beautiful* 25,40; 36,12.
benanansa *s. f. happiness, success, good luck* 1,22; 7,48; 44,30; 45, 6.
beutat *s. f. beauty* 1,54; 3,36; 9,40; 24,40; *pl.* 13,31; 16,43; *personified* 35,23; 40,26.
biaissar *v. refl. to turn away* 24,30.
bistensar *v. tr. to delay* 30,38.
biza *s. f. north wind* 44,16.
blanc *adj. white* 7,12; 8,37; 12,17; 28,37; 36,36; 44,3.
blandir *v. tr. to court, woo* 28,26; 45,31.
blasmador *s. m. blamer, accuser* 30, 15.
blasmar *v. tr. to blame, criticize* 15, 15; 30,48; 39,49; blasmar que no *with subjunctive, to criticize that it does not happen* 40,71; blasmat m'er 22,26.
blastenh (*n. s. - ens*) *s. m. blame* 39,32.
blon *adj. blond* 44,48.
bo *adj. good* 1,3,4,5,7 *etc.*; bo saber 10,18; saber bo *to be pleasing* 25,4; 35,19; *welcome* 9,24; 23, 46; bona domna *as address* 21, 41; 36,46; 44,53.
bocha *s. f. mouth* 1,41; 9,27; 15,7; 35,20; 39,39; 41,30; 40,47.
bosc *s. m. forest, wood* 24,1.
boschatge *s. m. wood* 23,16; 40,1; 42,2.
botonar *v. intr. to bud* 39,2.
braire *v. intr. to shriek, yell, bray* 36, 21.
bratz *s. m. arm* 24,35; 27,45; 35,20.
breu *adj. short (time)* 30,34.
breumen *adv. shortly, soon* 10,52.
bric *adj. foolish; miserable* 24,44.
brolh *s. m. wood, grove* 9,2; 41,3.
brolha *s. f. leaf, foliage* 9,1.
brolhar *v. intr. to bud* 42,4.
bruire *v. intr. to roar (of water)* 29, 38.
bru *adj. dark, brown, sombre* 8,40; *melancholy* 40,65.

C

Ca *see* cha.
cal *pron. adj. who, which, what, what kind* 10,8,9; 17,10,33; 7,47; 20, 44; cal que *whoever, whichever* 5,4; 13,10; 42,54; *any, something* 10,18; 25,52; 32,10; *subst. whoever* 12,30; 42,12; *whatever, no matter what... or* 6,15.
calfar *v. tr. to heat, warm* vida B.
can *interrogative adv. when (direct question)* 20,32; *conj. when, whenever* 1,27,53; 2,37; 3,9; 5,2; 9,9; 4,51; 4,13,58; 9,40; 15,37; 16,10; bel m'es can... 9,1; *since, if* 20,31.
can *interrogative adv. how, how much, as much, as (exclamation)* 22,9; 40,65; 43,45; tan can *as much as* 12,40; tot can 8,27; 21,28; 24,38.
captenemen *see* chaptenemen.
car *interrog. why* 3,6; 39,15; — *conj. for, since, because* 2,39; 7,39; 13, 16; 17,24; 35,26; 40,73; 42,32; per so car 1,8; 37,23; *then* 1,20, 43; 3,36; 4,37; me taina car no 39,21; 18,30; meravilhas ai, car... 43,7; *while* 8,26; fatz esfortz car 29,7; 35,3; *introducing a noun*

clause as subject 10,12; 15,28; 21,39; 31,59; *introducing noun clause as object* 1,11; *introducing a wish* 31,33.
carentena *s. f. fasting, fast, penance*; faire lonja c. 2,40.
cel *s. m. sky, heaven*; salhir al cel 35,30; re sotz cel 24,14.
cel *fem.* cela cilh 8,22; 19,51; 22,30; *m. acc.* celui cel 10,20; 40,71; *f.* celei cela *demonst. pron. that, that one* 16,32; cel que *he who, she who* 18,15; 37,51.
celar *v. tr. to conceal, hide* 4,36; 35, 38; c. alcu *to conceal someone's secret* 20,21; *refl.* 10,28; a celat *secretly* 6,58; 35,15.
cen *adj. hundred* 6,50; 13,22; 15,49; 31,28; cen aitans 21,33.
cenher (*past. part.* sens 39,7) *v. tr. to girt on, around.*
certa *adj. reliable, sure* amor certana 22,46; esser certa de 37,61?
cessar *v. to cease, stop* 40,55.
cest *n. pl. m.* cist *pron. subst. this* 13,52.
chabal *adj. superior, chosen, excellent* 15,5.
chabaleyar *v. intr. to be excellent, to act wisely* 24,47.
chadena *s. f. chain* 2,12.
chadorn *s. m. bait* 12,8.
chaitiu *adj. miserable, wretched* 10, 40; 17,9; 43,46,56,58.
calenda *s. f. Christmas* 26,48; *May-day* 7,13.
chaler *v. intr. impers. to be concerned about* 13,48; 28,44; 41,23; tornar en no-chaler *to be unimportant, indifferent* 21,8; *to consider worthless, unimportant* 42,27; 45,23.
chambi *s. m. exchange* faire chambīs de *to change, exchange* 40,60.
chamiza *s. f. shirt* 44,14.
chamjar, cambiar 28,23; *v. tr. to change* c. ma (sa) razo 9,32,33; c. los datz ad alcu *to spoil the game for someone, to cheat, to deceive* 35,40; *refl. to alter, vary* 1,39; 28,23.
chan *s. m. song, singing* 7,8; 14,1; 15,2; 19,6; 21,27; 22,4; 26,5; 33,7; 41,8; *song of a bird* 10,3; 33,1; 39,4; 40,4; 41,3; 42,2.
chanso *s. f. song* 28,67; *type of lyric,* canso 6,24; 8,1; *the poem itself* 4,61; 6,62; 8,53; 10,51; 18,32; 33,44.
chansoneta *s. f. little canso* 16,49.
chantador (*n. s.* chantaire 30,22) *s. m. singer* 13,55; 31,2; 36,5; *adj.* 28,6.
chantar *v. tr. to sing* 6,61; 22,8; 33,44; (que...) 22,32; *without object* 14,7; 20,1; 21,1; 25,36; 36,2; 45,1; sai chantar 19,49; 27, 59; 24,6; 45,4; *opposition* chantar plorar 36,3; (*of the singing of a bird*) 9,5; 41,5; 45,11; *subst.* 15,1; 22,1; 30,24; 37,56.
chap *s. m. head* 42,39; no saber ni chap ni via 45,5.
chapa *s. f. cloak, cape* desoz la ch. del cel (38, 12).
chapdelar *v. tr. to rule, guide* 25,21.
chapdolhar *v. intr. to stand out, tower* 42,21.
chaptenemen *s. m. manners, behavior* 17,37; vida B; saber far ch. *know how to behave* 27,2.
chaptener *v. tr. to defend* 43,27; *refl. to behave, hold one's own* 3,62; 21,16.
char *adj. dear, precious, valuable; adv.* tener c. 19,53; 39,25.
chara *s. f. face* frescha ch. colorida (*of the beloved*) 30,52; aver la ch. destrecha 3,56.
charamen *adv. seriously* esser auzitz ch. 40,58.
charcer *s. f. plur.* las charcers *prison* 31,22.
charn *s. f. flesh* 30,52.
chassar *v. tr. to hunt* 16,7.
chascu *pron. adj. each, each one, every one* 15,11; 28,28; 40,3; *subst.* 1,31; 7,28; ch. per se 22, 18.
chastel *s. m. castle* 38,22.
chastiar *v. tr. to blame, reproach, instruct* 24,28; 40,70; ch. alcu de 30,19.
chastic *s. m. reproof, correction* 24, 33.

chaussar *v. to shoe* sotlars be chaussans *well fitted shoes* 26,33.
chauza *s. f.* *thing, object, being;* (*of speech*) 4,41; c. de *in the case of* 30,41; tota ch. *living creatures* 4,45.
chauzimen *s. m.* *choice,* per autre ch. 6,36.
chauzir *v. tr. to choose* 1,55; 13,28; 22,33; 38,8,9.
chauzit *s. m.* *choice* aver lo ch. de 27,35; al seu ch. *according to her choice* 27,53; a totz ch. *answering all desires* 33,16?
chavaler *s. m. knight* 33,41.
chavar *v. tr. to hollow out* 16,40.
chazer *v. intr. to fall* 16,38; 25,2; 26,2; 43,3; ch. en mala merce 43,37.
clam *s. m. protest, complaint* esser de c. = se clamar de 18,17.
clamar *v. tr. to cry out, call* c. merce 2,31; 4,34; 7,57; 17,12; 40,54; *refl. to complain* 12,7; 18,17; 25,60; ad alcu 28,9.
clar *adj. clear, radiant, fine* 3,34; lo c. vis 1,51; 37,12?; lo tems c. 41,2. *adv. clearly* vezer c. 1,56; levar sa votz autet e c. 39,3.
clardat *s. f. brightness, light* (d'amor) 7,4.
clarzir *v. tr. to make light, illuminate* 3,37.
clau *s. f. key* 31,23.
claure *v. tr. to enclose, close* olhs claus 29,44; l'amor qu'es en me clauza 4,35; *enclose* 27,36; 39,7.
cle *adj. inclined* 36,50.
co *see* com.
cobertamen *adv. secretly* 10,27; razo C.
cobir *v. tr. to assign, fix* esser cobit ad alcu *to be a part of* 23,35; 40,61.
cobrir *v. tr. to cover, hide* 4,36; 6, 55; 35,1. *part.* cobert *covered* (de) 9,3; *secret* 20,16; 39,47.
cocha *s. f. trouble, need* a la c. *in pressing need, in time of trouble* 14,26; *urgency* 8,31.
cochar *v. refl. to hurry, hasten* 30,47.
col *s. m. neck* 27,45; 36,50; razo C.

colhir (*l. Pres.* colh 25,66; 41,27; *3. Pres. Subj.* colha 42,30) *v. tr. to gather, cull* 23,28; 42,30; *to grasp, harbor* 25,66; *to receive, take* s'amor colh 9,16; c. en grat 9,15; a tal ira 41,27.
Color *s. f. color* (*of flower*) 28,4; (*of the face*) 31,42; 39,38; 44,59.
colorir *v. tr. to color,* colorit (*beautifully*) *colored* 30,52.
colp *s. m. blow, stroke* 1,47; 45,28.
colpa *s. f. fault* 16,17; faire c. ad alcu de 16,30.
com, co 3,62; 12,8; 14,5; 43,38; *adv. how* (*exclamatory*) 27,49; 39,9; 40,13; 45,8; (*indirect question*) dire c. 40,32; saber c. 8,44; 18,7; 33,23; 36,15; membrar, sovenir c. 16,10; 33,16; 41,25; meravilhar, meravilhas es c. 1,10; 28,60; 39,17; estar en cossire c. *with subj.* 27,5; garnitz soi c. *with subj.* 21,48; se metre en grans c. *with subj.* 21,4; aissi com = com (conoisser aissi c.) 31,40; *comparison, as... as* 40,30; 19,1; 21,21; 40,27; si aissi enaissi c. 3,8,33; 7,10; 21,53,57; tan aitan c. 3,64; 5,26; 10,20; 16,48; 27,36; 33,35; atretal c. 1,46; com si (*with subj.*) 25,32; *as, like* 31, 51.
coman *s. m. command, order* far lo c. d'alcu 29,20; sui faihz a so c. 31,4.
comanda *s. f. command* 26,31.
comandamen *s. m. command* 31,53.
comandar *v. tr. to order, command;* a faire 4,5; a Deu vos coman 14,10; 45,43; *refl.* se c. az alcu 36,51.
comensamen *s. m. beginning* 1,4; 3, 8; 5,6.
comensansa *s. f. beginning* 1,5.
comensar *v. tr. to begin* 1,1; *intr.* 21,9; 33,7; *subst.* al c. *at the beginning* 19,33.
comjat *s. m. parting, farewell* 6,54; dar c. vidas A & B.
companha *s. f. company, fellowship* 6,8; 25,63; esser de bela c. 19, 34,54.

GLOSSARY

companho *s. m. companion* 6,7.
comte *s. m. count* 21,18.
comunal *adj.* amor c. *common, vulgar love* 15,18; amdui c. *both together* 28,39.
concluire (*3. Pres. Ind.* conclui 29,30) *v. tr. to condemn* 29,30.
confondre *v. tr. to ruin* 1,32; 5,23; 25,28; 43,30.
conhde *adj. charming, genial, comely* c. e gai 7,11; 16,46; 18,5; *opposed to* avara 3,45; bela e conhda 15,41; tals se fai conhdes e parlers 33,12; c. et ensenhatz 35,28.
conoissen *adj. learned, knowing* far se c. de *to spy out something* 1, 28.
conoisser (conoistre 22,15 Na) *v. tr. to know, recognize, realize* 13,14, 50; 22,15; 30,27; 31,39; 42,45.
conort *s. m. comfort, consolation* 13,7; 14,23; 22,28,32; *see Proper Names.*
conortar *v. refl. to console, comfort oneself* 17,52.
conquerre (*Part.* conquis 1,50; 37, 14; 44,27; conques 5,22; 31,47) *v. tr. to win, triumph, conquer, overwhelm* (amor, joi, bela semblansa) 1,50; 22,2; 44,27; esser conques (*through love*) 31,47; 37, 14.
contendre *v. intr. to contend, struggle* 4,17; 13,54; 19,21.
contener *v. refl. to contain oneself* 18,7.
contra *prep. against* (*place*) 31,44; 43,2; c. mon *upward* 43,40; *against* 7,43; *inimicably against* 13,51; 42,37.
contranher *v. tr. to cripple* 19,42.
contrastar *v. intr. to oppose, dispute* 4,44.
cor *s. m.* (*n. s.* cor *or* cors) *heart, part of the body*: traire lo cor de se 36,24; per la bocham feretz al cor 41,30; batre lo cor 41,46; la razitz del cor 40,8; l'aiga del cor 42,43; lo cors mi fon 43,8; 44, 55; foram de dos cors unitz 40, 64; - 43,13; 44,33; *the innermost, core* er sui vengutz del or

al cor 41,38; *heart: as center of all feeling* 17,44; 18,4; 23,3; 24, 39; *as source of song* 15,2; *as center of joy and pain* 2,36; 10, 6; 14,9; 25,20; 31,19; 41,4,6; 43,4; 44,1; *of sentiment* 1,23; 3,9,25; 7,5; 9,35; 31,10; 41,10; 44,9; *of hate* 27,22; 29,36; 30, 30; 35,31; 40,75; 42,36; *of disposition, attitude* 4,50; 15,12,14; 24,17; *of desire, purpose* c. volon 43,16; aver c. de, que 4,22; 12, 32; 19,38; 25,9; aver en c. 29, 47; dar, donar c. de 9,15; 17,5; 36,56; metre en cor que 26,23; metre so cor a 31,5; cor volatge 19,16; 23,34; va cor e doptos 22, 35; *of courage* 1,35. *Personification of the heart* 3,21,53; 4,37; 9,22; 10,6; 12,25; 22,6; 23,12; 24,32; 26,10; 29,56; 31,3; 35,30; 37,37; 40,46; 41,42; 44,64. De Cor *see Proper Names.*
coral, -au 15,4; 21,44 *adj. of the heart, sincere* amor c. 15,4; 28, 43; 41,31; amic c. 21,44.
coras *adv. when* c. mais 33,36; *whenever, with subj.* 27,64.
coratge *s. m. heart* 19,10; 20,47; *spirit, mind, courage* 8,15; 20,14; 23,48; 25,79; 37,8; 42,3.
corelhar *v. refl. to complain* 7,25,28.
correr *v. intr. to run* 39,21; 44,34,73. corren *swift, rapidly* 10,50.
corn *s. m. horn* 31,36.
cornut *s. m. horned* 6,20.
corona *see Proper Names.*
corrossar *v. refl. to become angry, annoyed* 35,31.
cors *s. m. body* 8,36; 12,16; 16,45; 28,37; 30,51; 36,36; 40,28; c. gen 1,49; 27,47; c. covinen 15, 41; gai 27,37; 33,15; *opposed to,* esperit 33,25; 44,35; cor e cors i ai mes 31,5; 39,23; mos c. *I* 10, 48; lo seu c. *her* 20,5; *address to the lady* bels, francs, gens c. 30,51; 31,54; 44,59.
cort *s. f. court* 33,40.
cortes *adj. courtly, well-mannered, noble* 22,16; 33,21,43; c. gatge

GLOSSARY

cortesia 20,43. *s. m.* 13,56; 22,20. *see Proper Names.*

cortesia *s. f. courtly manner, nobility* 21,7; 33,17; c. m'es que *with subj. it seems to me a good deed* 17,30; *personified* 22,13.

cosselh *s. m. advice, counsel, help* 6,64; 7,17,23; 14,24; 17,10,51; 42,37.

cosselhar *v. tr. to counsel, advise, help* 6,1; *intr.* 7,20.

cossentir *v. tr. to permit, consent to, grant, allow* 40,49.

cossi *adv. how* 4,12; 7,21; c. que *with subj., however* 26,21; 31,52.

cossir *s. m. misery, trouble* 14,3.

cossirar *v. tr. to ponder, think* 4,51; 13,22; 25,43; 44,62; 25,76 (com) 22,18; *to worry, be anxious* 7,33; 33,4; 39,9,10.

cossire *s. m. worry, perplexity* 27,4; 35,1.

cossirer *s. m. worry, perplexity* 7,37; 17,1; 23,4; 33,27.

costum *s. m.* or **costuma** *s. f. usage, custom* 42,29; per c. e per usatge 23,40.

coven *s. m. condition, stipulation* 12,31.

covenir *v. intr. to be due to someone, to be fitting, proper, suit* 3,18; 16,44; 17,50; cove que 2,30; 13,8; 18,13; 19,18; 21,55; *without subject, with reflexive pron.* 4,6; 7,50; 25,50.

covinen *adj. lovely, agreeable, pleasing* 15,41; 16,45.

cozer *v. tr. to cook* vida A.

cozi *s. m. cousin* 17,29; 27,20.

creatura *s. f. creature* tota c. *all living beings* 13,42.

creire (*1. Pres. Ind.* crei 24,23; *3. Pr. Ind.* cre 3,17; 36,26; crei 7,23) *v. tr. to believe, with an object:* 3,17; 5,7; 7,60; 10,24,27; 12,16; 18,19; no·m crei que 24,28; c. cosselh 7,23; 42,37; c. alcu 29,33; 37,62,64.

creisser *v. intr. to grow, increase* 8,56; 40,5; 42,4; 44,6.

crestia *adj. Christian* tot'arma crestia- na 37,57. — **crestiana** *s. f. Christian* 37,64.

criar (cria 45,11) *v. tr. to cry, call (of a bird) sing* 36,21; 45,11.

crim *s. f. crime, offense* 40,12.

criminal *adj. criminal, heinous* pechat criminal 28,48.

crit *s. m. cry* 27,26; *song (of a bird)* 40,4.

cubert, -tamen *see* cob-.

cuda *s. f. thought, imagination* dire per c. 8,38.

cui *see* que.

cuidar *v. tr. to think, believe (with Inf.)* 9,44; 13,1; 33,13; 43,9; *(with objective clause)* 1,42; 4,3; 7,52; 16,5; *(subjunc. in the acc. clause)* 20,13; 25,11; 26,16; 29,32; 33,22; no·s cuit que... 20,30; *to intend, plan* 4,13; 36,3; 37,31.

cura *s. f. sorrow, care* metre sa c. 8,18; penre c. de 13,5; 44,19; *to worry* 24,16.

D

Da *prep. from, out of* 15,2,3; mover d'a sos pes 42,41.

damnatge *s. m. ill, harm, loss, sorrow* 6,14; 19,8; 23,8; 25,73; 42,45.

dan *s. m. harm, pain, injury* 13,35; 20,9; 30,9; 36,42 *etc.*; esser dans ad alcu 15,16; 21,11; 26,20; 33,39; aver d. 28,17; 31,20; 37,39; vas me versa tot lo d. 29,28; e us prec de mon d. 45,29.

dar *v. tr. to give* 28,51; 31,38; (jauzimen, plazer) 3,11,26; (s'amor) 6,3; 13,17; (cor e talen) 17,5; (per prezen) 20,42.

dat *s. m. die* chamjar los datz 35,40.

daus *prep. from, from the direction of* 39,7.

de *prep. (place) place from which* B. de Ventadorn, *see* aire; *distance* de prop, de lonh, de pres 40,34; 41,50; *designation of place* aicels d'eviro 6,48; *(time) point of departure* de l'or'en sai 43,18; *measure of time* d'un mes 39,40?; d' autra vetz 37,62?; *time where, in*

GLOSSARY 201

which de noih prionda 44,51; point of departure 1,22; 3,10; 6, 5,49; 10,45; separation 1,60; 2, 12; 8,19; 9,34; comparison, parallel 6,50; 19,20; 24,20; 25,24; partitive 12,39; 1,59; 2,27; 3,4, 66; 5,21; 6,16,27; 10,19; possession 1,46; 20,49; point of departure, cause of a happening 1,47; 2,37; 3,6,44,54; 4,28,42; 5,5; 6, 54; 7,55; 8,4,18; 9,5,37; 10,29 etc.; about a conversation 2,24; device 1,56; 3,41; 6,49; 8,21; 10, 32; 19,10; form and manner 10, 41; 12,20; 18,10; 19,5,54; 20,7; 23,9; 41,11; more precise delimitation of a substantive 1,54; 6, 48; 7,10; of a verb 1,16,17,31,47; 4,38; 19,10; 40,64.
dechazer *v. intr.* to fall into ruin, be cast down 7,18,21; 15,17; 42, 21; tr. to harm, ruin 10,42; subst. 42,48.
defendre *v. tr.* to defend 8,14; to protect 26,42; to forbid 6,34; refl. to defend oneself 19,32; (vas) 3, 54; (de) 4,24.
defes, deves *s. m.* enclosure 10,3; 23, 15.
deis *conj.* since 44,20.
dejeonar *v. tr.* to eat 9,28.
delechar *v. refl.* to rejoice, delight (en) 12,6.
delgat *adj.* slender 30,51.
delir *v. tr.* to destroy, ruin 13,46; 40,21.
delonc *prep.* beside 5,3.
demandar *v. tr.* to request, claim 4, 58; 26,10; 28,31; 31,49; 39,44; 41,52; to ask 14,4; 20,49.
demenar *v. tr.* to express (joi) 2,5.
demorar *v. intr.* to tarry, delay, be joyful 41,29.
demostrar *v. tr.* to show 39,18.
den *s. f.* tooth esser feritz per las dens 40,20. [per las dens—metonymic expression for mouth.]
denan *adv.* before, in front of (*place*) pas li d. 29,44; el fron d. 31,36. *prep.* before (*spatial*) 17,40; 20, 18,33; (*temporal*) 30,32. Denan-Totz see Proper Names.

denhar *v. tr.* to be pleased to (*with infin.*), deign 4,31; 39,55; 40,42.
depenher *v. tr.* to paint 39,23.
deport *s. m.* sport, amusement, pleasure 7,31; 21,27.
deportar *v. intr.* to desport, amuse oneself 25,36; 35,2.
depus *conj.* since 5,22.
derrer *adj.* last 33,34; *subst.* li d. the worst 23,31.
des, d'eus 30,49; deis 44,20 *from*; d. adenan *from now on* 30,49; d. abans *from before* 33,32; d. que *as soon as* 44,20.
desa see deza.
desazonar *v. tr.* to spoil 23,22.
deschantar *v. tr.* to sing evil of someone, to ridicule 13,48.
deschapdolhar *v. intr.* to be of small worth 26,37.
deschaptener *v. tr.* to abandon, to leave in the lurch 43,28.
deschauzit *adj.* base, coarse 23,25; 40,12.
descobrir *v. tr.* to reveal, disclose, uncover 1,23.
desconoisser *v. tr.* not to see, not to perceive 27,10.
desconortar *v. refl.* to despair, grieve 25,34.
descreire (3 pres. subj. descreya 7, 24) *v. tr.* to disbelieve 7,24; razo D.
desduire *v. refl.* (d'alcu) to divert, amuse oneself 29,29.
desse *adv.* immediately 16,12; 43,7.
desenar *v. intr.* to be out of one's senses, lose one's reason 2,46.
dessendre *v. intr.* to descend 4,25.
desfiansa *s. f.* challenge, provocation ses d. 45,35 var.
desliau *adj.* faithless 13,47.
deslonhar *v.* (*not refl. with infin.*) to go away, withdraw, retire 40,38.
desmentir *v.* to belie, be false to esser desmentitz de 40,44.
desmezurar *v. refl.* to act without restraint 44,17.
desnaturar *v. intr.* to change its nature 44,2.
desobre *prep.* on 44,44.
desotz *prep.* under 24,5.

despolhar *v. refl. to undress* 26,30; 27,43; 41,17; 42,42.

destinansa *s. f. fate, destiny* 45,7.

destinar *v. tr. to allot, determine, be destined* esser destinatz a 35,41.

destolre *v. refl. to turn away, withdraw* (de) 29,42.

destorber *s. m. vexation, trouble, disagreeableness* 23,20.

destrenher *v. tr. to force, press* 3,51; la cara n'ai destrecha 3,57; 39,15; 41,44; *to compel* 18,14; 12,25.

destruire *v. tr. to ruin, destroy* 29,21; 43,30.

Deu *s. m. God* Deus 7,46; 17,35; 20, 32; ai a Deus 22,9,53; 31,33; 44, 49; per Deu 39,13,45; 45,18; per Deu li quer, li sia que, aya... 9,26; 17,58; 21,42; per amor de D. 10, 17; a D. vos coman, vos do 14, 10; 42,54; D. lau (que...) 2,12; 19,49; partit de D. *apostate, damned* 13,53; perdre D. 7,24; 17,28; si Deus be·m do 20,8; Deus que·l mon chapdela 25,21; Deus que tot lo mon garanda 26,22.

devedar *v. tr. to forbid* 43,36.

dever *v. tr. to owe* dever fe ad alcu 16,27; *with infin. must, should, ought, be obliged to* 1,7,61; 3,59; 6,37,39; 10,37; 13,23,37; 16,26; 17,35 *etc.*

deves *prep. from* 37,2.

deves *s. m. see* defes.

devi *s. m. spy, seer* 1,27.

devinalha *s. f. spying* 35,42.

devinar *v. tr. to find out* 17,35.

devire *v. tr. to divide, share* ab lauzengers non ai ren a d. 35,37.

deviza *s. f.* a ma d. *for my part* 44, 29.

dezacolorar *v. refl. to discolor oneself* 3,58.

dezadolorar *v. refl. to remove the pain from something* 3,3.

dezasegurar *v. tr. to take away the certainty* 13,32.

dezautreyar *v. tr. to renege, to refuse* 7,16.

dezenansar *v. tr. to lower, to harm* 44,41.

dezeretat *adj. disinherited, robbed* (d' amor) 6,22.

dezesperar *v. refl. to despair* (de) 25, 12; 43,25.

dezir (*or* -ire 3,28; 5,14) *s. m. desire, longing* 9,36.

dezirar *v. tr. to desire, long for* 3,17; 9,8,35; 12,18; 15,38; 25,39; 30, 54.

dezire *s. m. longing* 27,49; *plur.* 4,56.

dezirer *s. m. desire, longing* 23,12; 36,31; 39,16; 43,8,16.

deziron *adj. desirous of, full of longing* 5,10; 43,46.

dezonor *s. f. dishonor* (amar a d.) 6,17.

dia (*n. s.* dias 15,49) *s. m. day* 45,19.

dih, ditz *acc. plur.* 33,17; *s. m. speech* 8,45; 18,9; 41,11; bels dihz 16, 36; 33,17.

dins *adv. inside, within* 30,30; d. en in 35,31; *prep. in* 20,25.

dire 4,49,61; 12,21; dir 2,10; (*1st. pers. pres. subj.* dia 30,26) *v. tr. to speak, say* 1,11,59,63,64; 2,24; 3,40; 5,8; *etc.*; *to recite, sing* (chanso, vers) 4,61; 15,54; *with dat.* 13,21; *objectless* 17,50; no d. oc ni no 6,56; per me·us o dic (*as a particular experience*) 12,34; res no·n es a d. *there lacks nothing* 27,41; 35,21; no·n sai que d. 30,3.

dissendre *see* dessendre.

dissiplina *s. f. discipline* tener en d. 18,11.

divers *adj. varied, different* 28,4.

do *s. m. gift* 9,26; 28,56.

doblar *v. tr. to double* 6,14; *refl.* 4, 56; 28,27; *intr. to double, multiply* 5,20; 30,20; 42,4.

dol *s. m. pain, trouble, grief* 14,9; 25,20; 27,27; faire d. ad alcu 7, 26; dols me pren de 10,12; 17, 57; d. e dan 30,9.

dolen *adj. harmful, grieving* 2,36; 10,40.

doler *v. intr. to suffer, to pain* 27, 16,34,54; *refl.* 41,43; 42,31; *impers.* 9,5,6; 25,3. — *subst. m. pain* 4,28.

doloirozamen *adv. painfully* viure d. 3,63.

GLOSSARY

dolor *s. f. pain grief* 3,13; 4,40; 6, 11; 22,41; 36,16; *etc.*; viure a d. 28,13.

domna *s. f. woman, lady* 1,33; 2,24; 3,15; 5,21; 6,3 *etc.*; domnas e chevalers 33,41; ma d. 6,34; 7, 41; 9,12; 10,18; 18,16 *etc.*; d. *address to the loved one* 3,42,48; 4,49; 6,57; 7,54; 8,4,41 *etc.*; bela d. 1,49; 22,49; 28,50; bona d. 21,41; 31,49.

domneyador *s. m. man who courts ladies* 19,19.

domnei *s. m. courtship, service of ladies* 21,26.

domneyar *v. intr. to court ladies* 29, 9; 42,16.

Domnedeu *s. m. Lord God* 31,13; perdre D. 7,24.

don *relat. adv. from where (place from where)* 4,56; 7,37; 8,3; 9, 5,20 *etc.* (*partitive*) 12,39. — *in relation to a person* 3,59; 30,7.

donador *s. m. donor* 19,31.

donar *v. tr. to give, to give away* que·m don o que·m venda 26,28; be 3,61; (s'amor) 7,42; (cosselh) 6,64; (cor ad alcu) 9,15; 36,56; (un joi) 30,59; (mal ad alcu) 9,25; si Deus be·m do 20,8; Deus li do mal'escharida 23,49; Deus no·m do mais faire vers ni chanso 6,23; ams los olhs li don a traire 29,23; a Deu vos do 42,54; *refl.* se d. espaven 20,15; *no object* no sia qui dona qui tol 27,63. — *s. m. liberality, generosity* 13,4.

donc, doncs *adv. thus* 5,32; 13,37; 20,23; *introducing a question* 10, 40; 27,48; 17,17,33; 36,9; *within the question* 27,50; 35,35.

donzela *s. f. maiden* razo C.

doptansa *s. f. danger, peril, doubt, care, shyness (see note)* 1,14,57.

doptar *v. intr. to doubt* (de) 21,43; *tr. to fear* 39,26; 43,31; esser doptans vas alcu 26,26.

doptos *adj. timid* 22,35; esser d. vas alcu 3,35.

dormir *v. to sleep* 4,37; 39,42; 41, 18; 45,9; *s. m.* 2,8; 41,19.

dorn *s. m. hand's breadth* 12,13.

dos *n. m.* (dui 29,58); *adj. two* 2,22; 6,27; 15,30; 22,10; 28,55; dos tans 30,11; 33,14.

doussamen *adv. gently, in a sweet way* 26,17; 36,23.

doussetamen *adv. in a sweet way* 5, 15.

doussor *s. f. sweetness, kindness* 40, 33; 43,4; 44,10.

doutz, doussa *adj. sweet...* baizar, chan, esgart, sabor, semblan, sentir, temps de mai, verdor, votz *etc.* 1,43,51; 7,10; 9,28; 10,3; 13, 33; 17,43; 28,1; 31,10; 33,1; 39,43; *about the loved one* 13,33; 15,39; doussa res *address to the loved one* 3,45; 30,57; *the poet about himself* 33,42; Dous Esgar *see Proper Names.*

dreih *adj. straight, erect* 16,45.

dreih, drei 21,34 *s. m. right* gardar d. ni razo 20,27; d. l'en fatz 42,26; aver d. *to be right* 21,34; *to have a legal claim* 7,30; 43,50; aver d. que *to act correctly, justly* 20,36; dreihz es que *with subjunc.* 12,3; 19,37,40; 25,61; 40,44.

drogoman *s. m. interpreter, messenger* 21,49.

drudaria *s. f. love (as manifested in the fact)* 17,15; parlar de d. 21,6; amar per d. 25,49.

drut *s. m. lover* 6,31; 19,14; 28,41; *faithful friend* 12,41.

duc (*var.* dutz 26,43) *s. m. duke* 21, 18; 26,43.

dur *adj. hard* 8,5; 16,34,40; 30,33.

durar *v. intr. to hold out, endure* 4, 39; *to last* 19,46; (*with dat.*) 13, 24; 15,49; 17,45; 33,35; 44,56; 45,19; (*spatial*) *to reach* 24,24; *tr. to bear* 40,66; 39,17 (que no *with subjunc.*).

E

E (*before a vowel* et) 1,6,21; 3,20; 4,11; 7,35 *etc.*; *proclitic* e· 1,1,9 *etc.*; *conj. and* e... e... 21,45; *in negation* no... mas... e 4,57; *joining contraries* 3,45,46; 7,47; 20,

9; 36,39; *introducing a question* 1,29; 4,1; 10,8; 28,33; 31,11.
efan *s. m. child* 28,25; 31,45; 39,34.
efansa *s. f. childhood, childishness, foolishness* 1,21.
egal, engal *adj. equal* 15,32; *subst.* non ai par ni e. 41,39; *adv.* mezurar e. 28,40.
egansa *s. f. equality* no·us trob e. *your like, your equal* 1,54.
eis, eus 23,30; 29,30; 30,49 *pron. self; with pers. pron* eu e., el e. 16,13; 25,72; 42,30; *after prep.* d'eus lo sieu tort 23,30; 29,30 d'eus adenan, deis que *see* des.
eisernir *v. tr. to point out, relate* 40, 17.
eissernit *adj. picayune* 40,17 (Raynouard *gives* 'distingué'. Levy *rejects this and thinks the meaning incomprehensible here, see note*.)
el *pers. pron., nom. sing. masc., fem. tonic* ela 4,11; 9,38; 10,24; 17, 11,33; *ilh* 6,6; 8,39; 9,32; 10, 33; 16,25; 17,4,34; 23,35; *etc.*; *m. acc.* lui; *fem.* leis; *m. nom. pl.* ilh; *fem.* elas 2,27; 37,26; *m. acc. pl.* lor 13,7; 28,12; *fem.* lor 2,28,47; *atonic m. dat.* li, l' (en), ·lh; *fem.* li, l' (en), · lh (lo li *it, to her* 17,19; lo ·lh 9,21); *m. acc.* lo, l', ·l; *fem.* la; *dat. pl.* lor; *m. acc. pl.* los, *fem.* las. — leis 3,21,22; 13,41; ela 4,31 *the beloved*; lui *in reference to* rossinhol 39,5.
el — en lo.
emblar *v. tr. to take away, to steal* 19,43; 39,43.
emendar *see* esmendar.
empero *adv. however* 36,18.
empreizonar *v. tr. to imprison* 9,17.
en, e 18,1; 27,16 *prep. in, on (place)* (a) *place where* 3,64; 4,46; 12,9; 31,36; 43,48; 44,40; en pes 20, 40; (b) *place to which* 12,8; 16, 39. (*temporal*) 4,40; 5,4; 7,59; 10, 1; 13,2. en *with part. while* 13, 17; 14,7; 28,52.
en, n', ·n, ne 23,31; 44,29 *adv. of it, of them; from her* 31,59; una en 30,6; 43,29; *referring to the sentence content* 8,48; 17,22; 30,39.
en, ·n, *standing before a name: lord (title)* 12,41,42; 29,60.
enaissi *adv. in such a manner, thus, so* (com) 3,7,32; 29,57; 43,28.
enamorar *v. tr. to fill with love* 3,25; *s. m. falling in love* nostr' enamorar 40,59.
enan *adv. before, previously* 28,29; *forwards* salhir e. 36,45; *much more* 28,45; enans que *rather than* 7,7.
enans *s. m. advantage* 26,19; 28,66.
enansar *v. tr. to help, to advance, further* 1,29; 45,42,52; *intr. to proceed* 1,58; 16,51.
enardir *v. refl. to embolden* (de faire) 1,16.
encara 37,48; enquer 29,50; 45,37; enquera 3,1; 16,54; anquer 7,16; *adv. still* 16,54; 29,50; 37,48; 3, 1; 7,16.
encendre *v. intr. to enkindle* (3,9), 17,48.
enchantar *v. tr. to bewitch* 39,33.
enchaussar *v. tr. to pursue* 29,46.
enclaure 4,35 *see* claure.
encobir *v. to desire, covet* 30,50.
encolpar *v. tr. to accuse* 16,25.
encontra *prep. against* 25,73; *in comparison with* 22,2.
encontrada *s. f. region, county* vidas A & B.
encorelhar *see* corelhar 7,28.
endormir *see* adormir 33,2.
enemic *s. m. enemy* 1,40; 13,43; 39, 34.
enemistat *s. f. enmity, hostility* 22,40 (*pl.*).
engenh *s. m. cunning, deceit* 18,1; 26,15.
engenoir *v. to beget, produce, conceive* 40,16.
engres *adj. violent, enraged* 20,10.
engrevir *v. refl. to trouble, burden* 40,52. (*See Appel's note p. 229 of his edition.*)
enic *adj. sulky* 24,4.
enjan (engan *or* enjan *see* 14,19) *s. m. deceit* 15,23; 21,9; 29,10; 37,28;

GLOSSARY

faire e. 14,19; 29,39; amar ses e. 28,22; 31,17.
enjanar *v. tr. to deceive, cheat* 19,41; 22,48,54.
enliamar *v. tr. to fetter* 3,42.
enoi *s. m. vexation, annoyance* 1,25; 22,40; 45,13; enois es de far 4, 33; far e. ad alcu 1,30; 31,12; 41,47.
enoyos *adj. vexatious* 12,33; 13,47; 22,19; 1,29; 28,68.
enquera *see* encara.
enquerre (*part.* enquis 1,18; 49,20) *v. tr. to seek* 16,13; *to ask about* 1,18; 27,21; *to woo* 17,6,7; (d' amor) 44,20.
enraizar *v. tr.* 44,25 (*See Appel's note p. 265 of his edition.*)
enrequir *v. to enrich* 14,20; 27,62.
ensenhar *see* ess-.
entendre *v. tr. to direct to* (en) 15,6; *to understand* (un vers) 15,51, 53; (letras) 17,53; *to hear* 4,32; se e. en *to direct his effort to* 4,19; *to woo* en una domna 27,11.
ententa *s. f. mind, effort* 37,7.
enter *adj. whole* 33,19; *perfect* 8,42; 23,59.
entrar *v. intr. to enter* (en) 24,11; 27,4.
entre *prep. between* 24,35; *under, between* 1,34; 22,33; 33,41; triar d'entre 31,34.
entreliar *v. intr. to bind oneself* 17, 39.
entre(s)lonhar *v. refl. to remove oneself, go away* 36,44.
entremetre *v. refl. to impose, force, press* 32,46.
entrepenre *v. tr. to seize* esser entrepres de 31,46.
entresenh *s. m. sign* 39,47.
entro *prep.* e. lai *up to* (*temporal*) 13,2; e. que *until* 25,84.
enveya *s. f. envy* 1,40; *desire* 3,28; 7,40; 29,3; 42,32.
enveyar *v. tr. to envy* 21,18; *to covet* 7,39; 24,14.
enveyos *adj. envious* 28,54; *s. m.* envier 8,41; 22,11.
enves *prep. toward* lai e. *there by* 12,1; *opposite* 10,11; *against* 4,44.

envezat *adj. glad, joyful* 35,29.
envilanir *v. refl. to make contemptuous* 13,49.
enviro *adv. round about* aicels d'e. 6,48.
era, eras *see* ar.
erba *s. f. grass* 5,3; 39,1; 42,1.
erebre *v. tr. to transport, fill with rapture*, ereubut de *transported by* 12,44.
error *s. f. unrest, trouble* 6,9; 13,25.
essai *s. m. attempt, trial* 10,28.
essayar *v. to try* 36,4.
esbait *adj. dismayed* 33,3.
esbaudeyar *v. refl. to rejoice* 24,6; 29,1; 42,7.
esbaudir *v. intr. to rejoice* 2,3.
esbruir *v. tr. to make known, to announce* 1,11.
escaudar *v. tr. to heat* vida A.
eschafit *adj. slender* 40,29.
escharida *s. f. fate, destiny* 23,49.
escharir *v. tr. to allot, make fall to* 27,60.
escharnir *v. tr. to mock, insult*, mal escharnit *to whom an evil fate has fallen* 40,65.
eschaufar *v. tr. to warm, heat* 40,39.
eschazer (*3 pres. subj.* eschaya 7,53; *3 cond.* eschazegra 3,26) *v. intr. to fall to* 12,29; *to become the lot of* 7,53; 10,9; 42,13; *to suit, intr.* 3,26; *refl.* 7,50; 10,5,33; 18,13; 37,46; *to go with, match* 17,41.
esclairar *v. tr. to brighten* son semblan 44,65; *refl. to light up, shine* mos cors s'esclaira 29,56; 37,37.
escola *s. f. school* l'e. n'Eblo 30,23.
escolh *s. m. form* 41,35.
escolorit *adj. discolored, pale* 40,40.
escondire *v. tr. to deny* 40,68; *refl.* (de) *to refuse* 27,23; *subst. refusal* 35,39.
escondre *v. refl. to hide* 5,2; 26,4; 43,60; 44,42.
escoutar *v. tr. to listen to* 41,12.
escriptura *s. f.* l'e. *the holy scripture* 30,40.
escrire 12,28 (*1 pres. subj.* escria 17, 54) *v. tr. to write* 6,50; 17,54; e. en mal 12,28.

escuder *s. m. squire* faire e. de senhor 23,39. See Proper Names.

escur *adj. dark* 8,40.

escurzir *v. to darken* 7,2.

esdevenir *v. intr. to happen*, 16,17; 43,39; *refl.* 4,12; 17,34; si locs s'esdeve 36,52.

esdevi *s. m. spy* 20,12.

esduire *v. refl. to remove, withdraw* 29,45.

essenhador *s. m. he who teaches, a teacher* 2,35.

essenhamen *s. m. what is sensible* 1,20; *good manners* 1,52.

essenhar *v. tr. to teach* 13,57; 18,32; essenhat *sensible* 35,28; ben e. *educated, well-bred* 30,57; mal e. *uneducated (in conduct)* 22,16.

esser (*1 pres. ind.* so 6,47; 20,49; son 20,31 -n *before vowel*); sui 29,14,57; *6 pres. ind. pl.* son (-n *is constant*) 5,31; *3 pres. subj* sia 17,47,58; 21,46; 25,57; sei 5,35. *v. intr. to be* 10,49; 15,4; 19,47; qui fo 6,63; no es... mas 1,25; 10,43; 17,47 *to be in a place* 2,12; 5,31,35; 6,47,63 etc.; *to be constituted* (*with refl. pron.*) 22,3,44; 27,18; 33,32; 43,32; *connective, with subst.* 4,3; 6,18; 10,8 etc.; *with pres. part.* 5,12; 26,40; *with past. part.* 2,14,22; 4,15,43; 6,46 (*passive* 2,25; 22,26; 35,11; *refl. in dat.* 19,3); *with adv.* 5,9; 8,44; e. a far *to have to do* 4,17; 27,41; (non es a dire *see* dire); e. de *to be from, originate* 5,27; 9,37; e. d'alcu *to belong to someone* 20,49; e. de bel acolhimen, de bo pretz, *etc. to have a special quality* 10,41; 18,10; 19,54; 28,60; e. de salvatge 19,5; e. de dos cors unitz *to have two hearts united* 40,64; e. en *to be in* (en error, en la vostra merce) 6,9; 21,46; *to exist in* 15,30.

essernir *v. tr. to perceive clearly* 13,31.

essertanar *v. tr.* (alcu de) *to assure* 37,61.

esfortz *s. m. effort, undertaking* faire e. car *to force oneself to...* 12,38; 29,7; 35,3.

esgar *s. m. regard*, na Dous-Esgar, See Proper Names.

esgarar *v. tr. to look at* 5,19; 39,19.

esgardamen *s. m. heed, attention*, penre e. de *to think about something* 27,56; *to care for* 13,18.

esgardar *v. tr. to look at* 6,42; 15,48.

esgart *s. m. regard, look* 1,51.

esglai *s. m. fear, terror, grief* 7,26; 10,26.

esglayar *v. refl. to dismay, frighten* 7,29.

essien *s. m. knowledge*, mon e. *to my knowledge* 6,28; en essiens *knowing* 5,26.

esjauzimen *s. m. joy* 5,5.

esjauzir *v. refl. to rejoice* 13,3; 21,37; 40,9; de *to rejoice about* 23,55.

eslaissar *v. refl. to rush, hasten* (en, vas) 12,8,10.

eslonhar *v. tr. to prolong, remove, cause to become distant* 38,29.

esmai *s. m. care, trouble, dismay* 8,19; 17,1.

esmayar *v. refl. to alarm, deny* 7,3,6; 36,9.

esmansa *s. f. judgment, estimation* se penre e. 1,53.

esmenda *s. f. recompense, compensation* 19,24; 26,7.

esmendar, em- 30,49 *v. tr. to compensate, make good on* 20,25; *refl. to better oneself* 30,49.

espaa *s. f. sword* 45,28.

espandre *v. refl. to spread out* 26,3.

espaven *s. m. fear, terror* se donar e. *to be frightened* 20,15.

espaventar *v. refl. to be afraid* 37,20.

esper *s. m. hope* segon mon e. 24,11; bon e. 15,36; 21,40; 42,34; 45,37.

esperansa *s. f. hope* aver s'e. en 1,62; metre s'e. en 45,21; bon'e 25,27; 44,37; 45,51; e. bretona 23,38.

esperar *v. tr. to expect, hope for* 4,20.

esperdut *adj. distracted* 8,46; *benumbed* 19,1.

esperit *s. m. soul, spirit* 33,23; 44,34; faire chambi dels esperitz 40,60.

GLOSSARY

esperital *adj. of the spirit, spiritual* olhs esperitaus 15,47.
esplechar *v. tr. to accomplish* 39,45.
esplei *s. m. practice, exercise* 5,14.
esponda *s. f. edge of bed* 26,32; 44, 44.
esquern *s. m. mockery, derision,* esquerns er 6,18.
est (si'st = si ist 8,41) *dem. pron. this* 27,6; 40,24.
establir *v. tr. to establish* 40,28.
estar (*3 pres. indic.* estai 36,15; *1 pres. subj.* esteya 42,38,54; estei 24,39; *3 pres. subj.* esteya 29,41; *1 cond.* estegra 3,15; *3 cond.* estara 8,11) *v. intr. to be, exist, stand* 4,46; 24,39; 29,41; 42,38, 54; estar pres de... 20,22; n'estauc *I am far from* 16,21; 31,59; 42,28; *to refrain from doing* 26,6; *to be in a condition (with adj.)* 8,49; 12,4; 19,7; 20,39; 24,4; *refl. e. with adj.* 3,15; 19,7; *with adv. e.* len 3,10; e. mau ab alcu 13,39; e. ben, mal 1,33; 39,20; ben estan *excellent* 33,21; estai be, gen, mal (que) 4,7; 8,11; 17, 32; 20,1; (car) 10,12; *no subject* 7,35; 36,15.
estatge *s. m. being, existence* esser de bel e. 42,23; *stay, sojourn* aver son e. ab joi 23,10; faire lonc. e. *to remain far away from for a long while* 20,5; *period, while* 19,2.
estener *v. refl. to abstain from* (de) 4,18.
estenher *v. tr. to extinguish, destroy* 3,51; 39,16.
estraire *v. tr. to take away, remove* 8,42; *v. refl. to depart, escape* (de) 4,13; 29,47,59; 37,40.
estranh *adj. strange* 45,47; *hostile* 19,36; *strange* 25,13.
estranhar *v. refl.* vas alcu *to act hostily toward, to alienate* 25,67.
estrenher *v. tr.* (vas se) *to squeeze, press, hug* 36,35.
estuyar (*or* estruire?) *v. refl. to encircle, enclose, protest* 29,53.
esvelhar *v. refl. to awaken, arouse* 7,36.

eu 1,16,19; 3,15; 4,3,20; *etc.*; e· 3,7; 4,51; 6,64; 8,6; 26,27; 31, 51; *etc.*; *acc.* me *tonic* 3,50; 4,2; 17,10; 43,13,57; mei 24,31; *atonic* me 1,6; *etc.*; m' 1,9,17; *etc.*; ·m 3,7; *etc.*; *pers. pron., 1 pers.* eu oc 18,27; eu las ... agra 23,17.
eus *see* eis.
eviro *see* enviro.

F

Fachura *s. f. condition, quality, form* 24,40; 12,41. *See Proper Names.*
fachurar *v. tr. to enchant* 8,21; 12, 41.
faih *s. m. action, deed* 1,8; 23,59.
faire 4,5; 12,45; 29,7; far 3,30; 6, 16; 4,47; *1 pres. indic.* fatz 22, 7; fau 13,21; 21,21; *3 pres. indic.* fai 10,19; 17,33; 25,78; *etc.*; *6 pres. indic.* fan 28,24; 37,22; *3 perf.* fetz 3,8; 6,54; 8,25; *etc.*; fei 24,22; *part.* faih 8,2) *v. tr. to make, produce* 2,23; 22,34; 25, 42; 27,48; 31,4; 35,23; cors befaih 30,51; f. chan *to sing (of the nightingale)* 33,1; *to write poetry* f. vers, chanso 6,24; 8,2; 15,54; 26,36; que Deus aya faih de me rei 5,28; f. escuder de senhor 23, 39; *with double acc.* ric. ome m'a faih 15,42; *with acc. and nom.* se faire devis, rics. *etc.* 1,27; 20,12; 21,21; 33,12. — f. lonc aten, badatge, ben ad alcu, longa carantena, colpa ad alcu, do, dol, enoi, esfortz, esglai, esmenda, lonc estatge, falhimen, ira, mal ad alcu, meravilha, onor, paor, parven, plazer, mala preizo ad alcu, so pro, rancura, bo saber ad alcu, bel semblan, so talen, lo voler d'alcu; *see* aten, badatge, *etc.* — *to do* 4,5,6; 6,15,54; 21,39; que farai? 10,40; 35,35; 40,13; non fatz mas gabar e rire 4,57; faire que pros, *etc.* 8,25; 22,57; mal o fara si no... 26,29; s'ela tan fai que perdonar me volha 42,46; *with refl.* que·m farai? 17,9; 36,

28; no sai que·m fan 13,21; 18, 12; 39,12; *substitute word* 3,8; 15,48; 29,62; 31,44; 36,8; no *object* no farai 17,20; *with infin.* 1,40,48; 3,43; 4,8,19; 19,39; 23, 56; 25,18; 37,33; *with a and infin.* me fari' a pendre 4,21; be fari' a aucire 25,41.

faisso *s. f. face* cobrir sa f. 6,55; *pl. features, form* 8,33; 13,29; *features of the face* 28,57.

faissonar *v. tr. to fashion, form* 35, 22.

falhimen *s. m. fault, offense* 1,25; faire. f. 3,55; 6,44; 37,22.

falhir *v. tr. to refuse, deny, to forsake* 40,56; 35,36; *intr. to fail* 10,38; que lhai falhit 27,51; vas alcu 1,15; *part.* falhit *who has transgressed, offended* 23,41.

fals, faus 15,26; *adj. false* falsa laus umana 22,45; *of one who speaks falsely* 15,26; *faithless* 8,41; 20, 10; 22,14; 23,25; 29,16; 31,34; 41,16 — fausa *s. f. falsifier, faith breaker* 2,37; 41,26.

fatz *s. f. face* 16,42; 40,30.

fe, fei 21,10 *s. f. faith* 10,36; 41,10; 45,48; *trust* 4,15; amar per bona f. 21,10; 31,17; tot o fi per bona fe 16,28; juraria per ma fe 25, 54; fe qu'eu dei 16,27; 42,33; a la mia f. 17,20.

feblezir *v. to weaken, become weak* 40,25.

felo *s. m. adj. bad, villainous* 6,31; cor f. 29,36; 42,36.

femna *s. f. woman* 43,33.

fenestral *s. m. window* 28,36.

fenher *v. refl. to become lazy, to diminish* 18,10.

fenir *v. tr. to finish, end* 8,29; *s. m. end* 1,8.

fer *adj. cruel, hostile* 16,34; 19,36; *wild* la fera mar 26,39; *bad, evil* 40,21.

ferir *v. to strike, hit, wound* 1,48; 40,20; 42,31; 31,25; 41,30; *refl. to strike oneself* 23,28; *intr.* 16, 39.

fermansa *s. f. assurance, guarantee* 45,20.

feuneyar *v. intr. to act faithlessly* 29, 27.

feunia *s. f. wickedness, malice* far f. d'alcu *to deal badly with someohe* 45,25; *indignation, anger* 17, 23.

fi *adj. faithful, reliable, sincere* 9,35; 20,21; 29,14; fina *true, sincere (concerning the beloved)* 13,33; 15, 39; 18,18; fin' amansa 1,13; fin' amor 7,11; 15,4; 18,6; 22,46; 27,66; 42,21; 44,15; fin amic, amador; aman 15,30; 21,44; 24, 12; 31,34; 37,30; esser fis de *to be sure, certain of* 37,16; *true, honorable* 15,50; 16,43; Fis-Jois, *see Proper Names.*

fi *s. f. end* 1,7; *peace* 29,50.

fiansa *s. f. trust, faith* 45,48; aver f. en, de 1,38; 25,25; 44,26; m' avetz trait en f. 45,35.

fiar *v. refl. to trust* (en alcu) 28,12; 43,26; 45,33.

finamen *adv. truly, faithfully* 2,39; 20,46; 31,40.

finar *v. intr. to cease, to become peaceful* 18,4.

flama *s. f. flame* 3,64; *flame of love* 3,9; 12,11.

flanc *s. m. side, hip, pl.* 40,29.

flor *s. f. flower (collective)* 5,2; 7, 12; 10,2; 24,2; 25,6; 27,7; 28, 3; 29,2; 39,2; 41,1; 42,1; 44,3.

florir *v. intr. to blossom, flower,* florit *in bloom* 40,1; lo tems. f. *blossom time, spring* 27,8.

foc *s. m. fire* 12,12; 40,39.

fol *adj. foolish, mad* 15,16; 25,66. *s. m.* 7,38; 15,33; 42,29; 43,38; *adj. subst.* 4,2; 5,8; 6,26; 13,54; 17,13; 23,36,53; 42,26; 44,17; 45,20,33; *the poet to himself* 7, 38; 17,13; fols no tem tro que pren 30,21; ai be faih co·l fols en pon 43,38.

folatge *s. m. folly, madness* 42,44; faire f. 19,4; 25,77; dire f. 23, 56.

folatura *s. m. fool* 24,34.

foleyar *v. intr. to act foolishly* 40, 43; 42,29.

folh *s. m. foliage, leaves* 9,4; 41,1.

GLOSSARY

folha *s. f. leaf,* 3,33; 31,44; *foliage* 9,3; 10,2; 25,1,6; 27,7; 28,3; 39,1; 42,1.
folhar *v. intr. to leaf* 24,1; (*the poet about himself*) 24,8.
folhat *s. m. pl. foliage* 24,5.
folia *s. f. madness, folly* 1,21; 2,11; 30,20.
folor *s. f. folly* 2,14; 6,25; faire f. 25,38.
fon *s. f. fountain* 5,3; 43,24.
fondre *v. intr. to melt, destroy* 43,8; 44,55.
for *s. m. manner* 41,5; *fashion.*
forfachura *s. f. offense, abuse* 24,26; en la mia f. *for abuse on my part* 8,8.
forfaire *v. tr. to be guilty of* 8,27.
formar *v. tr. to form, create* 16,48; 30,53,58; 40,26.
formir *v. refl. to care for, to concern oneself about* (de) 1,31.
forn *s. m. oven* 12,12. vidas A & B.
fornegeira *s. f. bakeress* vida B.
fors, for 41,45 *adv.* de for *outside* 41,45; fors de *out* 2,12; 23,18; *except* 38,14.
forsa *s. f. strength, force* 31,6; 42, 12; venser a f. 35,6; per f. *by force* 28,56; *fortress* 8,14 (*see Appel's comment p. 50 of his ed.*).
forsar *v. tr. to compel* (de faire) 4, 46; forsat *compelled, against the will* 40,73; *forced* 6,38.
fort *adv. strong, great* 7,32; 12,12; 14,23; 25,30; 35,29; 40,36.
foudat *s. f. folly* 2,43; 6,30; 7,43; 16,14; 22,23.
fraire *s. m. brother* 27,20; seu f. *his equal* 29,32.
franc *adj. noble* (*of mind and conduct*) 20,41; 28,62; *sincere* 29,14; f. vis 37,12; *said of the beloved* 15,39; 19,34; 31,54; 37,35; *of the poet himself* 33,42; 41,36.
Frances, *see Proper Names.*
franchamen *adv. in a noble manner* 20,43; *sincerely* 20,47.
franher *v. tr. to shatter, break to pieces* 25,69; *refl.* se fr. *to break* 18,8.

frê *s. m.* rein, tener en so f. 17,4; si·m tira vas amor lo fres 31,7.
freih *adj.* (*fem.* freja) *cold* 37,1; 44, 16. *s. m.* (*n.* freis) *cold* 40,37.
frejura *s. f. cold* 26,3; 44,4; *time of cold weather* 13,6.
fresc *adj. fresh* (erba, verdor) 28,2; 39,1; (color, chara, fatz) 30,52; 39,38; 40,30; 44,59; (*said of the beloved and their bodies*) 3,34; 12,17; 27,37.
frezir *v. intr. to get cold, grow numb* 40,53.
fron *s. m. forehead* 5,24; 16,42; 31, 36; 35,20.
fugir (*3 pres. indic.* fui 29,46) *v. tr. to flee* (alcu) 29,46; 42,23; *intr.* 40,40.

G

Gabar *v. intr. to boast* 40,43; *to jest* 4,64 (*praising*); *to jest, to mock* 4,57 (*censuring*).
gai *adj.* (*fem.* gaya 7,14) *happy* 1,12; 7,11,14; 18,5; 28,6; auzel g. 24, 5; cors gai 12,17; 16,46; 27,37; 31,54; 33,15; *adv.* (?) 10,48.
gaire *intensifier of the negation* no ... g. 4,11; 15,1; 29,40; 30,24; no ... g. de *scarcely, barely, hardly* 12, 39; 13,27; si ... g. *some while, a long time* 44,56.
galiar *v. tr. to cheat, deceive* 24,27.
ganda *s. f. evasion, subterfuge* 26,15.
garan 38,11 *see note.*
garandar *v. tr. to embrace* 26,22.
garar *v. tr. to protect, pay attention to* 22,24.
gardar *v. intr. to see, look at* (*a place*) 6,43,47; *tr. to look at* alcu 17,42; *to consider* 5,1; 20,27; *to attend to, watch* (alcu de) 41,49; *no object* gardatz; *as an introduction to a question* 18,25; *refl. to beware of* 12,11; g. que no *with subjunc. to preserve from* 41,46; *to guard* 29,53.
garir, *see* guerir.
garnir *v. tr. to prepare, part.* garnit *ready, prepared to* (de) 27,65; 33, 30; (com fassa) 21,47.

gatge *s. m. pledge,* dar un g. 20,43; rendre so g. 42,39.

gazanhar *v. tr. to win, gain, get* 32, 48; 40,11 *(the beloved);* 41,48 *refl.* se g. *to get for oneself* 19, 44; 25,65.

gazardonar *v. intr. to reward, recompense; v. tr. to give a reward to someone* 23,37.

gel *s. m. frost, ice* 44,11.

gelos *adj. jealous* 24,34. *s. m.* 41,45.

gens *s. f. people* 31,12; (falsa, fola, malvaza, vilana, *etc.*) 7,22; 15,16; 22,14; 37,41; autra g. 7,6; tota g. 5,29; 6,18; 13,9; *pl.* avols gens 1,34.

gen *adj. (fem.* genta 7,44; 37,5) *pretty, charming* 1,49; 4,27; 7,44; 17,60; 20,6; (tems, termini) 26,4; 28,1; gen es *it is welcome* 15,35; *to be proper, suitable* 5,23; 42, 49; gent estera que 20,1; a leis non estara g. *it will not be fitting for her* 17,32. *Compar.* gensor *(nom.* genser) *more beautiful, more charming* 1,55; 3,56; 12, 16; 20,37; *Subst.* la genta *(designation of the beloved)* 37,5; gensor *a more beautiful* 35,23; la gensor *the most beautiful (the beloved)* 6,51; 7,14; 28,15; 39, 37; 44,74 — gen *adv. beautiful, nice* 3,43; 6,42; 7,56; 13,44; 16, 33,46; 21,36; 30,58; 31,25; 39, 54; *(ironic)* 29,29.

generation *s. f. origin, birth* vidas A & B.

genh *s. m. meditation, form of thought* 18,1; *trick* 39,48.

genolh *s. m. knee,* a genols *kneeling* 26,34.

genolhos, a. g. *kneeling* 20,40.

gequir *(1 pres. indic.* gic 24,9) *v. refl.* se g. de *to leave, forsake, abandon* 24,9; 43,59.

ges *s. m. something (in the question)* 14,5; *generally an intensifier in the negation* no ... ges *not at all* 10,45; *nothing* 22,36; 43,44,57; *emphatic negation* 2,25; 4,7; 8, 46; 16,2; 31,55.

getar *v. tr. to throw* g. a so dan 45, 29; *to deliver from a particular state, condition* (d'ira mortal) 41, 32.

gola *s. f. throat, chest* 16,42.

gota *s. f. drop* 16,38.

grâ *s. m. grain* 30,46.

graile *adj. slim, thin* 40,29.

gram *adj. ill-disposed* (vas alcu) 12,4.

gran *adj. great, big* 4,33; 6,40; 9,29, 40; 10,19; 17,8; 29,3; 31,48; 33, 11; gran re *much* 3,4; *subst.* se metre en grans *to strive very hard* 21,3.

gras. *adj. fat, round (in praise of the body of the beloved)* 36,36.

grat *s. m. favor, will, gratitude,* per mon g. *for, according to my pleasure* 18,22; colhir en g. *to receive in a friendly way* 9,15; mal grat n'aya ... 19,50; *thanks, gratitude* 16,26; aver g. de 6,37; rendre gratz ad alcu 35,17; saber g. 45,38; se venir a g. *to suit, agree with oneself* 32,8.

grazir *v. tr. to approve of, to welcome, to praise* 1,7; *to be grateful for, to welcome* 13,13; 20,3; *part.* grazit *agreeable* 40,41.

greu *adj. difficult* 2,26; 6,8; 40,10, 25; greu m'es que ... 26,8; 29, 51; 37,17,27; *adv. with difficulty, painfully* 1,13,36; 2,15; 8,14; 13, 28,55; 36,5; 40,74.

greuyar *(3 pres. indic.* greya 29,49) *v. intr. to be harmful, painful* 29, 49.

groi *adj. yellow* 44,3.

guerra *s. f. war, strife (in love)* 13, 38.

guerrer *s. m. enemy* 25,44.

guerreyar *v. tr. to make war* 7,31,32; 29,19.

guerir, garrir *v. tr. to cure* 1,44; 10, 22; 27,15; 40,77; *intr. to heal* 1,47; 36,29.

guidar *v. tr. to lead, guide* 23,11.

guiren *s. m. surety, pledge* 42,44.

guiza *s. f. manner, way,* se captener a g. d'amor *to behave after the manner of love* 21,16; se tener de g. *behave in the proper way* 44, 18.

GLOSSARY

guizardo, -zer- *s. m. reward* 8,28; 9,29; 31,52; rendre g. 4,27; aver g. 6,39; dar g. 28,52.
guizardonar, ga- *v. tr. to reward* 9,30; 23,37.
gurpir *v. tr. to abandon, quit* guerpisca 24,31.

I

I *adv. there (place)* 5,31; 6,63; *there, that way (to the beloved)* 16,24; *refers to stressed idea (lovers)* 21,59; 31,6; *about a person, "chez elle"* 45,49; *"chez vous"* 45,30; *referring to preceding ideas* 1,56; 3,55; 6,44; 19,20; *to following ideas* 7,44; 8,25; 15,31; 31,38.
ins *adv.* i. en *within* 7,5; 27,22; 41,14; *in, herein* 23,3; d'ins da *from within* 15,2.
ira *s. f. anger* 28,46; *grudge, chagrin, grief, trouble* 8,19; 18,8; 22,41, 42; 40,75; 41,27; i. mortal 28,46; 41,32; faire i. ad alcu 7,26.
irat *adj. angry* 12,5; 16,34; *grieved, sad* 22,32; 30,30; 33,37; 35,16.
ironda *s. f. swallow* 44,49.
issilh *s. m. exile, misery* 43,56.
issir *v. intr. to go out* 30,45.
ivern *s. m. winter* 7,13; 26,45; 44,11.

J

Ja *adv. ever, now* 5,10,25; 7,45; ja no *never* 2,10; 4,4; 8,47; 10,27; etc.; *not at all* 7,30; 8,3; *not even* 19,45; ja no mais *never more* 6,23; 37,63; si ja no *if not* 28,53.
jai *s. m. joy* 37,58.
jarric *s. m. oak thicket* 24,1.
jasse *adv. always* 32,26.
jauzen *adj. rejoicing, glad* 1,12; 3,16.
jauzidor *s. m.* (jauzire) *a pleasure-taker* 9,42; 25,47; 27,13.
jauzimen *s. m. enjoyment, joy* 3,11; 5,5; 10,5,19; 15,13; 30,7.

jauzion *adj. (fem.* -onda 44,53) *full of joy* 5,16; 43,6.
jauzir (jauvir) *v. tr. (3 pres. ind.* 21, 12) *to enjoy* 23,51; *to take pleasure from* 1,32; *(from the beloved f.)* 3,59; 9,41; 25,22; *rfl.* se j. de 13,40; (d'alcu) 21,12; *(from the beloved f.)* 18,22; no ... jauzit *without joy, joyless* 40,9.
jauzire *see* jauzidor.
jazer *v. intr. to lie, repose, rest* 27, 46; 36,32; vau j. 45,10; *(next to the beloved)* 37,49; *s. m.* 28,52.
jëonar *v. intr. to fast* 9,27.
joc *s. m. game, play* 30,10.
jogar *v. intr. to play* (d'alcu *with someone*) 29,29.
joi *s. m. joy* 2,48; 17,41,47; 19,44; 20,22; 22,48; 25,72; 27,12; 28,8; 30,29; 31,28; 40,5; 41,8; 43,60; *play on the word* joi 1,1-9; 23, 8; 10,14; 33,3; 39,5-8; 42,3-8; fi j. 28,35 *see proper names,* ric j. 35,38; j. d'amor 15,6; 22,46; atendre j. 15,52,54; 30,59; s'atendre en un j. 10,6; auvir j. 45,14; aver j. 7,27; 12,40; 13,20; 21,32; 22, 31; 35,2; 41,6; 44,10; conquerre j. 22,2; enquerre j. 1,18; 27,21; esperar j. 4,20; sentir j. 3,66; tornar alcu en j. 41,32; aver jauzimen d'un j. 10,6; jois torna en error 13,25; vos etz lo meus jois 33,33; li meu jornal son joi 41, 8; trametre jois e salutz 12,36; de joi 12,20; 41,11. Joi *personified* 27,17.
jonher *v. tr. to join, to unite* j. las mas *to fold the hands* 44,58; mas jonchas 20,39; 36,50; 42,40.
jorn *s. m. day* noih e jorn 7,33; 40, 7; ja pois viva j. ni mes 31,14; lo j. que *on the day on which* 13,17; *whenever* 35,19; ja'l jorn que—no *nor whenever* 25,45; 44, 31; lo j. *each day* 31,27; un jorn *some day* 12,10; chascun j. *each day* 15,11; 28,28; tot j. 4,42; 29, 11; totz jorns *daily, always* 9,16; 40,35.
jornal *s. m. day, day work* 41,7; a j. *daily, always* 28,34.

212 GLOSSARY

jos *adv. below* 25,2.
josta *prep. beside, near, among* 26, 32; 29,2; 41,1.
joya *s. f. joy* 8,22; 10,44; 44,1.
joyos *adj. joyful* 8,17.
jurar *v. tr. to swear* 17,46; (sobre sainhz) 25,53; ome jurat e plevit 33,31.

L

Lai *adv. there* 45,52; (*next to the beloved*) 18,30; *to that place* 10, 51; 12,3; 17,3; 22,63; 36,18; 44,34; lai on *there where* 8,13; 18,3; 24,13; 35,10; *in the circumstance when* 28,64; 39,54; *there where* 4,26; 6,47; 26,30; 27,43; 31,57; *wherein* 29,18; de lai *thither* 25,76; lai vas (enves) 12,1; 22,62; entro lai en *until* 13,2.
laih *adv. hateful, bad* 1,63; l. m'estai 8,11.
lairo *s. m. thief* 29,31; 39,11; a l. *stealthy, furtive* 20,17.
laissar *v. tr. to leave, abandon* 23,42; *give up, stop* 28,67; *to leave behind* 43,15; laissar *plus inf.* 25, 22; 27,27; 43,3,19; no·t laisses levar al ven 17,16; lais m'en *I give up* 6,35; 20,8; se l. de far 42,9; no·m lais que no 24,33.
lancan *conj. when* 24,1; 25,1; 26,1.
landa *s. f. plain* 23,16; 26,1.
lansa *s. f. lance* 1,46; 45,28.
lansar *v. tr. to throw, refl.* 44,43; *remove violently* 25,29.
las *interj. alas* 4,37; 28,33; 40,13; eu las! 23,17; 30,3,5; *see* ai.
lassar *v. tr. to bind, fetter* 17,2; 22, 52; 40,8.
latz *s. m. sling* 27,45.
latz *s. m. side* 22,47.
lau 21,4; *s. m.* laus *s. f.* 22,45; *praise* 3,40; rendre laus 35,17.
lauzar (*1 pres. ind.* lau 13,12) *v. tr. to praise* 1,8; 16,47; 21,22; Deu lau *thank God* 2,12; (que ...) 19, 49; l. alcu re ad alcu *to tell someone that something is right, to demand* 15,35; se l. de *to be happy with* 3,23; 13,12; 21,33; *inf s. m. praise* 13,30; 22,27; 33, 18.
lauzenger *s. m. liar, slanderer* 13,35, 39; 19,42; 20,10; 23,52; 27,25; 31,35; 35,37; 37,42.
lauzeta *s. f. lark* 43,1.
lauzor *s. f. praise* (22,45 var.)
lê *adj. smooth, slippery* 12,17; 36,36
legir *v. tr. to read* 16,37; 17,56.
leih *s. m. bed* 26,32; 28,36; 41,18.
leis *see* el.
lemozî *see Proper Names.*
len *adj. slowly* 39,24, *adv. lazy, disinclined* 3,10; *idle* 15,48.
lenga *s. f. tongue* 17,39; 40,45; *personified* 40,18.
lengueyar *v. intr. to chatter* 40,47.
leô *s. m. lion* 31,55.
letra *s. f. letter pl.* 17,53.
leu *adv. light* 40,31,74; be leu *perhaps* 13,36; 21,14.
leuger *adj. frivolous* 23,23.
levar *v. tr. to raise up, to remove* 17, 16; *to raise up* la votz 39,4; un crit 27,26; ochaizos 29,26.
leyal 41,16; -au 15,39; *adj. loyal, faithful, sincere* 28,41.
lezer *s. m. leisure* 45,3.
lïar *v. tr. to bind, to tie* 24,45.
lige *adj.* ome l. *servant* 42,38.
linhatge *s. m. lineage* 23,26; *behavior* 29,22.
lo *sing. mas. nom. and acc. art., when contracted* ·l, *f. nom.* la 1,3,55; *etc.; when contracted* ·lh 4,48; 17,39; 20,37; 21,31; 24,2; 45, 18; *acc.* la, *pl. m. nom.* li, *when contracted* ·lh 1,50; 24,4; *etc., acc.* los, *fem.* las.
loc *s. m. place* 4,38; 16,39; 27,44; 29,41; *applied to the love* 4,19; 35,27; *occasion* 19,47,48; 36,52; 37,46; en l. de *in place of* 44,23.
lonc *adj.* (*fem.* longa 6,4) (*spatial*) *slim, slender, big* 16,45; (*temporal*) *long, a long time* 2,40; 16, 5; 19,2; 12,29; 30,46; 23,32; 27, 1; 29,52; (lonja paraula d'amar) 39,51; *adv.* lonjas *a long time* 7, 60.
lonh *adv. far away* 44,36; *distant* 25,

GLOSSARY

29; esser de l. *to be distant* 41, 50.
lonhar *v. tr. to remove, expel* (alcu de) 20,11; *refl. remove oneself* 26, 40; 29,42; 33,25.
lonhor *adj. longer (temporal)* 2,41.
lonjamen *adv. for a long time* 6,4; 10,13; 16,21; 17,45; 31,59.
lor, lui *see* el.
luzir *v. intr. to light, to gleam* 7,1.

M

Mâ *s. f., s. m.* 35,20; *hand* 30,53; jonher las mas, mas jonchas 20, 39; 36,50; 42,40; 44,58.
mai. *s. m. may* 7,10; *see* mais.
mainh *pron. adj. (fem.* manhta) *many* 3,44; 6,53; 8,9,42; 18,1; 39,10; 44,70.
mais, mai 10,41; 18,26; 27,1; 36,8; *adv. more; used as a comparative* 2,9; 3,49; 4,10; 5,24; 6,35; 13, 32; 17,23; 19,35; 29,62; m. val que (*with a conjunction*) *it is better that* 6,28; *the best* 13,56; *with a verb and subs.* 4,2; 19,16; *with a verb and prep. phrase* 10,41; no m. (mas) *no thing further, only* 17,47; 35,14; *further* 5,18; 13,55; 2,11; 29,56; *ever* 36,8; coras m. *any further* 33,36; no m. *no more* 27,1; ja m. no, ja no m., no ja m. *no longer, never* 6,24; 42, 35,41; 43,26; no anc m. *never, at no time* 43,42; *adjectival use* re m. *anything more, anything else* 18,26; 40,6; re m. no *nothing further* 24,14; *substantival use*, m. de (*with noun*) 12,37; 15,13; 19,8; 41,6,33; *with a number* 6,50; 26,6; on m. de *even more* 5,21; no i a m. del morir 25,24; que·n puesc m. *what more can I do?* 31,21.
mal, mau 13,39; 21,45; *adj. bad, evil* 1,34; 3,15; 14,11; 28,60; *wicked* 9,18; 23,26; m. pes 35,1; mals traihz 23,5; ses mal resô *without hurting the reputation* 20,18; mala merce *denial of grace, ungracious* 41,26; 43,37; mal grat, *see* grat

harmful 45,7. *Adv. badly, wickedly* m. me vai (de) 36,6,7; m. o fara si no 26,29; estar m. ab alcu 13,39; mal m'estai que, car *it appears bad to me that* 8,11; 10, 12; *characteristic negation* mal sal es *it is not well done* 42,25; mal sembla *it does not appear* 43,45. *Subst. evil* 3,4; 5,13; 6,27; 9,24; 36,38; 40,24; m. d'amor 35,8; maus m'en ve 15,11; per m. de *through fault of* 28,68; dire m. de 1,63; 12,19; faire m. (ad alcu) 10,36; 21,45; penre m. *see* penre, sentir m. 27,16; traire m. 4,8; 17,11; 37,33; voler m. ad alcu 28,47.
malamen *adv. unfortunately* 22,53.
malastruc *adj. unfortunate* 37,50.
malvatz *see* mauvatz.
maltraih *s. m. hardship* 4,28; 8,18; 23,5; los mals traihz.
manal *adj. by hand*, vida B.
mandar *v. tr. to send* 12,39; 42,50; lo coratge en ostage 25,87; ...ostage 25,83; *to inform* alc re ad alcu 20,4; 39,28; m. faire 26,29; ...que 21,37; 45,54; m. fin e plaih 29,50.
maneyar *v. tr. to caress* 36,34.
manh, manhta *see* mainh.
manjar *v. tr. to eat* 38,23.
mantel *s. m. coat, cloak* razo C.
mantener *v. tr. to maintain* 30,13.
mar *s. f. sea* 26,39; *without article* 27,36.
marrit *adj. troubled, stricken, grieved* 33,37; 40,37,73.
martire *s. m. torment, suffering* 35,7; 44,76.
mas *conj. but* 1,13; 3,16,40; 4,7; 6, 5; 7,36; 8,13; *etc.*; m. pero 23, 45; no ...m. *not ... but* 3,27; 15, 11; no ... m. *not ... except, only* 4,57; 8,38; 10,43; 15,20; 27,58; 31,23; 37,26; 45,19; re m. ... no *no other than* 13,30; als no ... m. 3,21; no ... m. car *not ... especially since* 2,39; 7,51; 28,54; 43,40; no i a m. del morir 25,24; non es enois ... mas d'ome 1,27; tuit ... mas *all except* 28,7; que val

... mas 31,12; mas cant 4,2; *then, thus, naturally* 9,10; 20,10; 22, 26; 33,37; 40,77 (*in the manuscript interchanged with* car); 4, 37; 42,15.

matî *s. m. morning* 10,4; 45,9.

mauvatz 7,17; 19,31; 42,37; *f.* mauvaza 7,22; *adj. and subs. bad; subs.* 37,20.

mauvais *adj.* 23,50; 24,17; *bad, evil, wicked.*

maya, calenda m. *may festival* 7,13.

mayor *adj. greater* 39,6; lo m. *greatest* 10,29.

me, mei *see* eu.

mei *adv. in the middle of,* per mei *throughout* 9,2; 26,1; en m. *in the middle* 12,11.

meitat *s. f. half* 6,29.

melhor (*n. s. masc. and f.*) melher 5,30,35; 15,52; 22,4; 33,5; *adj. better* 7,30; 13,9; 19,22; 31,18; 25,81; 41,35; *with article or possessive pronoun, best* 5,30,35; 33, 5; 39,46; *subs. f.* 22,33,34; 31,18.

melhs *adv. better* 7,35; 13,44; 27,8; 31,2; 35,1; 36,8; *for intensification* 3,31; 13,49; 22,60; 28,22; lo m. *best* 40,28; mo m. *my best* 13,28; *the best people* 27,13; (22, 34; *var.*).

melhuramen *s. m. improvement* 30, 28.

melhurar *v. tr. to improve* 24,19; *refl. to improve oneself, to become better* 24,18; 30,34; *intr. to become more worthy* 7,7; 8,56; 13,14; 16,51; 21,58; 22,6; 44,8.

membransa *s. f. intelligence* aver m. que (*with subj.*) *to be mindful of doing* 1,37.

membrar *v. intr. to be mindful* mi membra com 41,25; membrat m' es de *I remembered* 6,53.

menar *v. tr. to lead* m. alcu ab se 36,58; *to move along* 29,18.

mendic *adj. miserable, poor, wretched* 24,17.

menhs, mens 39,31,57; *adv. less* 19, 20; 39,57; *subs.* 3,66; 16,44; 39, 31; 40,19.

menor *adj. smaller* 6,27.

mentaver (*1 pres. ind.* mentau 13,29) *v. tr. to praise, to mention* 13,29.

mentir *v. intr. to lie* 1,63; 35,40; 39, 54,56; m. ad alcu de alc. re 1,19; 15,28; 37,15.

meravelha *s. f. wonder, marvel,* faire m. 7,44; m. es (com) 1,10; (se) 31,1; m. ... as ai (car) 43,7.

meravelhar *v. rfl. to wonder, to marvel* (si) 7,41; 12,15; (com) 28,59; 39,17.

merce 10,15; 14,12; 17,12; 31,23; mercei 7,55,57; 21,42; *s. f. grace* 14,12; 16,36; 31,23; 43,41; mala m. *ill favor, pitilessness, mercilessness* 41,26; 43,37; aver m. d'alcu 3,5; 21,42; clamar m. 4,34; 7,57; 17,12; esser en la m. d'alcu 25, 58; penre alcu a m. 19,26; merce us prenha de 3,50; trobar m. 4, 4; 10,14; 31,24; per m. prec ... 22,17; per merce·lh sia que 17, 58; merce *grace* 36,46; 41,39; merces *thanks* 10,15; moutas merces! 40,51; rendre merces 35,17.

merceyar *v. intr. to ask for a favor* 26,27; 29,11; se m. vas alcu 7, 58; *tr.* 7,56.

merchadanda *s. f. tradeswoman (selling love)* 15,25.

mertsar *v. intr. to haggle, to bargain for* 4,29.

mes *s. m.* (*undeclined*) *month* 5,1; 10, 1; 30,2; 31,14; 39,40.

messatge *s. m. message, news* 16,4; 23,50; *messenger* 25,81; 42,24.

messatger *s. m. messenger* 17,49; 33, 26; 42,50; *the address to the messenger of the song* 10,50; 18,29; 22,61; 33,43; 44,73; *secret name?* 6,63; 39,57.

mescreire *v. tr. to mistrust* 43,31.

messonger *s. m. liar* 15,26; 23,55.

mespenre *v. intr. to fail* 10,38; 16, 29; (en amar) mespres *guilty* 31, 15.

mester *s. m. to be one's duty to do* 1,31; *occupation, employment* 33, 5; m. m'a *it is necessary to me* 22,50; 23,7.

metre *v. tr.* (meira *1 pers. sing. condit.* 10,49) *to put, to place, to*

GLOSSARY 215

spend, to apply, to bring 22,47; 27,44; 31,22; 42,42; la flama me mis al cor 3,9; m. cor e cors en 31,6; m. so coratge en plaih de *to take pains to, to strive to* 25, 80; se m. en plaih 8,3; 10,49; 16,14; se m. en agaih 8,43; se m. en grans 21,3; m. sa cura, s'ententa, son esper, s'esperansa 8, 16; 15,36; 37,7; 45,21; m. en cor ad alcu que 26,23; m. en soan 45,22.

meu 2,23; 17,41; *stressed pron. poss. tonic masc. sing., my, nom. sing.* meus 42,47; 43,18; *f. sing.* mia 8,8; 16,16; 17,22; 21,30; 45,18; *pl. nom. m.* mei 41,7; lo meu *what belongs to me* 40,35.

mezeis *pron. self* me m. 30,16; 43,14.

mezura *s. f. measure* sen e m. *sense and moderation* 8,24; 13,23; 16, 32; razos es e m. *it is right and cheap* 13,41.

mezurar *v. intr. to measure* m. egal 28,40; (*See Appel, p. 170*).

midons *s. f. my lady, nom.* 5,34; 20, 24; 27,50; *acc.* 4,42; 10,37; 15, 45; 16,15; 17,31; 21,33; *etc.*

mil *num. adj. thousand* (14,30) *subs., a thousand men* 6,46.

miracle *s. m.* (*var.*, -cla) *wonder, feat* 12,38.

mirador *s. m. mirror* 25,42.

miralh *s. m. mirror* 43,20,21.

mirar *v. rfl. to look at, to reflect oneself* 12,16; 25,45; 43,21; en leis ma mortz se mira 9,39.

mô *pers. pron. my, nom. sing. masc.* mos 1,17; 3,21; 4,45; *acc. sing. masc* mô, mon 2,32; *f. sing.* ma 4,61; 6,11,34; 17,42; m' 1,62; *pl. nom. masc.* mei 4,56; 9,36; 25,70; *acc. f.* mas 42,40.

molhar *v. tr. to make moist, wet* 42, 43.

mon *s. m. world* 1,55; 10,43; 12,16; 21,31,56; *etc.* tot lo m. 22,47; 25, 82; 43,14; Deus que·l mon chapdela 25,21; mais volh que·l mons mi falha 35,36.

mon *s. m. mountain* contra m. *against the heights* 43,40.

montar *v. intr.* 44,7; *to climb.*

morir *v. intr. to die* 3,53,64; 5,11; 25,24; (lo segles, pretz mor) 7, 18; 13,4; m. per amor, per ben amar 10,7; 41,13; m. de cossirar 39,9; de dezire 27,49; de dol 27, 27; de dolor 31,27; de feunia 17, 23; de talan 37,34; 45,8; se m. 17,17; 35,4; 40,76; 44,54.

morn *adj. dark, gloomy* semblan m. 12,5.

morsel *s. m. morsel, a bite, a tidbit* 38,23.

mort *adj. dead* 40,31,72; 31,9; mort m'a *has killed me, has slain me* 2,38; 4,53; 14,11; 25,28; 43,22, 54.

mort *s. f. death* 3,51; en leis ma mortz se mira 9,39; mortz m'avenha, venh'a sel ... 3,40; 40,71; per m. li respon 43,54.

mortal *adj. mortal* ira m. 28,46; 41, 32.

mostrar *v. tr. to show* 15,37; *to indicate, to point out* 4,42; 30,40; 40,58.

mot *s. m. word* 26,11; *words of a text* 26,37; 27,5; escrire los motz *to write what one has to say* 17, 55; no saber m. de *not to have a presentiment of* 12,9.

mout *adv. very much* (*stands before verb*) 2,36; 3,12; 6,44,45; 15,36; *etc.* m. mais de *much more* 15,13.

mover *v. tr. to move* 43,1; se m. *to move about, to stir* 10,11; *to remove oneself, to go away, to retire* 42,41; *to begin* 1,1; 39,4; *intr., to come out, to induce* 2,35; 15, 2,3,23; 21,27.

mudar *v. tr. to change, to alter* 8,15; se m. 30,5; no posc m. no *I cannot refrain from* 13,5; 29,4.

mut *adj. dumb, mute* 19,7.

N

N', 'n *see* en.

na (*before the name*) *Lady* 19,50.

nadal *s. m. Christmas* 15,46; 28,38.

naisser *v. intr. to be born* 20,37; 30, 17; *to break out* 5,3; 42,4.

natura *s. f. nature, being, essence* 13,

51; 24,8; *personified* 16,48; 40, 27.
natural *adj. natural, truthful,* fol n. 15,33; joi n. 28,35; amor n. 41, 15; *well-formed, well-turned* vers n. 15,50.
nau *s. f. boat* 44,40.
nauza *s. f. vexation, annoyance, worry* 4,33.
ne *see* en.
negre *adj. black* noih negre 3,37.
negu *pron. adj.* n. no ... no *not any* 17,41,51; 26,25; 41,24; n. ome *no one* 21,12; 35,33; *s. m.* n. no *nobody* 13,3.
neis *adv. even* 13,43.
nems *adv. much too much* 40,47.
nesci *adj. silly, foolish* 17,13,37; 26, 12.
neu *s. f. snow* 7,12; 8,39; 28,38; 44,12.
ni (*before i,* ne? 14,8) *conj. binds the parts of the sentence in a negative statement* 1,25; 5,1; 6,56; 8,24; 10,15,16 (*verbal clauses*); 4,37; 13,20; 15,43; *in sentence with* greu 1,36; *joins negative sentences* 4,39; 13,21; 14,8; 15,44; *joins negative clause to affirmative clause* 2,10; 6,7; *joins clause to assumptive clause* 1,28, 30; 27,59; *of the initial clause* 4,22; 7,29; *in the relative assumptive clause* 1,23; 16,41; 25, 3,45; *clause of concession* (tan can) 24,24; *in a clause which depends upon one of the above clauses* 7,42; 13,21; 31,14.
nien *s. m. nothing* 5,13; faire de n. 15,42; 27,48; no ... n. *not at all* 31,24; *in no way, in no measure* 30,56.
noih *s. f. night* 3,37; 27,43; la n. *at night* 33,2; 41,17; n. e jorn *night and day* 7,33; 40,7; tota n. *throughout the entire night* 44,43; de n. prionda *in the deepest night* 44,51.
noirir *v. tr. to bring up, to nourish* 40,74.
no (*before consonant*), non (*before vowel*) *adv. not* 1,11,25; *etc.*; anc no, ja no, nulh no, *see* anc *etc., verb implied* 6,15; 20,35; 3,27; *through association* (*after comparative*) 12,37; 13,13; 22,4; 24, 36; 29,62; 36,8; (*after* blasmar) 40,72; no-chaler, no-jauzitz, no-saber, *see* chaler, *etc.*; *no* oc ni no 6,56.
nom *s. m. name* (*in contrast to the thing*) 15,20 per nom que *in the meaning that* 17,15.
nonca *adv. never* (*without* no) 17,14.
nos, ·ns *pers. pron. we, us* 2,27,28; *etc.*
nostre *poss. pron. our* 40,59.
novel *adj. new* 13,6.
novela *s. f. news* 25,13.
nualha *s. f. laziness* 35,12.
nul *pron. adj.* n. ... no *none, not any* 4,20; 6,7,31; 26,19; 44,61; n. ome no *no one* 1,18,60; 3,66; 4,43; nula re no *not at all* 15,31; n. anyone 6,38; 18,14; 31,2; *anything* 4,10.
nut *adj. naked* 8,39; 44,14.

O

O *conj. or* 1,56; 6,15; 27,51; o ... o *either ... or* 1,24; 37,29.
o *dem. neut. pron., prefiguring the content of sentence* 1,10; 7,52; 30,38; *referring back to content of sentence* 4,6,16; 8,38; 16,13; 28,19; *as reference* re mai 18,27; *to adj.* 29,40; *uncertain reference* 28,42.
oblidar *v. tr. to forget* 16,11; 19,52; 23,17; se o. *to forget oneself* 43,3.
oblit *s. m. neglect* 40,5.
obrir *v. tr. to open* 31,23.
oc *adv. yes* no poder dir oc ni no 6,56; *in the answer* eu oc 18,27.
ochaizo *s. f. pretext, occasion* 36,17; aver o. *to have an occasion for reproach* 9,20; *reproach* trobar o. ad alcu 29,26.
ochaizonar *v. tr.* alcu de *to accuse, to make reproaches to him* 9,19; 20,36; 23,30.
oimai(s) *adv. now, from now on* 16, 6; 17,35; 19,13; 28,49.

GLOSSARY 217

olh *s. m. eye* 1,50,56; 6,41,49; 8,20; 15,7; 16,42; 25,70; 28,58; 29,34; 37,12; 39,20; 41,41; olhs espiritaus 15,47; volh perdre·ls olhs del fron si... 5,24; ams los olhs li don a traire si... 29,23; mas olhs claus *since my eyes are closed* 29,44; virar sos olhs ad alcu 35,15; de sos olhs no·m ve 36,27.

ome *s. m. man* 8,51; 19,1; *servant, vassal* 12,23; 20,48; 35,13; 42,49; o. lige 42,38; ric o. 15,42; *one* 1,15,47; 19,43; (*to hide the specific person*) 41,44; *anyone* 1,27; 6,37; o.... no, nul ome... no *no man, no one* 1,18; 3,66; 4,43; 24,20; 29,33; nul ome any man 18,14.

on, o 14,24?; o 27,43; 29,18; *adv. where* 14,24; 31,57; 44,42; (*referred to person*) 10,14; 37,7; on que *wherever* 24,39; 42,38; viatge per on 20,17; no·m posc saber vas on... tam ben amar pogues 5,17; *whence* 29,18; 43,56; on mais *the more* 5,21; on plus... plus 5,19; 30,33; on plus... mais 19,7; on melhs... e peihz 7,35; on plus *the most* 25,12.

oncas *adv. ever, still* 9,10.
onda *s. f. wave* 44,40.
onor *s. f. honor* 2,27; 10,8; 12,22; 21,4; 22,1; *the honor through which a man receives the love of a lady* 3,19; 13,16; 19,25; 44,22; faire o. 12,32; 28,14; 36,10; 39,30.
onrar *v. tr. to honor* 6,45; 16,10; onrat paradis 20,29.
ops *s. m. (undeclined) need* ops es *it is necessary* 3,47; ops a *it is necessary* 22,3; 33,19; a ops de *for, in favor of* 13,45; a sos ops *for her* 29,53; a ops d'amar *for love* 39,24.
or *s. m. edge, brink* 41,37,38.
ora *s. f. hour* a las oras *at times* 36, 43 a l'ora que *when* 41,37; en cal c'oras *whenever* 5,4; de l'or en sai que *since* 43,18.
orgolh *s. m. pride, arrogance, presumption* 25,62,69; 29,10; 42,20, 21; aver o. 41,33; (vas alcu) 9,10.
orgolhar *v. rfl.* vas alcu *to be arrogant, to be overbearing* 9,9; 25,7; 26,9; 42,22.
orgolhos *adj. proud, haughty* 3,46; 28,63.
ors *s. m. bear* 31,55.
ostatge *s. m. security, hostage* mandar alcu o., en o., 25,83,87.
ostatge *s. m. domicile, dwelling, hospitality* 20,25.
outra *prep. beyond* 26,38.

P

Pais *s. m. (undeclined) land, country* 20,11; 37,2.
pan *s. m. bread* vida A.
pan *s. m. free end of a skirt, coat* razo C.
pantais *s. m. (undeclined) confusion, agitation* 40,25.
paor *s. m. fear, fright* 1,14; 6,35; 22,25; 31,43; aver p. que 13,34; 44,55; faire p. 7,17; 19,30; perdre vergonha e p. 13,52; per p. reman 21,38; si no fos per p. 39,22.
par *adj. like, equal, similar* non ai p. ni engal 41,39; tot p. a p. 40,63; *s. f. mate, companion* 40,3.
paradis *s. m. (undecl.) paradise* 37,4; 20,29.
paratge *s. m. rank* 42,18.
paraula *s. f. speech, talk, word* 23,46; 39,51; *pl.* 1,39; 4,32.
pareisser *v. def. intr. to appear* 24,2.
paren *s. m. father, relative* 17,29; 27,20.
parer *v. intr. to appear, seem, be visible* 3,4; 10,2; 5,2; 39,1; 41,1; *to seem, to appear (plus subs.)* 1,20; 43,33; 44,4; (*with adj.*) 8,40; 28,62; 40,30; 42,26; *to appear that* 20,19; p. de *appear to come from* 39,52.
parladura *s. f. speech* (13,50; *with contempt*).
parlar *v. intr. to speak, to talk* 1,16; 13,44; 19,47; 40,18 p. de 21,6; 23,44; 39,27; —*s. m. speech* 17,60; 40,56.

parler *adj. talkative* 33,12.
part *s. f. part, share* 30,13 vas cal que, autra p. 13,10; 24,15; 31,8; daus totas partz 39,7; calque part que m'esteya 42,54.
part *prep. on the other side of* 10,51; 26,39; *beyond* 26,48.
partida *s. f. part, share* 23,19.
partimen *s. m. parting, separation* 30, 35.
partir *(1 pres. ind. part.* 40,73; partis 37,9;*) v. tr. to leave, separate, depart, divide* 2,44; 12,13; 20,30; 30,43; 33,38; 40,73; 43,53; *intr. to depart* 37,9,54; mos cors mi vol de dol partir 14,9; 25,20; partit de Deu 13,53; —*s. m. leaving* 17, 48.
parven *adj. visible, clear, evident* 31, 41; faire p. 27,12; se faire p. *to show* 3,65; —*s. m. appearance* 15,20.
parvensa *s. f. appearance* 30,29.
passar *v. intr. to pass by* 29,44; *to elapse* 4,54.
pascor *s. m. Easter, spring* 28,1.
pasmar *v. intr. to faint, pass out* 40, 67.
patz *s. f. (undecl.) peace* 22,39; 35,8.
paubramen *adv. poorly* 10,33.
paubre *adj. poor,* —*s. m.* 42,18.
pauc *adj. small, little, slight, few* 3,3; —*s. m. few* 17,13; 39,45; us paucs de jauzimen 10,19; ab p. de 5, 14; per p. *almost, nearly* 4,21; per p. no *almost, nearly* 16,12; per p. ... no *hardly* 39,21; 41,28; *few* pauc (*sing.*) de cortes 22,20; ab paucs d'amics 39,14; *adv. little* 13,24; 42,20.
pauza *s. f. pause* 4,48.
pauzar *v. intr. to rest, come to rest* 4,37; 18,4.
pe *s. m. foot* 26,35; en pes *standing* 20,40; no·m volh d'a sos pes mover 42,41.
pechat *s. m. sin* 28,48; 30,32.
peihz *adv. worse* 28,26; *subs.* p. traire *to endure the worst* 7,35.
peira *s. f. stone* 16,40.
peis *s. m. (undecl.) fish* 12,8.
pena *s. f. pain, suffering* 2,26; 25, 74; 28,17; 35,24; 40,66; 44,45; a penas *hardly* 29,13.
penar *v. refl. to exert oneself* 38,26.
pendre *v. tr. to hang* 4,21.
penedensa *s. f. repentance* 30,31.
penedre *(1 pres. ind.* penet 42,44; *3 pres. cond.* penedera 10,26;) *v. refl. to repent, to regret* 42,44; *to feel remorse, repentance* 10,26.
penre *(1 pres. ind.* pren 6,26; *3 pres. subj.* prenda 19,26; 26,21; prenha 3,7; 18,21;) *v. tr. to take (from a choice of two or more)* 6,26; 22,48; p. alcu per servidor 31,50; p. alcu a merce 19,26 *to catch, to capture* 16,7; *to take prisoner* 5,15; 10,10; 12,15; 22, 52; 29,57; 31,21; *refl.* se p. (en l'alma) *to be caught on a hook* 12,9; p. cosselh 17,10; cura 13,5; 44,19; esgardamen 13,18; 27,56; esmansa 1,53; bon uzatge 20,23; venjansa 45,27; cossi que vostr' om mal prenda 26,21; (*without object*) 15,21; 30,21; *trans. or intrans. to arise, originate* (dols, enveya, merces, pietatz, talans m'en pren) 3,50,52; 10,12; 15,9; 17, 57; 18,21; 42,32; (*without subject*) *to get on, to fare* enaissi·m pren 3,7.
pens *see* pes.
per (pel 10,3; 20,9; 33,1; pels 24,3;) *prep.* A) *locality: through, across, over, by, in order to, on account of* 41,30; 9,2; 10,3; 20,17; 24,3; 40,20; 41,3; 44,50; *in time:* lo tems vai per jorns, per mes e per ans 30,2; *because of, on account of* 10,40; 8,47; 16,10,33; 24,22; 25,56; 35,5. B) *for, for the sake of, on acount of:* non ai de sen per un efan 31,45; chascus per se 22,18; per me·us o dic 12,34; penre per servidor 31,50; gazanhar be per mal 41,48; 3,48; 5,8; 6,20; 20,42; 22,17. C) *occasion, purpose* 6,30; 7,18,51; 8,38; 9, 44; 10,7,39; 16,17,28; 21,38,55; 22,45; 26,31; 33,1; *way and manner* 1,45; 10,28; 21,10; 25, 49; *occasion and purpose, on ac-*

count of, for the sake of 1,5,12, 39; 4,55; 6,35; 7,48; 8,45; 9, 14,37; *etc.* per Deu, per amor de Deu 9,26; 10,17; per ver *truly* 43,41; per aisso *therefore* 7,3; 29, 21; per so—car 1,7; per pauc (no) *almost, nearly,* (*see* pauc), per far *in order to do* 29,20; 31, 12; per que *wherefore, why* 7,38; 36,9; 40,18; 17,34; (*relative*) 1, 37; 7,8; 31,20.

perdô *s. m. pardon* en p. *in vain* 10, 13; 30,18.

perdonar *v. tr. to pardon* 6,40; 9,21; (*without obj.*) 23,54; 42,46.

perdre *v. tr. to lose, to suffer a casualty* 39,46; 42,48; *to lose the beloved* 3,60; 8,6; 45,32; be m'an perdut 12,1; p. Deu (*see* Deu) perdre·ls olhs 5,24; p. benan-an-sa, dormir, joi, valor, *etc.* 8,55; 13,52; 22,45; 25,62; 30,8; 35,42; 41,19; 45,6; p. afan, amor, preyar 12,33; 29,52; 30,12; se p. *to destroy oneself, to perish* 40,11; 43, 23.

pero *conj. but, however* 7,50; 10,34; 13,26; 19,19; 25,51; mas p. 23, 45.

pertraire *v. tr. to prepare* 8,26.

pes *s. m. thought* mal pes 35,1; 44, 41.

pes *see* pe.

pessamen *s. m. thought, care* 6,10; 27,57; venir en p. *to occur (an idea)* 17,24.

pessar, pensar *v. intr. to think, to care* 7,33; (d'alcu) *to think of someone* 16,2; (d'alcuna re) *to think about something* 25,46; *to be considering, deliberating about* 19, 41; 41,8; 22,18; se p. que *to think that* 3,7; se p. d'alcu que 8,4; —*s. m.* 41,24.

pessat *s. m. thought* 6,13.

pensiu *adj. pensive* 33,4.

petit *adj. small, little* 4,48; 33,10; —*s. m. less* 25,65; 43,10; 44,38.

peyor *adj. worse* 2,42; 25,44; 29,38; —*s. m.* d'amor tot lo p. 13,45; *s. n.* aver lo p. *to have the worst* 30,11.

pezansa *s. f. sadness, pain, trouble* 1,30; 25,33; 44,32; 45,13.

pezar *v. intr. to grieve, displease, trouble* 5,25; 14,23; —12,24; 22, 55; 25,3; 35,9; —(car, si) 15,28; 31,58; 40,45; (*without subject*) peza li de 7,27; 21,2.

pic *adj. colored, bright, shimmering, uncertain* 24,25.

pietat *s. f. pity, mercy* 3,52; 30,39.

plâ *adj. even, level, plain, smooth* via plana, *straight-away* 22,61; *smooth, delicate* 30,51; razo plana *frank, clear talk* 37,55; per p. essai *to test* 10,28.

plâ *s. m. plain* 23,16.

plai 10,49; 17,27; 18,20; plaih 8,3; *s. m. law suit, legal action* 6,12; 17,27; mandar ad alcu fin e p. *treaty and peace* 29,50; metre en p. *to be occupied, to be busy* 25, 80 se metre en p. *to trouble oneself* 8,3; 10,49; 16,14; querer p. (ad alcu de) *to complain* 18,20.

plaideyar *v. intr.* (ab alcu) *to negotiate* 42,49; *tr.* (alcu) *to begin a quarrel, make reproaches to* 29, 25.

planher *v. intr. to bewail, lament* 7, 34; 25,61; 28,7; se p. de *to complain, bemoan* 19,45; 27,54.

plasmar *see* pasmar.

plazen *adj. pleasing, charming* 3,22.

plazer (*3 pres. ind.* plai 7,51; 36,19; 37,56; platz 22,55; 24,37; 35,10; *3 pres. subj.* playa 7,54;) *to please* 3,29; 7,51; 9,6; 12,24; 13,16; 17,55; 18,28; 19,26; 22,50 *etc.*— *s. m. pleasure, favor, liking* 2,23; 4,26; 10,25; 25,57; 40,52; 42,40; 43,51; *that which pleases* 21,48; (*pl.*) 1,59; 3,27; 12,45.

plê *adj. full.* 44,1.

plevir *v. tr. to pledge* 36,48; ome jurat e plevit 33,31; plevidas 14, 30.

pleyar *v. tr. to bend, refl.* 29,17.

plor *s. m. tears* 2,21.

plorar *v. intr. to cry, weep* 3,56; 25, 70; 28,7; 31,19; 44,70; (*as antonym of* chantar) 36,3; *tr.* pl. aiga dels olhs 6,49.

ploya *s. f. rain* 27,3; 44,5.

plus (pus 44,45) *adv. more* 6,47; 24, 36; 31,3; *more, longer* 4,47; *most* 15,38; 25,8,68; 27,9; 42,22; can p. *when most* 4,13; *when even more* 9,9; tan no ... que p. no 4, 30; com p. *the more* 21,57; on p. *see* on, *adj. intensification* 1, 63; 3,2; 6,52; 7,32; *etc. s. m. more* 21,39; 37,13,29; 43,43; al p. qu'ilh pot 45,42; lo plus (*than the kisses*) 13,18.

pluzor *s. m.* li p. *majority* 6,19.

poder *v. tr. to be able, can* (*with inf.*) 1,24,36,47; 3,30; 4,35; *etc.*, d'ome qu'es aissi conques, pot domn'aver almorna gran *ought to* 31,48; *with complementary inf.* 4. 14; 17,6; 21,35; 27,29; ieu [que·n]. posc mais? 31,21; *without obj.* d'aitan com poira 5,26; s'ilh podia 45,40; al plus qu'ilh pot m'enansa 45,42; —*s. m. force, power* 15,8; de mo p. *with my power* 10,32; aver en p. 21,56; 42,10,47; 45,24; aver p. de, que 4,23; 25, 10; 43,17; metre fors'e p. a 31,6.

poderos *adj. powerful, in a position to do* 28,64.

Poi *see Proper Names.*

pois *adv. afterwards, then* 6,53; 7,34; 28,63; pois ... pois que 31,14. *conj. since, after* 30,45; 31,15 (poisque); 28,25; 45,6; *when* 12, 33; 22,21; *since* 6,25,33; 7,28,56; 9,12; 10,15; 31,31.

poizonar *v. tr. to give a magic love potion to drink* 8,21.

pon *s. m. bridge* 43,38.

portar *v. tr. to bear, carry* 31,36; en p. *to carry away* 39,11; p. la chanso, lo vers ad alcu 4,63; 6, 62; 10,50; 23,57; messatge 23, 50; port sa beautat el cor 24,39; p. amor ad alcu 28,27; 41,15; *to bear, to suffer* (afan) 40,10.

poyar *v. intr. to rise, climb up, ascend* 43,40; 44,7.

prat *s. m. meadow* 7,9; 23,15; 24,3.

prec *s. m. prayer, plea, entreaty* 41, 12; *please* 43,50.

preizô *s. f. prison* 9,18; 20,45; 22, 51.

prendre *see* penre.

preon, prion *adj. deep* 26,39; de noih prionda 44,51; *adv. deeply* 5,9; li sospir de p. 43,22.

pres *adv. near* esser de p. 41,50; p. de *near by* 20,22; 26,32; 36,33; 44,33.

pretz *s. m.* (*undecl.*) *price, worth, merit, nobility* 40,49 esser de bo p. 18,10; *merit of a person* 1,58; 13,14; 16,51; 44,7; p. e valor 2, 45,48; 27,39; *fame, glory* (p. ed onor e lau) 21,4; *personified* 13,4.

preyar *v. tr.* p. alcuna *to beg a lady for a love favor* 2,25,28; 30,33; —19,39; 40,42; (*without object*) 2,30; p. alcu que (*accusative of the person*) 3,1; 19,27; 27,61; 33, 39; 36,1; (*object clause without que*) 1,37; 20,25; 24,33; (*dative of person*) 22,17; e·us prec de mo dan 45,29; —*s. m. pleading* 10, 15; 12,33.

prezan *adj. estimable, distinguished, excellent* 21,25,41.

prezar *v. tr. to esteem, regard, prize, value* 35,26; p. mens 39,57.

prezen *adj. public, publicly* a p. 6,57.

prezen *s. m. gift, present* dar per p. 20,42.

prezentar *v. tr. to present, offer* 37, 11; se p. denan alcu *to appear before* 17,40; 20,33.

prezenter *adj. ready to serve* 33,40.

prim *s. m. at the beginning* al p. de 40,59.

primer *adj. first* 33,33.

prion *see* preon.

privat *adj. intimate* 6,6; esser p. de 16,18; 22,60; p. a 22,24; p. ed aizitz 33,24; semblan p. 35,35; —*s. m. intimate, friend* 22,60.

pro *adj. able, capable, valiant, worthy, excellent* 1,36; 8,25; 28,50; 37, 19.

pro *s. m. advantage, profit* 10,9; pros m'es *it is profitable for me* 22, 27; 30,27; far so p. 6,16,32; aver (lo) p. de 6,59; 7,40; 43,12; 45, 30; p. tener *to be useful* 10,16;

15,31; 17,28; 26,24; 43,29; pel meu dan e pel seu p. 20,9.
proeza *s. f. excellence, perfection* 21, 28.
prometre *v. tr. to promise* 7,15.
prop *adv. near* de p. 40,34.
pur *adj. pure* 13,33; 18,18.

Q

Que *I. interrogative pronoun: (forms: masc. nom.* qui, *obj.* cui, *neuter* que, qu' 26,14) *examples*: Amors m'en det ... sabetz que 3,27; Amors e que·us es vejaire 4,1; als no sai que dire mas ... 25,37; no ve qu'amors l'atenda 26,14; no sai de que ni de cui (dei chantar) 29,5; que·m n'es si fer, si...? 40, 21.
II. relative pronoun (before vowel qu' 1,15; 3,19; 6,54; *etc.*) qued 22,34; 39,40; 41,9; *other forms: nom. sing. masc. without reference* qui (*but* que 13,56;) *related* que *to the person* 3,64; 8, 51; 10,20; *and* qui 7,32; *also to thing* 14,23; *nom. sing. fem.* qui *to the thing* 9,17; que 4,43; 16, 38; *to the person* 2,38; 29,19; *obj. sing.* cui *without reference and related to the person* 16,51; 25,30; 30,53; *but* una res per que ... 10,37; que *related to the person and thing, to a thing after a preposition* 10,6; 22,52; 33,11; *but* cui 2,45; 22,48; *nom. pl. masc. related to the person* que 6,2; 7, 26; *to things* que 6,42.
III. relative adverb: (tro) aras que 5,9; una mala res c'anc no·n me valc Deus 14,12; aicel jorn que 15,47; 25,45; tals ... qu'eu n'ai dos tans 33,14; cen aitans qu'eu no sai dir 21,34.
IV. conjunction, than (after a comparative) 2,9,28; 3,47; 4,10; 6,36; *etc.*
V. conjunction: that (before vowel qued 9,6; 39,40; *rel.* ques 13, 39;) *introduction of the noun clause* 3,29; 4,8; 7,46; 8,9; *of object clause* 1,4; 3,2,50; 4,3; 7, 42; 24,35; *introducing the sentence beginning with a prep.* 1,18, 39; *etc. of assumption 'when also' (with conj.)* 5,28; *of request* 19, 45; 26,28; *so that, such that, under such circumstances that* 6,56; 12,27; 31,56; 33,9; 42,28; que no *such that no, without that (with ind.)* 39,12; 43,48; *(with subj.)* 1, 19; 37,13; nonca — c'ans no *(with subj.)* 17,16; *through association in an uncompleted sentence*, o si que no 37,63; per nom que, *see* nom.
tan que 2,11,28; 3,18; 5,7; *etc.* tan no ... que 17,4; aitan que 9, 36; d'aitan que 6,46; si que 6, 59; 39,40; aissi que 3,17; *then* 1,15,40; 3,15; 4,6; 6,55; *etc.*, ab que, per que, pois que, sol que, *see* per, *etc.*
querer, querre *(cond.* queregra 3,48) *v. tr. to seek* 16,31; 20,16; 43,44; chascus auzels quer sa par 40.3; *to wish, to ask for* q. alcu re ad alcu 6,64; 9,26,29; 25,31; 35,14; 39,28; 42,16; q. *(with inf., to wish)* 23,44; 45,32; q. que 3,48; 7,42; 9,26.

R

Rai *s. m. ray (of the sun)* 7,2; 43,2.
ram *s. m. branch* 9,3; 29,17; colh lo r. ab que's fer 23,28; 42,30.
rama *s. f. branch* 3,31.
ramel *s. m. branch* 38,2.
rancura *s. f. complaint* 8,29; faire r. d'alcu *to make a complaint against someone* 8,52.
rancurar *v. refl.* se r. de *to complain* 7,25; 12,7.
randa *s. f. outermost, end* tot a randa *completely* 26,36.
rayar *v. intr. shine* 7,5.
razitz *s. f. root* la r. del cor, 40,8.
razô *s. f. right, reason*, razos es e mezura 13,41; gardar dreih ni r. 20,27; a r. *with reason* 30,16; aver r. que *(with subjunctive) to have reason to do* 42,31; *thing,*

subject, affair, ilh me chamja ma r. 9,33; *subject of the speech* r. e chauza 4,41; la bela r. *speech (in contrast to action)* 6,60.

razonar *v. refl.* se r. per *(with nom.)* *to declare oneself for, to confess oneself as* 20,48; *intr.* r. de *speak of* 23,45.

rê *s. f. thing, matter*; d'una re *in relation to something* 1,17; 6,9; totas res *everything* 12,28; tal, aital re *such a thing* 16,25; 35, 33; gran re *many* 3,4; ren al(s) *something else* 12,7; 41,8,52; nula re *nothing* 15,31. re *something* 4, 58; 10,25; re no, no re *nothing* 21,25; 22,28; re mai *something more* 18,26; re mas — no *nothing further than* 13,30; en re *in some way* 29,27; e (n) re no *in no way* 18,15; 27,16; re no *not at all* 41, 18; 45,52; *being, person* 14,11; 45,27; doussa res *address to the beloved* 3,45; autra re, re autra *another person* 3,49; 30,55; nula re *any person* 4,10; re mais *some other person* 5,18; re no *no one* 4,49,52; 36,49.

reblandir *v. tr. to serve, pay homage to* 26,8; 39,26.

recire (reciza *3 pres. subj.*) *v. tr. to cut off, sever* 44,25.

reclamar *v. tr. to demand, appeal for* 3,20.

reconoisser *v. tr. to recognize*; *refl.* reconogutz me sui *I realize* 19,3.

recordar *v. tr. to recall* 33,28.

recreire *v. refl. to yield, to give up* (d'alcu) 43,53; *to renounce, to desist from* 19,6; 29,51; 36,37; 41,28; 42,8; 43,59; *(relatively)* 29,51.

reduire *v. intr.* (a mal lignatge) redui *to degrade oneself* 29,22; al r. *eventually* 13,25.

reflorir *v. intr. to be again blooming* 24,7.

refrimar *v. intr. to resound* 23,14.

refudar *v. tr. to refuse* 36,40.

rei *s. m. King* 5,28; 15,40; 17,7; 21, 19,50; 26,43,46; 33,38; 45,41.

rëina *s. f. Queen* 33,45.

reire *adv.* traire alcu en r. *or* reiretraire *v. tr.* alcu *to retard, to draw one back* 37,44? *See Appel's Note.*

remaner *v. intr. remain* 2,14; 13,11; 42,20; *(with adj.)* 40,40; *refrain* 19,48; 21,38 (car) en 35,12; *to cease, to end* 1,2; 21,13.

remirar *v. tr. to view, to contemplate, to look upon* 1,56; 9,40,41; 27, 32; 33,15; 35,19; 40,34; *(without an object)* 16,41.

rendre (*in Limousin* redre) *v. tr. to give back* 8,22; *to give* (guizardo) 4,27; (laus e merces e gratz) 35, 17 (so gatge) 42,39; *to give oneself* 19,9; 26,27; 31,56.

renhar *v. intr. to act, to behave oneself* 13,51.

renovelar *v. intr. to renew, to become young* 40,2.

repairar *v. intr. to return* (vas alcu), 29,48.

repaire *s. m. dwelling, dwelling place* 44,52.

repenre *v. tr. to blame, to find fault with* (alcu) 15,34.

repentir *v. tr. to repent, refl. to desist from, denounce* 37,17.

reperdonar *v. tr. to pardon again* 9, 22.

replenir *v. tr. to fill* 40,33.

reponre *v. refl. to hide oneself, to bury oneself* 23,21.

reptar *v. tr. to blame, to reproach* 29,25.

requisit *adj.* requisitz li serai 10,21. *See note.*

rescos *adj. p. p. hidden, concealed*, a r. *furtive* 28,51.

resô *s. m. response, echo*, 20,18.

respeih *s. m. expectation* 7,36; *delay, postponement* 19,32.

resperir *v. tr. to re-enliven, to reanimate* 40,24.

respondre *v. tr. to answer* 26,11; *(with an object)* 14,8; per mort li r. 43,54.

respos *s. m. answer*, esser de mal r. 28,60.

restar *v. intr. to remain* 26,48.

retener *v. tr. to retain, to keep hold on* alcu (e. g. a loved one) 3,29;

GLOSSARY

18,28; 43,55; 45,44; r. los precs d'alcu 41,12; r. alcu de *to hold back someone from something* 16, 20.
retraire *v. tr. represent, paint (with words)* 12,37; 37,25; 44,63; *to find fault, to reproach* 4,16; 7, 43; 29,24; 43,34; r. alcu per ... *to wish to name someone about* 7,46; se r. *to say something to oneself* 8,10.
revelar *v. intr. to be obstinate* 25,23.
revelhar *v. intr. to re-awaken* 33,3.
revenir *v. tr. to revive, to restore, to refresh* 17,44; 41,4.
reverdeyar *v. intr. to become green again* 24,7.
reverdir *v. intr. to become green again* 9,2.
reviure *v. intr. to come to life again* 31,28.
revivar *v. tr. to allow to come to life* 40,31.
revolver *v. tr. to surround* 27,36.
ric *adj. rich* 15,42; 24,20; se faire ric de ... *to be proud of* 21,21; esser rics d'amor 33,13; 5,5; 7, 39; 8,26; 35,38; *s. m. rich* 42,18.
ricor *s. f. wealth* 10,35; 44,23.
rire *v. intr. (1 pres. subj.* ria 45,39) *to laugh* 1,41; 4,57,64; 27,59; 35, 3; 44,68; *s. m. laugh* 30,8.
rossinhol *s. m. nightingale* 2,9; 9,4; 10,4; 29,1; 33,1; 39,3; 40,4; 45, 11.
rossinholet *s. m. nightingale* r. sauvatge 23,2.
roza *s. f. rose* 40,30.

S

Sâ *adj. sound, healthy* saus ni sas 30, 44.
saber *v. intr. to be pleasing,* s. bo. 25,4; 35,19. *tr. to know (objective clause with* que) 1,58; 5,32; 6,5; 8,6; 9,39; esser sabens que 5,12; *(objective clause)* 2,41; 33, 26; *(indir. interrog. clause)* 3,62; 4,12; 5,17; 15,23; 17,25,34; 18, 12; 25,37; 33,36; 37,15; 45,45; *(incomplete interrog. clause)* 2,38; 3,27; *to know, to be acquainted with* 4,33; 13,56; 17,11,51; 33,8; 39,29; 43,9; no saber mot de *not to know at all* 12,9; saber lettras *to know how to read* 17,53; no sai domna ... c'amar no la pogues 12,26; saber grat 45,38; *to know that* tan la sai bel'e bona 9,23; si'ns saubes d'un coratge 20,14; *to learn* 8,47; 21,60; *to know how to do, to be able to do* 1,59; 2,10; 4,25; 15,10,43; 16,48; 19, 49; 21,15; 39,33; *s. m. favor, bo* saber, *what is well pleasing* 10,18; *knowledge* s. en sen 6,2; 31,5; 42,51 no — s. *ignorance, folly* 15, 15.
sabor *s. f. taste, savor* 31,10,26; aver s. 28,8; 44,71.
sai *adv. here, towards here* 17,3; 25, 84,88; 33,22; 36,14; 45,51,55; *temporal, here on earth,* de l'or en sai 43,18.
sainh *s. m. saint, relic,* jurar sobre s-z 17,46.
sal *adj. whole, sound, unhurt* s. e. sa 30,44; sela en cui lo reis seria saus 15,40; mal s. es *it is not well done* 45,25; sordeis aver o s. *to have one's pains lost* 28,42.
salhir *v. intr. to jump* 36,45; 23,3; 35,30.
saludar *v. tr. to greet* 8,54; 40,50.
salut *s. m. greeting* (escrire, mandar, trametre) 6,50; 12,36; 16,3; 19, 15; 22,64; 35,43.
sanar *v. intr. to recover* 22,6.
sauvamen *s. m. rescue* 17,56.
sauvar *v. tr. to keep, to preserve* 41, 40,51.
sauvatge *adj. wild, shy* 19,5; 23,2; *cruel* 12,4; 42,36.
savai *adj. bad, hard* 7,22; 18,9; 37, 42; *s. m.* 7,19.
savi *s. m. wiseman* 24,47.
sazir *v. tr. to seize* 27,17.
sazo *s. f. time* 20,26; 28,49; manhtas s-z *often* 8,9; *season* 5,1.
se, 's *refl. pron.* 1,27,31,39,60 *etc. accented* 36,33,58; 43,23; *refl. in*

the place of a passive 4,56; 18,
8,9.
sê *s. m. breast, bosom* 36,24.
sebelir *v. tr. to bury* 40,72.
segle *s. m. world* 2,23; 7,18; 22,19.
vida A.
segon *prep. according to, corresponding* 24,8,11; amors s. ricor no vai
10,35; *subj.* s. que *after what, acc.
to what* 24,32.
segre *v. tr. to follow* (alcu) 29,45; 42,
22; *to be obedient* 3,32; la folha
sec lo ven 3,33; (l'usatge, las voluntatz *etc.*) 19,13; 22,41; 26,13;
35,22; *to follow, befall* 21,11.
segur *adj. sure, certain, confident* 8,
48.
semblan *s. m. appearance, look, aspect* 16,6; creire lo s. 29,34; esser
de bel s. 31,29; faire s. *to make
an appearance* 39,42,53; no faire
s. *to seem to know nothing* 35,4;
look, mien, glance 12,5; 24,25;
(faire, mostrar, *etc.*) bel s. 4,55;
15,37; 17,43; 26,18; 27,28; 36,
53; 44,65; (*plural* — bel s-s) 21,
35; 26,13; 33,28; 35,35; s = bel
s. 22,15.
semblansa *s. f. appearance*, faire s.
to make an appearance 25,35; 45,
54; per s. *to appear as* 1,45.
semblar *v. tr. to seem like* (*with acc.*)
44,11; *to seem, to appear; intr.*
(*with nom.*) 7,9; 15,46; 28,61; s.
de bon aire 29,40.
semnar *v. without an object; to sow*
2,33.
sen *s. m. wit, sense, understanding*
13,27; 15,7; 16,31; 17,13; 31,45;
35,45; s. e mezura 8,24; 13,23;
saber e s. 6,2; 31,5; 42,51; s. e
valor 10,47; 20,24; 27,39; amar
de tot so s. 3,41; baizera-lh la
bocha en totz sens *in all directions* 39,39.
senh (*nom.* sens) *s. m. sign, mark,
signal* 39,40.
senhor *s. m. lord, master* 12,42; 23,
39; 31,51; 39,14; *address* apelar
alcu s. 13,43; mo s. lo rei 21,50;
address to the listener 6,1; 28,9;
36,1.

senhoratge *s. m. rule, mastery, power*
20,41; 23,42; 42,15.
senhoreyar *v. intr. to be lordly* 5,7.
senhoria *s. f. lordship, suzerainity,
domination* 21,31.
sens *see* cenher.
sentir *v. tr. to feel, to perceive* 3,66;
10,20; 27,16; 31,9; 37,3; 40,75;
s. entre sos bratz 24,35; s. que
5,12; se s. *to be master, aware
of, oneself* 27,30; *s. m. feeling* 40,
23.
ser *s. m. evening* 10,4; 45,9.
ser *s. m. o serf* 24,44.
serê *adj. serene, cheerful* (tems) 41,2.
servidor (*n. s.* servire 12,23; 27,58;
35,13) *s. m. servant, attendant* 31,
50.
servir *v. tr. to serve* (alcu) 16,33;
23,33,36; *refl. instead of passive*
amors se vol soven servir 14,27;
intr. ad alcu 10,32; 13,37; *tr.
or intr.* 1,24; 13,42; 30,18; 31,
51; *s. m. servant, attendant* 10,16;
23,37.
servizi *s. m. service* 6,38; 33,30.
ses, senes 1,57; *prep. without* 1,14;
3,62; 20,18; 21,29; 22,40; 28,22;
39,14; *apart from* 35,8; esser ses
13,55; ses aucire *without killing*
12,25.
setmana *s. f. week* 22,38; 37,53.
seu *f.* sua, 8,56; *poss. pron. stressed,
his* 1,47; 6,41; 17,43; 19,27; *etc.*
si, s' *conjunction if* (*with indicative*)
1,30; 5,23; 6,13,21; 7,42,45,59,
etc. (*with subjunctive*) 2,41; 18,
25; 20,2,8; 22,44,50; *etc.* *although* 29,61; si no *if not, unless*
1,24,44; 3,52; 4,48; *etc.* si tot *although* (*with indicative*) 3,65; 22,
3,25; 27,7; mais que si *more than
if* 19,36; com si *as if* (*with subjunctive*) 25,32; *if, whether* (*indirect question*) 7,16,46; 18,26;
20,35; 45,3,46.
si *adv. so* 1,9; 7,11; 18,5; 27,17;
e si *and also, too* 33,34; si com
21,53; *as ... as* 28,24; si que *so
that* 6,59; 8,16; 23,4; 26,37; 27,
47; *introducing a contrast* 10,47;
13,24; 39,22.

GLOSSARY

sidons *s. f. his lady, mistress* 7,57; 23,53.
sirieir *s. m. cherry tree* 32,38.
siriesa *s. f. cherry* 32,40,43.
sivaus *adv. at least* 8,7; 15,12; 44,27.
so *demonstrative pron. neuter this, that (referring back)* 1,26; 24,23. *(referring to accusative or nominative clause)* 9,16; 29,15; 30,40; 36,16; so que *that which* 3,22; 6,54; 15,34; 16,7; 27,52; *referring to a person* 1,15; 22,54; 25,8,68; 42,13; per so (que, car) *therefore* 1,7; 9,11; 12,21; 15,5; 37,23; *so that* 29,43.
sô *f.* sa, s' *n. pl., m.* sei 29,32; *poss. pron. unstressed, his hers.*
sô *s. m. melody, tune* 27,6; 30,25.
soan *s. m. disregard, scorn* (tornar. mettre en s.) 14,22; 45,22.
soanar *v. tr. to scorn* 22,58; 36,40; 37,51.
sobra *adj. over, more excellent* 22, 5,7.
sobrar *v. tr. to overcome, to subdue, intr. to be in excess, to abound* 40,35.
sobre *prep. on* 17,46; *beyond* sobra *s.* 22,8; de sobre *on* 44,44.
sobrepenre *v. tr. to surprise* 26,45; alcu de *to accuse someone, to reproach someone with something* 16,15.
sobrer *adj. to possess in the extreme, excessively, extremely* 33,13.
sobresenhoreyar *v. tr. to have completely in one's power* 42,11.
socorre *v. tr. to help* 19,23.
socors *s. m. help* 22,49.
sofertar *v. refl. to endure* 39,31.
sofranher *v. intr. to lack, be absent* 19,40; 25,71; 41,40.
sofridor *s. n.* sofrire 9,43; 27,14; 35,9; *s. m. sufferer.*
sofrir *(1 pres. ind.* sofris 1,10) *v. tr. to suffer, to bear, to endure* 9,44; 28,19; 35,8; 36,42; 44,47; (car) 1,10; se s. de *to abstain from* 1, 60; 13,1; *pres. part.* sofren *one who suffers because his beloved associates with someone else* 6,20.

sojorn *s. m. rest, repose* 2,8.
sojornar *v. refl. to have a pastime* 12,6; 37,49.
sol *adj. alone* 10,42; 15,49; 30,42; 39,41; *between prep. and substantive* ab sol 7,31; 27,28; de sola 7,40; *adj. only* 37,11,60; *also, only* 40,42,50; sol no *not even* 27,30; sol *with the subjunctive when, only* 15,45; 19,47; 30,49; 31,39; 41,51; *with subjunctive only, when* 1,3; 4,31; 41,40; ab sol que *with subjunctive provided that* 9,7; 39,55.
solamen *adv. only* 3,21.
solatz *s. m. comfort, consolation, entertainment* 13,9; *pleasantness of conduct* 17,59; 37,45; *joy, pleasure, delight (in relations with others)* 21,8; 22,31; 25,64; 35,2.
solelh *s. m. sun* 7,1.
solelhar *v. intr. to shine, to glitter* 7,4.
soler *v. defect. to be accustomed, want to* 21,3; 25,16; 27,18; 40,19; *(present used with preterite meaning)* 25,64; 29,62; 40,39; 41,25; 43,27.
sonar *v. intr. to sound, to echo* 23,14; *tr. s.* alcu *to address, to appeal to someone, to speak to him* 21,36.
sopleyar *v. intr. to implore* (vas alcu) 24,15.
sordeis *adv. worse, more evil* ... sordeis o aya sal 28,42; *subst.* tot per s. d'amor 13,53.
sordeyar *v. intr. to become worse* 7,8; *to be worse* 7,7.
sort *s. f. lot, luck, fortune (through which fate will be prophesied)* 25,26.
sospir 43,22; sospire *s. m. sigh* 4,53; 44,72.
sospirar *v. intr. to sigh* 7,34; 9,38; 31,19; 40,7; s. per 9,37.
sostener *v. tr. to endure, to bear, to stand, to suffer* 2,26.
sostraire *v. tr. to revile* 18,16.
sotil *adj. tender, delicate, slender, slim* 27,37.
sotlar *s. m. shoe,* 26,33.

sotz *prep. under* 8,37; 9,4; 24,14; 25,19; 28,36.
sotzmâ, a sotzmana *secretly* 37,47.
soven *adv. often* 3,43,56; 16,39; 29, 25; 36,18.
sovenir *v. intr.* me sove de *I remember* 2,37; 3,6,60; 8,18; 36,20; 41, 20; (com) 16,9.
suau *adj. soft, gentle, mild, lovely, delightful* lo tems s. 13,2; *adv. softly, gently, mildly* 21,36; *s-lowly, softly* 29,37.
sus *prep.* de sus de *down from* 42, 39.

T

Tâ *adv. so, thus* 40,36.
tafur *adj. rascally, knavish* 8,45.
tainar *v. intr.* me täina car *I wait with impatience that* 18,29.
tal *adj. such* (t. que, don) 1,62; 4, 19; 12,31; 16,25; 19,9; 21,17; *etc.* (*with the same meaning*) 8, 31; (t. per que) 27,27; *after subst.* 12,44; *s. m., s. f. such a one that* 17,7; 20,12; *many a, who* 21,14; 33,12; 36,25; tals n' i a que 41, 33.
talan 4,50; 15,9; 21,1; 26,12; 30,4; 36,54; 56,59; 37,34; talen 3,30; 5,20; *s. m. sense, mind* 30,4; aver bo t. de 18,23; aver bo, fi t. ad alcu 4,50; 28,32; aver mal t. 29, 36; *sense, inclination, desire* 18, 2; 26,12; 31,16; 35,25; 39,18; 44,68; *demand, longing for* 36,54, 59; morir de t. 37,34; 45,8; *demand, wish* 5,20; 15,9; 21,1; *far so t. d' alcu* 3,30; dar cor e t. 17, 5; 36,56.
talhar *v. tr. to cut, to carve* 39,23.
tan *adj. so much* (*pl.*) 8,1; *so many* (*sing.*) 8,2; *s. m. so many* 4,59; dos tans *twice as much* 30,11; t. de (*with noun*) 2,27; 13,16; 19, 25; 21,23; 25,33; 26,15; *so much* (*that,* que) 2,10; 27,30; *intro. of the objective phrase* 35,39; 42,46; (*temporal*) *so long* 28,19; t. can *as much as* 12,40; (*spatially*) *as wide as* 24,24; t. com *as much as* 19,43; *as long as* 33,35; (*with subjunctive*) 30,44; *adv. so, so very, with adj.* 1,12; 2,26; 6,8,40; 8,26; 9,43; 10,20; *etc. with adv.* 6,42; 7,58; 10,33; *etc. with verb* 3,18,56; 4,52; 9,30; 17,3; 21,2; *with verb and adj.* 3,34; 5,6; 7, 2; 9,23; *etc. with verb and adv.* 16,33; 27,10; t. — per que 31,20.
tanher *v. refl. to be fitting, proper, to appertain* 14,15.
tart *adv. late* 19,11.
tarzar *v. tr. to hold out, to put off* (son amic) 39,50.
tarzer *v. intr. to be silent* 40,47.
tastar *v. tr. to taste, relish* 32,45.
te *see* tu.
techir *v. tr. to make grow, thrive, to further, promote* 40,36 (*Levy, petit dictionnaire, suggests "provided with"* (muni).
temer *v. tr. to fear, dread* 27,3 (alcu) 45,31; (*the beloved*) 15,43; (que) 3,51; (*with infinitive*) 1,15; (*without object*) 10,39; 30,21; sui temens del anar 39,58.
tems *s. m. time* 30,1; 39,46; aquel tems *at that time* 5,7; *time of year* (t. doutz, florit, clar e. sere, suau, de pascor) 7,10; 13,2; 27, 8; 28,1; 40,2; 41,2; *see* tostems.
tendre *v. tr. to reach out* 26,35.
tenen, a un tenen *at once* 17,21.
tener *v. tr. to hold, to keep* 4,14; 17,2; *to possess* 33,11; 45,16; t. alcu car no (*with indicative*) *to hold something* (*to do*) 21,52; *to hold to one place* 41,22; *to hold, keep in one condition* 5,10,16; 7, 11; 10,48; 12,14,15; 17,4; 18,5, 11; 44,39; t. pro *see* pro; *to hold, estimate,* ad afan, a vilania 28,20; 45,50; t. char (*adv.*) 19,53; 39,25; t. vil 42,19; *to hold, to consider* (que) 1,4; *to take to be,* t. per (*with acc.*) 6,19; 23,23; 24,12; 27, 15,24; *refl.* se t. ab amor (2,16) se t. de guiza *to hold something, as due to oneself* 44,18; se t. de far *to abstain from* 21,15; 43,11; per pauc me tenc que no (*with in-*

GLOSSARY 227

dicative) 39,21; *intr. to reach* 24, 24.
tensonar *v. intr. to dispute, to quarrel, to fight* (ab alcu) 23,53.
termini *s. m. time, term* 19,30; *season* 26,4.
terra *s. f. land* 5,30; 26,38; 45,47; *earth* 24,24.
tezor *s. m. treasure* 41,21.
tirar *v. tr. to pull, to draw* 26,41; 31, 7; *to vex* 18,15.
tolre (*1 pres. ind.* tolh 25,72; 41,19; *3 pres. ind.* tol 27,63; *p. p.* tout 2,48; 29,15; 43,13; tolgut 8,7) *v. tr. to take away* 17,60; 27,25; 42, 51; (*from the world*) 2,48; so m'a tout tot mon afaire que 29,15; *to take away a person* 43,13; (*the beloved*) 8,7; 9,14; 42,52; *refl. to take something away* (joi, dormir) 25,72; 41,19; *to withdraw oneself* (ad alcu) 9,13; (d'amor) 24,9; 25, 9; *to cease* (de faire) 42,10; *without an object* 27,63.
tornar *v. tr. to turn, to remove to one place, to one condition* 20,28; *return to* 41,32; 42,34; t. en soan, en no-chaler 14,22; 42,27; *refl. to turn oneself* 27,31; *intr. to return* 2,11; 12,3; 16,19; 22, 63; 25,84,88; *to turn to, to turn out to* (a plazer, a dan, en error, en no-chaler) 10,25; 13,25; 21,8; 39,36.
tort *s. m. wrong, injustice* 6,40; 18, 20; 23,30; 29,24,30; *pl.* 8,32; aver t. 3,20; 9,21; 16,30; 20,35; (ad alcu) 10,29; 25,32; faire t. ad alcu 17,33; a t. *to wrong* 30,38.
tost *adv. quickly, immediately* 4,53; 18,30; 40,24.
tostems *adv. always, forever* 3,14; 15, 12; 24,37; 30,54.
tot *pron., adj. all* 3,41; 6,59; 17,22; tota gens 5,29; *all* (*pl.*) 1,8; 2,13; 6,48; 8,32; 9,24; *etc. every* 4,37; 5,13; 13,42; t. jorn 4,42; 29,11; totz (tems *see* tostems); *adj.*: *instead of*: *adv. at all* 12,18; 25, 34; 27,10; 33,3; me t. sol 10,42; *with the superlative the most* 13, 45.

tot *adv.* 13,53; 26,36; 28,37; 44, 2; *see* si tot.
tot *s. m. pl. all the men* 5,32; 10, 41; totas *all women* 5,34; 37,9; *neuter all* 16,28; 27,60; t. can *all which* 8,27; 21,28; 23,13; 24,38; lo t. 6,30; del t. *at all* 16,35; per t. *everywhere* 22,21; (*to all people*) 19,15.
träidor *s. m. traitor* 28,11; *adj. treacherous* 6,41.
träir (*3 pres. ind.* träis 22,54; *3 perf. subj.* träis 1,42; *participle* träit 4,15; 12,35; 23,27; 27,24; 40,13, 69; 45,35) *v. tr. to betray, to deceive, betray.*
traire (*1 pres. ind.* trai 7,35; 17,11; 25,74; *1 pres. subj.* traya 7,38; *participle* (traih 8,19) *v. tr. to pull, to draw, to draw out, to pull off* (los sotlars) 26,33; *to attract* 31, 3; *to pull, to tear out* (los olhs, lo cor) 29,23; 36,23; t. de mort *to deliver from death* 38,30; t. d'ira 8,19; *to suffer, to endure* mal t., t. mal 4,8; 7,38; 10,20; 17,11; 44,60; t. peihz 7,35; t. pena 25,74; 44,45.
träiritz *s. f. traitoress* 23,26.
trametre *v. tr. to send, transmit, dispatch* 6,51; 12,36; 17,49; 19,15; 31,58.
trassalhir *v. intr. to tremble* (*from love*) 13,19.
trassio (*variant,* träizo) *s. f. treason* 28,61.
trebalha *s. f. torture, pain, suffering* 35,46.
tremblar *v. intr. to tremble, to shake* (*from fright*) 31,43.
trencar *v. tr. to cut* (*without an object*) 40,75.
tres *number three* 2,22.
trespassar *v. intr. to die* 40,76.
triar *v. tr. to pick out, to select, to choose,* 40,27; *to recognize, to perceive, to discern* 39,35; trian *recognizable* 31,33.
trichador (*s. n.* trichaire 29,16; 37, 27) *s. m. cheat, deceiver* (*in love*) 31,35.

trichairitz *s. f. (female) deceiver, cheater (in love)* 2,47.

tro *prep. to, as far as, till, until,* t. aras que 5,9; t. part calenda 26, 48; *conjunction until (with indicative)* 12,11; 16,40; 23,34; *(with subjunctive)* 16,35; t. que *until (with indicative)* 12,9; 30,14; *(with subjunctive)* 29,48.

trobar *v. tr. to find* 4,2; no.us trob egansa 1,54; t. ochaizos ad alcu 29,26; t. merce 4,4; 10,14; 31,24; *with double accusative* 2,42; 39, 13,41; *(by reading) to find* 16,37; *to find, to be of an opinion* 13,22.

trop *adv. too much* 9,29; 10,39; 12, 10; 16,5; 19,39; 29,12; 40,43; 43,40.

tropel *s. m. troop, band, heap* 38,13.

truan *s. m. tramp, vagrant;* anar t. 36,57 *(See Note) adj. deceitful, faithless* 19,7.

truandar *v. tr. to deceive, to treat meanly* 26,17.

tu *acc.* te 43,21; verbunden te 16,49; *personal pron. you (familiar)* 4,62; *address to the beloved* 36,29.

U

ufana *s. f.* ostentation 22,22.

umâ *adj. human, transitory* 22,45; *humane, good, kind* 22,30; de u. *granted in friendship* 37,45.

umil *adj. humble, mild, gentle* 31,54.

umiliar *v. refl. to bow, to humble oneself* 29,12; umilian *humble* 26, 34; 33,42.

un, u; *f.* una *number one* 4,54; 10, 43; 28,55; 45,19; *one and the same* 30,4,5; 42,18; us ... ab l'autre 22,39; us no *not one* 19,45; 21,10; 22,11; 39,15,35; 43,29; *article* 1,17; 3,3; 4,46; 6,9; 2,37; 4,40; 5,5; 6,3; 7,4; *etc.*; *substantive one* (l'us ab l'autre) 7,20; una *a woman* 30,6.

unir *v. tr. to unite* 40,64.

uzatge *s. m. usage, custom* 13,26; 19, 13; aver, penre bon u. 20,23; 25, 75; per costum e per bon u. *according to custom and usage* 23, 40.

V

va *adj. unreliable* 22,14,35.

vair *adj. many colored, unreliable* semblan v. e. piec 24,25.

vaireyar *v. refl. to change tobe unconstant* 24,30.

valen *adj. able, fit, clever, worthy, noble, proficient, excellent* 1,36; 5,33.

valer (*3 pres. ind.* vau 13,38; 21,29; *3 pres. subj.* valha 2,18;) *v. intr. to be worth (with the qualifications* gaire, mais, plus, re, tan) 6, 28; 15,1; 21,29; 30,24; 35,18; 45,17; 28,55; 30,42; mais val *with the subjunctive: it is better than ...* 6,28; viure que.m val? *What is it worth to me? What help is it to me, to live?* 28,33; que.m val *what aid to me?* 40, 70; *help, aid* 1,24; 10,37; 13,38; 14,12; 39,48; 40,54; 43,49; 19, 23; 35,44; *help, to make good, to repay, to requite* 4,30.

valor *s. f. worth, ability (of man)* 2, 45,48; 8,55; 10,47; 31,11; *(of the beloved)* 13,34; 25,46; v. e sen 20,24; 27,39; *help, aid* 8,30.

vanar *v. refl. to boast* (de) 22,21; 37,60.

vas *prep. toward (direction) (local)* 8,34; 12,30; 13,10; 16,19; 21,52; 22,62; 39,21; estrenher vas se 36, 35; se' eslaisser vas 12,10 *(friendly)* esser oclis vas 29,19; 37,6; valer v. alcu 10,37; vas on posc amar? 5,17; *(hostile)* 3,54; 8,5; (doptar) 3,35; 21,44; 26,26; (orgolh) 9,10,11; *against someone* 1, 15; 7,58; 10,28; 19,38; 23,41; *in proportion to* 5,14; 8,40; 33,11; 41,16.

vassalatge *s. m. bravery, valor* 20,32; far v. *to do knightly deeds* 42,14.

ve *(in* ve·us) *interjection — see!* 12, 5; 27,65; 31,53.

vejaire *see* veyaire.

velh *adj. old* 28,31.

velhar *v. intr. to watch, to keep watch* 7,33.

GLOSSARY

ven *s. m. wind* 3,33; 17,16; 27,3; 31,44; 37,4; 44,5.
venal, -au *adj. venal* 15,25.
vendre *v. tr. to sell* 26,28; *to sell dearly, to sell for a high price* 12, 31; 19,28; *to do evil* 4,29.
venir *v. intr. to come* 16,4; 20,17; 25,18; 36,18; li venh a so plazer 42,40; anar e venir *go here and there* 18,2 (*temporal*) 30,1; *to arrive* a tal cocha m'es venguda 8,31; *to come here, to arise, to originate (from)* (jois, mals, gratz mi ve, *etc.*) 1,6; 12,34; 15,11; 16, 26; 17,18; *etc.*; mortz venh'a ... 3,40; 40,71; *to arrive at, to* (vengut er al partimen) 30,35; v. a plazer, a joi, *etc.* 4,26; 15,45; en pessamen me venc 17,24.
venjansa *s. f. revenge, vengeance* penre v. 45,27.
vensedor *adj. conquerable* 39,13.
venser *v. tr. to conquer, to overcome, to surpass* 1,9; 4,45; 5,19; 7,31; 35,6; ela·m vens a tota sa volontat 30,36; *to excel, to exceed* 5, 34; 39,8.
ventar *v. intr. to blow (wind)* 37,1.
ventura *s. f. good luck,* vida B.
ver *adj. true (neuter)* mais es ver 21, 24; *s. m. true, truth* 1,64; 3,44; (See *Appel*) — vers es 5,32; 8,9; 17,19; 45,46; dire lo ver de 2,24; 10,30; 15,22; saber lo ver 45,2; per ver *truly* 43,41.
verai *adj. sincere, genuine, truthful* 10,6; 18,10.
verdor *s. f. green, verdure* 28,2.
verdura *s. f. green, verdure* 24,2; 44, 12.
verger *s. m. garden, orchard* 23,15; 24,3.
vergonha *s. f. shame* 16,22; 22,25; perdre v. e paor 13,52.
vergohnos *adj. ashamed* 3,57.
verjan *s. m. branch* 29,2; 39,2.
vermelh *adj. red* 7,9,12; 44,3.
vers *s. m. verse, type of lyric* 29,8; v. e chanso 6,24; 8,2; *where the word appears in poems*; 1,1; 13, 6; 15,50; 21,57; 22,7; 23,57; 26, 36; 31,58.

versar *v. tr. to turn* (vas me versa tot lo dan) 29,28.
vert *adj. green* 7,9; 41,1; 42,1.
vertader *adj. true, truthful* 33,20.
vertat *s. f. truth* 15,27; 29,31; sai de v. 6,5.
vertut *s. f. marvel, wonder* faire v. 12,38,43.
vestidura *s. f. clothing* 8,37; 44,13.
vetz *s. f. time* una v. *once* 37,18; manhtas v. 6,53; 39,10; 44,70; cen v. 13,22; 22,32; 31,27; car una v. no ... 39,15; autra v. 1,48; d'autra v. *another time* 37,62 (See *note*).
veyaire *s. m. view, opinion* v. m'es que *it seems to me that (with indicative)* 18,24; 37,21; 44,67; (*with subjunctive*) 35,30; 37,3; no m'es v. que (*with subjunctive*) 29, 55; que·us es v.? 4,1; si no. us es v. *when it still doesn't appear to you (it is still the case)* 29,61.
vezer (*1 pres. ind.* vei 5,21; 7,47,59; 21,2; *3 pres. ind.* ve 16,41; 36, 27; *1 pres. subj.* veya 7,60; 29, 43; 42,28,52; *3 perf.* vit 27,33; *participle* vis 44,31; vegut 8,23, 51; 33,9) *v. tr. to see* (alcu) 5,21, 22; 7,59; 29,33; 33,36; *take a* 10,52; 15,38; 20,6; 26,44; 7,48; (ad alcu); 19,19,31; 20,26; 25,6; 27,7; 28,41; v que ... 43,29; *to see at a glance* 1,13; 6,14; 24,20; 36,5; 41,2; cal vos vi e cal vos ves! 7,47; v. far 1,8,32; 7,1; 9,1; 10,2; 13,4; (*with the dative of person*) 6,32,55; (*without an object*) 1,56; (v. clar) 13,20; v. en un miralh 43,19; *s. m. sight* 41,24.
vezi *adj. near, close* 18,25; *s. m. neighbor* 1,34.
veziat *adj. cheerful, gay* 35,29.
via *s. f. path, road, way*; vai s'en via plana 22,61; no'n saup ni chap ni via 45,5; tota via, *always, constantly* 21,47,58; 21,59 see note.
via see vida.
vianda *s. f. food, meat* 26,24.

viatge *s. m. trip, journey, way* 20,16;
fors sui del dreich v. 23,18.
viatz *adv. quickly, swiftly* 18,31.
vida 23,9; 30,43; *s. f. life* 33,35;
esser d'avol v. 23,9; a ma v. *time of my life* 30,43.
vil *adv. common, low, vulgar* 42,19.
vilâ *adj. bad thinking and behavior* 22,13,57; 37,41.
vilanamen *adv. in a base, mean, lowly way or manner* 42,16; vertat en dic v. 15,27.
vilanatge *s. m. baseness;* dire v. 23, 24; faire v. vas alcu 42,35.
vilania *s. f. discourtesy, baseness, villainy* 1,26; 22,23; faire v. 25,78; *cowardice* 17,38.
virar *v. tr. to turn, to change* 44,43; (los olhs, l'esgar, lo cor) 35,15; 44,64; *to turn oneself, to change* 13,10; 27,31; *to alter, to vary, to turn* 1,39; 18,1; *to turn towards* 40,6; *to turn away from* 9,34; *intr. to turn, to turn aside* 30,1.
vis *s. m. face* 1,51; 3,58; 31,42; 37, 12; *view, opinion, sight* so m'es vis *it seems to me* 1,26; no m'es vis que *with subjunctive* 42,5.
viu *adj. living, alive* 41,28.
viure *v. intr. to live* 3,12,64; 28,33; 31,11,14; 40,15; 38,24,28.
volar *v. intr. to flee, to fly* 44,50.
volatge *adj. fugitive, transitory, flighty* 19,16; 23,24.
voler (*1 pres. ind.* volh 9,8; 25,68; *1 pres. subj.* volha 25,5; *3 pres. subj.* volha 9,7) *v. tr. to want, to wish* 12,18; 15,34; 35,45; 37,26; *to wish to have* 6,33; 10,46; 17, 27; (*either the lover or beloved*) 9,8; 19,14,53; 25,68; 27,9; 30,6; 41,9; *to strive after* 12,22; 13,35; (*see:* be, mal) *to plan, to scheme, to intend* (*as opposed to execute*) 22,8; v. mais *see* mais; v. que (*with subjunctive*) 5,27; 21,30,55; 45,2; v. faire *want to do* 1,23; 40,26; *to do according to his own nature* 1,31; (14,27); *to be about to do* 14,9; 40,76.
voler *with the dative of the reflexive pron.* 10,30; 27,52,64; *without an object* 12,26; (volgues o no volgues) 15,29; *s. m. wish, desire* 4,22; 10, 23; 18,3; be-volen *s. m. well wisher* 13,45.
volon *adj. longing, desiring* 43,16.
volontat *s. f. will* 15,32; 24,13; 30, 37; (*plur.*) 35,32.
volonters 33,6,44; -er 23,47; *adv. willingly, gladly, readily* 1,19.
volontos *adj. willing* 3,24.
volp *s. f. fox* 32,38.
volver *v. tr. to turn* — voutz sui en la folor 6,25; *refl. to turn oneself, to turn* 18,1; 27,31.
vos — *enclitic* ·us — *pers. pron. stressed and unstressed* — *address to the listener* 6,2; *etc.; to love* 3,1; 4,1; 7,49; 10,8; *etc.; to the beloved* 1,54; 3,54; 13,11; 16,10; 19,52; 20,46; 28,59; 30,54; 31,55 *etc.*
vostre *poss. pron. stressed and unstressed* 1,49,50,58; 7,23,51; 13, 15; 20,41,45; *subst.* 33,29.
votz *s. f. voice* (*of the nightingale*) 23,1; 39,4.
voupilhatge *s. m. cowardice* 20,34 (*see note*).
vouta *s. f. kind of singing* 30,25.

PROPER NAMES

Alegret 4, 62 *jongleur*.
Alvernhatz 12, 42; l'A. 16, 27; mon A. 29, 58. *hidden name*: *Raimon V of Toulouse (1148-1194)*?
Amor *see glossary*.
Anjau 21, 54 *Anjou*.
Arnaut de Meruoil vida B *Troubadour from last third of twelfth century. There is a definitive edition edited by R. C. Johnston,* Les poésies lyriques du troubadour Arnaut de Marueil, *Paris, 1935.*
Aziman 21, 51; 26, 47; 36, 60 *hidden name, see glossary*.
Belcaire 12, 42; 29, 60 *Beaucaire*.
Bel-Vezer 1, 57; 8, 49, 54; 12, 41, 43; 28, 65; 29, 60; 41, 49, 51; 42, 33, 50 *hidden name*.
Bernart 2, 1, 15, 29, 43; 7, 57; 14, 1, 13, 25; 32, 8, 22, 36, 46; B. de Ventadorn 2, 1; 15, 53.
Bornel *see* Giraut de Bornelh.
bretô *adj. Breton* esperansa bretona 23, 38.
Conort 16, 1; mo C. 16, 53; 20, 2; 22, 28, 32; 45, 38; Bel C. 16, 9 *hidden name*.
Corona 23, 57; 35, 43 *messenger*: *a jongleur*?
Cortes 31, 57 *hidden name*.
Dalon vidas A & B *in Dordogne. Dalon was the seat of a Cistercian abbey in Dordogne.*
De-Cor 22, 64 *hidden name*.
Denan-Totz 28, 66 *hidden name*.
Dous-Esgar 19, 50 *hidden name*.
Eblo vida A; 30, 23 *the Lord of Ventadour; see introduction*.
engles *adj. English* 26, 43. — *s. m. Englishman* 26, 46.
Engleterra *s. f. England* vidas A & B.
Enrics d' Engleterra *Henry II of England (1133-89)* vidas A & B.
Escudor 36, 55 *Bernart's jongleur*.
Espanha 17, 22 *Spain*.
Fachura 12, 41 *hidden name*.
Ferran 4, 62 *messenger*: *a jongleur*?
Fi-Joi 19, 52 *hidden name*.
Fons Salada 21, 49 *messenger*.
Frances 10, 51; 16, 50 *hidden name*.
Fransa 44, 36; 45, 41 *France*.
Garsiô 6, 61 *jongleur*.

PROPER NAMES

Giraut de Bornelh   vida B   *Troubadour of the last part of the twelfth century. He has been edited by Adolf Kolson (Halle 1910, 1935) 2 vols.*
Gui d'Uisel   vida B.   *Troubadour. The critical edition is by S. Santangelo, Poesie di Gui d'Uisel, Catania, 1909.*
Iseut   44, 48   *Heroine of the legend of Tristan and Iseut.*
Lemozi   14, 7, 19; 45, 43   *troubadour or jongleur?*
Mauren   10, 51.
Messatger   6, 63, 39, 57   *hidden name.*
La Mura   8, 53   *town within the territory of Vienne.*
Narbona   23, 58   *Narbonne.*
Narcisus   43, 24   *Narcissus son of the river naiad, Liriope. Ovid, Metamorphoses, iii, ll. 338 ff.*
norman   s. m.   *a Norman* 26, 46; 33, 45. — *adj.* dux normans 26, 43; terra normanda 26, 38.
Normandia   21, 54   *Normandy.*
Peire   2, 8, 22, 36, 46   *troubadour: Peire d'Alvernhe?*
Peire d'Alvergne   vida B   *Troubadour who wrote from c. 1158-1180. There is a critical edition by Rudolf Zenker, Die Lieder Peires von Auvergne, Erlangen, 1900.*
Peirol   32, 1, 15, 29, 43   *see note for canso 32.*
Peitau   21, 53   *Poitou.*
Peläus   1, 46   *Peleus, see note.*
Piza   44, 24   *Pisa.*
Lo Poi   21, 60   *Le Puy-en-Velay, former capital of Velay (now Haute-Loire)?*
Proensa   12, 36   *Provence.*
Raimon de Toloza   vida A   *Raimon V de Toulouse (1148-1194).*
lo rei   15, 40; 17, 7; 21, 50; 26, 43; 33, 38   *Henry II?*
la reina des Normans   33, 45   *Eleanor of Aquitaine, (c. 1122-1204) daughter of Guillaume X last Duke of Aquitaine. She divorced Louis VII of France in 1152 to marry Henry Plantagenet who became King Henry II in 1154.*
Romeu   22, 62; 45, 53   *hidden name.*
Torena   21, 53   *Touraine.*
Tristan   *the lover of Iseut*   44, 46.—*hidden name*   29, 61; 43, 57; mo T. 4, 63; Amics Tristans 42, 53.
Huguet   33, 43   *messenger: a jongleur?*
Ventadorn   2, 1; 12, 1; 13, 55; 15, 53   *Ventadour.*
Viana   22, 62   *Vienne.*
Vianes   5, 29   *The region of Vienne.*

BIBLIOGRAPHY

Critical Edition

Carl Appel, *Bernard von Ventadorn, Seine Lieder mit Einleitung und Glossar,* Halle a. S., 1915.
   Reviewed by: Giulio Bertoni, *Archivum Romanicum,* I, (1917), pp. 110-115.
                Salverda de Grave, *Neophilologus,* III, (1917), pp. 64-69.
                Walter Küchler, *Die Neueren Sprachen,* XXVI, (1919), pp. 180-185.
                Karl Vossler, *Literaturblatt,* XXXIX, (1917), col. 183-190.

Books

Carl Appel, *Die Singweisen Bernarts von Ventadorn,* Halle a. S., 1934.
   Reviewed by: E. Hoepffner, *Revue des Langues Romanes,* LXVII, (1934), pp. 152-155.
                Kurt Lewent, *Zeitschrift für franz. Sprache und Literatur,* LVIII, (1934), pp. 348-355.
                H. Spanke, *Literaturblatt,* LVII, (1937), pp. 120-122.
Jean Audiau, *Les Troubadours et l'Angleterre,* Paris, 1927.
Salvatore Battaglia, *Jaufre Rudel e Bernardo di Ventadorn, Canzoni, Testo, versione e introduzione,* Napoli, 1949.
André Berry, *Bernart de Ventadorn, Choix de Chansons, présentées et traduites,* 1958.
Hans Bischoff, *Biographie des Troubadours Bernhard von Ventadorn,* Göttinger Diss., Berlin, 1873.
A. Bosset, *Les Troubadours Limousins,* Limoges, 1949.
Giosuè Carducci, *Un poeta d'amore nel secolo XII, Nuova Antologia,* 15 Gennaio e 1 Marzo 1881, (*Opere di G. Carducci,* vol. VIII, Bologna, 1893, p. 389, and *Opere,* Edizione Nazionale, vol. IX, 1936, p. 147).
H. J. Chaytor, *The Troubadours of Dante,* Oxford, 1902.
Martín de Riquer, *Bernartz de Ventadorn, selección, traducción castellana y prólogo,* in "*Poesía en la Mano*", Barcelona, 1940.
F. Gennrich, *Bernart de Ventadorn,* ebd. I, 1778.
   Der Musikalische Nachlass der Troubadours, vol. I, *Songs of Bernart de Ventadorn,* Darmstadt (published by Gennrich), 1958, pp. 31-44 (nos. 16, 34); p. 280 (no. 291 — addenda).

D. Ghezzi, *La Personalità e la Poesia di Bernart de Ventadorn*, Genova, 1948, in *Cultura e Vita*, S. 86.

E. Hoepffner, *Les Troubadours dans leur vie et dans leurs oeuvres*, Paris, 1955, Coll. Armand Colin.

Richard Hofmeister, *Sprachliche Untersuchung der Reime Bernarts von Ventadorn*, Marburger Diss., 1884.

A. Jeanroy, *La Poésie Lyrique des Troubadours*, 2 volumes, Paris-Toulouse, 1934, pp. 138-144.

A. R. Nykl, *Troubadour Studies: a critical survey of recent books published in this field*, Cambridge (Mass.), 1944.

Nicola Zingarelli, *Il primo poeta d'amore della Provenza, Bernardo di Ventadorn*, in *La Cultura Moderna*, Milano, 1923, and *Scritti di Varia Letteratura*, Milano, 1935.

Articles

Carl Appel, *A! tantas bonas chansos, Ein Lied Bernarts von Ventadorn* in *Miscellanea Crescini*, Padova, (1927), pp. 429-441.
Bernart von Ventadorn: Ausgewählte Lieder, in *Sammlung romanischer Übungstexte* no. 7, Halle, 1926.

Vincenzo Crescini, *Bollettino della Società Dantesca Italiana*, N. S., XXV, (1926), p. 166 ff.

J. L. Deister, *Bernart de Ventadour's reference to the Tristan story*, Modern Philology, XIX, (1921-2), pp. 287-296.

Moshé Lazar, *Classification des thèmes amoureux dans l'oeuvre de Bernard de Ventadorn*, Filologia Romanza, VI, (1959), pp. 371-400.

Kurt Lewent, *Weitere textkritische Bemerkungen zu den Liedern des Bernart von Ventadorn*, Zeitschrift für rom. Phil., XLIII, (1923), pp. 657-674.

Tullio Ronconi, *L'Amore in Bernardo di Ventadorn e in Guido Cavalcanti*, Propugnatore, XIV, I, (1881), pp. 19-77; 176-197.

D. Scheludko, *Ovid und die Trobadors*, Zeitschrift für Rom. Phil., LIV, (1934), pp. 140-160.

Oskar Schultz-Gora, *Zum Texte des Bernarts von Ventadorn*, Zeitschrift für Rom. Phil., XLII, (1922), pp. 350-370.

Antonio Viscardi, *Gli Studi sulla poesia di Bernardo di Ventadorn e i nuovi problemi della critica trobadorica*, in *Memorie dell' Accademia dell' Instituto di Bologna, Classe scienze morali*, series IV, vol. II, 1938-1939, pp. 5-46.

Karl Vossler, *Der Minnesang des Bernhard von Ventadorn*, in *Sitzungberichte der Kgl. Bayer Akad. der Wissenschaften Philosoph.-Philolog. und Hist. Klasse*, 2, München, 1918.
Die Dichtung der Trobadors und ihre Europäische Wirkung, Romanische Forschungen, LI, (1937), 253 ff; also in *Aus der romanischen Welt I*, Leipzig, 1940.

Nicola Zingarelli, *Ricerche sulla vita e le rime di Bernardo di Ventadorn*, Studi Medievali, Serie Novati, I, (1905), pp. 309-393. Also Appendix to the article, pp. 594-611.

Anthologies

J. Anglade, *Anthologie des Troubadours*, Paris, 1927, (re-ed. 1953).
P. Bec, *Petite Anthologie de la Lyrique Occitane du Moyen Age*, Coll. *"Les Classiques d'Oc"*, Avignon, 1954.
A. Berry, *Florilège des Troubadours*, Paris, 1930.
R Borchardt, *Die Grossen Trobadors*, deutsch von Rudolf Borchardt, München, 1924.
R. Bossuat, *La Poésie Lyrique en France aux XIIe et XIIIe Siècles*, in *Les Cours de Sorbonne*, Paris, 1952.
J. Boutière and A. H. Schutz, *Biographies des Troubadours*, in *Bibliothèque Méridionale*, I^e série, t. XXVII, Toulouse-Paris, 1950.
F. Brittain, *The Medieval Latin and Romance Lyric*, Cambridge, 1932.
Vincenzo Crescini, *Manuale per L'Avviamento agli Studi Provenzali*, Milano, 1926.
Martín de Riquer, *La Lírica de los Trovadores, Antología comentada, tomo I, Poetas del Siglo XII*, Barcelona, 1948.
István Frank, *Trouvères et Minnesänger. Recueil de textes pour servir à l'étude des rapports entre la poésie lyrique romane et le Minnesang au XIIe siècle*, Saarbrücken, 1952.
R. H. Hill and T. G. Bergin, *Anthology of the Provençal Troubadours*, New Haven, 1941.
Erhard Lommatzsch, *Leben und Lieder der Provenzalischen Troubadours*, 2 volumes, Berlin, 1957.
G. Marone, *Trovadores y Juglares: Lo Coms de Peitieus. Marcabrus. Jaufres Rudels. Bernartz de Ventadorn. La Comtessa de Dia*. Buenos Aires, 1948.
G. Ribemont-Dessaignes, *Les Troubadours, textes choisis et traduits, avec une préface*, Paris, 1946.

[A. B. G.]

ADDENDUM TO BIBLIOGRAPHY

Anthologies:

A. Berry, ed., *Bernart de Ventadour: Choix de Chansons*, Limoges, Rougerie, 1958.

Articles:

J. Frappier, "Variations sur le thème du miroir, de Bernart de Ventadour à Maurice Scève," *Cahiers de l'Association Internationale des Etudes Françaises*, 11 (1959), 134-158.

www.ingramcontent.com/pod-product-compliance
Lightning Source LLC
Chambersburg PA
CBHW021840220426
43663CB00005B/332